1991

In this world of sin and sorrow if virtue
triumphs over vice it is not because it is virtuous,
but because it has bigger and better guns.
                              W. Somerset Maugham
                              Then and Now

We never forgive those whom we have wronged.
                    La Rochefoucauld-Liancourt

"With the Hammer of Truth"

James Thomson Callender
and
America's Early
National Heroes

MICHAEL DUREY

University Press of Virginia
Charlottesville and London

THE UNIVERSITY PRESS OF VIRGINIA
Copyright © 1990 by the Rector and Visitors
of the University of Virginia

First published 1990

Library of Congress Cataloging-in-Publication Data
Durey, Michael.
    With the hammer of truth : James Thomson Callender and America's
early national heroes / Michael Durey.
        p.   cm.
    Incudes bibliographical references.
    ISBN 0-8139-1278-4
    1. Callender, James Thomson, 1758–1803. 2. Journalists—United
States—Biography. 3. Jefferson, Thomas, 1743–1826—Relations with
women. 4. Hemings, Sally. I. Title.
PN4874.C224D87   1990
070'.92—dc20
[B]   90-31096
                                                                        CIP

Printed in the United States of America

Contents

Preface

This is not the book I set out to write. I began research with the intention of exploring the Philadelphia phase of the career of the High Federalist and Tory William Cobbett. I have finished by writing a book on Cobbett's archenemy. James Thomson Callender initially came to my attention as a victim of Cobbett's venomous satire. Only one of the many radical immigrants actively to oppose "Peter Porcupine" in the 1790s, Callender was the most despised (and the most feared). I was intrigued by the fact that whatever their political sympathies, historians had presented opinions of Callender which conformed almost exactly to those of his worst enemy. Although his notorious publications regarding Alexander Hamilton's and Thomas Jefferson's private lives go far to explain this unanimity of interpretation, it was still unusual to find no one prepared to offer extenuating reasons for Callender's actions.

Yet even a cursory glance at the admittedly relatively meager evidence to be found in the collections held by the Historical Society of Pennsylvania and the Library of Congress showed that Callender, although always the subject of partisan execration, had not been consistently vilified by his contemporaries. The Jefferson-Callender correspondence, for instance, fails to confirm the Virginian's later opinions of their relations in the 1790s. Isolated letters to Tench Coxe and from James Carey make it clear that Callender was by no means a pariah but rather a colleague—even a friend—of partisan Republicans in Philadelphia.

My growing suspicions that Callender's own perspective had been either suppressed or ignored were strengthened when I began to examine contemporary evidence for some of the more unsavory revelations on his past. All were either untrue, one-sided, or inaccurate. Yet some historians seemingly had accepted these partisan assertions uncritically. It appeared to me that they had failed to judge the protagonists of the past by the same rules of evidence and of confirmation. Moreover, consideration of Callender's writings, both formal and ephemeral, unearthed a developing but consistent set of political values which reflected a relatively unexplored side of Jeffersonian Republicanism. By reducing Callender to a mere libeler, historians had lost an opportunity of uncovering a minority sensibility which hovered in the wings of the Republican party: an extreme egalitarian and democratic republicanism.

Thus, even if an elementary sense of justice had not convinced me to explore Callender's career in depth, his relatively novel political ideas and his great expertise as a pamphleteer and newspaper editor would have persuaded me to do so. The consequence is this book, which has the intention not so much of rehabilitating Callender as of presenting in the round his view of the world and of the events in which he became embroiled. Only the most inegalitarian would deny Callender a fair hearing.

For all its beauty and charm, Perth, Western Australia, is the most isolated capital in the world. To remain active as a historian of both Britain and the United States in such an environment would be impossible without the financial support of an institution committed to research in the humanities, the dedication of a sympathetic and efficient library staff, and the psychological prop of correspondence with scholars— both interstate and overseas—who share comparable interests and concerns. I have been the beneficiary of several Special Research Grants from Murdoch University, and my ability to consult printed materials has been enhanced by Murdoch University's library staff, who have continually amazed me by their success in obtaining even the most obscure historical references.

In their correspondence, and on rare occasions in personal discussions, scholars across the world have shared with me their ideas, insights, and inspiration. In particular, I wish to thank Lance Banning, John Brims, John Dinwiddy, Geoffrey Gallop, Iain McCalman, Michael McGiffert, Richard Twomey, James Walvin, Roger Wells, and Gwyn A. Williams. Special gratitude is extended to Geoffrey Bolton and Iain Brash, who both read and commented on the Edinburgh chapters, and to F. Barry Smith, who, modestly feigning ignorance of the subject, nevertheless offered wise suggestions on the whole of the penultimate draft of the manuscript. This book is the better for their assistance, although such errors as must certainly remain are my responsibility. Without the invaluable help of Stephen Walker, Callender's life in Edinburgh would still remain unknown.

I was fortunate to spend, with my family, several months of 1981 in the United States, where I first began research on Callender. In Philadelphia, Terry Parssinen and his family extended friendship and gracious hospitality, offered wise survival advice, and converted my son and me into enthusiastic fans of the Philadelphia Eagles. Richard Woodbury, of Concord, N.H., showed us the beauties of the countryside around Lake Sunapee.

My greatest debt, however, is to my wife and friend, Jill, and our children, Francesca and Robert. They have shared with me the pleasures and uncertainties of emigration to a strange country and have tolerated my eccentricities, especially prevalent when writing, with the greatest good nature. To them this book is dedicated, with my love.

Part One

Edinburgh

1

A Scottish Swift

I

The early life of James Thomson Callender is shrouded in mystery. Only vague snippets of information from his adult years give hints of his family, childhood, and youth. Unlike his great enemy of the 1790s in Philadelphia, the fellow immigrant but Tory William Cobbett, who positively reveled in retailing events from his past, Callender was extremely reticent in his writings. His only reference to his parents, for example, came in the last months of his life, when Callender mentioned that his father had been a tobacconist. Although his reserve about his early years is no proof that he had anything to hide, the fact that other sources provide no solid evidence of his family and background suggests either that Callender came from humble stock, as the occupation of his father suggests, or that some family or personal misfortune severely curtailed his career opportunities early in life. His parents possibly died when he was young, for in a poem dedicated to his mentor Lord Gardenstone in 1789 Callender referred to himself as "an orphan bard."[1]

Callender was almost certainly born in Scotland in 1758; no birth registration, however, has been located (the statutory registration of vital events in Scotland did not begin until 1855). According to one late nineteenth-century source, Callender's birthplace was Stirling, but his name cannot be found in the parish registers of that town or in those of the surrounding parishes. His first confirmed place of residence is Edinburgh, but this was in 1782 when Callender was already twenty-four years old.[2]

The only other hint of his family roots comes from Robert Anderson, Callender's contemporary and a successful man of letters, who in his *Life of Samuel Johnson* claimed Callender to be the nephew of the poet James Thomson. No evidence corroborates this assertion, although on the surface some tantalizing coincidences exist. It was common in Scotland for a son to be given as his second name the maiden

surname of his mother, and James Thomson had five sisters who grew
to adulthood, about one of whom nothing is known. She could have
married someone called Callender. If so, James Thomson Callender
would have had a maternal grandfather who was a Presbyterian minister, which might explain the strong impact of Calvinism on his character. Moreover, James Thomson the poet received the liberal financial
assistance of a local minister in order to pursue his education; a similar
arrangement might explain Callender's classical education.[3]

Callender's possible family connection with Thomson suggests a
motive for his later attacks on Samuel Johnson, who had criticized
Thomson in his *Lives of the Poets*. Callender certainly censured Johnson
for his comments on Thomson, but he also was critical of his supposed
kinsman's poetry. Moreover, an anonymous but probably unreliable
correspondent to Dr. James Anderson's journal the *Bee* stated in 1792
that Thomson had only two nephews, neither of whom could have been
Callender.[4]

The source of Robert Anderson's statement may have been Callender himself, who had good reasons for wishing to enhance his lineage.
Adjudging himself a poet but with no good family connections, Callender may have dropped hints of his kinship with Thomson, which
Anderson picked up. Such an attempt to boost his social standing—
Thomson's posthumous reputation was being promoted at that time by
some of the Scottish intelligentsia, including burgh reformers with
whom Callender was connected—would have been understandable
from a poor and struggling but ambitious young man in late eighteenth-
century Edinburgh.[5]

What little evidence does exist suggests that Callender had a
repressed and probably lonely childhood and that he was being nur-
tured for a career in the professions. In 1800 he confessed to having
been "bred up" in the Presbyterian faith. It is significant that his only
reference to his childhood relates to his religious upbringing and that he
was concerned with refuting the suggestion that Presbyterianism rejected the doctrine of original sin. Presbyterianism in Scotland at the
time of Callender's birth was divided between the Moderates, who
were Erastian and dominant in the Church of Scotland, and the Evan-
gelicals, who remained true to the brimstone Calvinism of the seventeenth century, in which the doctrine of original sin still retained
compelling force. It thus appears that Callender's early religious experiences were in the tradition of Evangelical Presbyterianism.[6]

Callender had a complex and contradictory character. He was self-
righteous, strongly puritanical with regard to personal morals, insuf-
ferably proud, with a deep and abiding mistrust of human nature. Yet
he became involved with a group who composed bawdy verse, wrote

satirical poetry himself, frequently drank heavily, and embraced low tavern life, both in Scotland and in America. These apparent contradictions strongly suggest a temperament continually at odds with an orthodox Calvinism imbibed in his youth, from which he never fully escaped. His religious upbringing instilled in him—as it did in his fellow radical Thomas Muir—a strong sense of right and wrong, a belief in the existence of an objective Truth, and a determination, often carried to excess, to defend his principles. Calvinism is a key element in an understanding of Callender's life.[7]

In Callender's youth Scotland was renowned for its comparatively advanced educational system. Most lowland parishes had parochial schools that gave a good, cheap elementary education and prepared promising boys for university. In the towns (burghs), high schools provided an education that usually stressed the teaching of Latin. "No other country in Europe offered so many openings for poor boys below the rank of gentlemen, and the intake of students from humble homes probably increased in the eighteenth century."[8]

There is no doubt that Callender benefited from the Scottish commitment to nearly universal education. He was to inform James Madison in 1796 that he was competent to teach English grammar, writing, arithmetic, and Latin, "none of them with eminent skill but not I think below mediocrity." His early published works confirm his ability to write correct standard English and are punctuated with quotations from, and allusions to, many writers of ancient Greece and Rome. (In "The Battle of the Books" Callender, who was a very capable classical scholar, would always side with the Ancients against the Moderns.) There is, however, no evidence of his attendance at any of the better Scottish grammar schools, nor does his name appear in the matriculation registers of any of the Scottish universities. Yet he would never have learned Latin if there were not some hopes of a subsequent career in one of the professions.[9]

Five major avenues of advancement existed for a young man wishing to become successful in eighteenth-century Scotland: the law, the Kirk, medicine, teaching, and the world of letters. All required a knowledge of the classics, for as Bruce Lenman has stated: "It was vitally important for the careers of many ambitious Scots . . . that various forms of classicism constituted an international cultural vocabulary, immediately accessible to, and therefore saleable to the ruling classes of what contemporaries called the polite nations." Only two of these professions, however, were expanding in the eighteenth century, for the Kirk was chronically oversubscribed with hopeful ministers, teachers were paid a pittance, and the law remained the preserve of the landed classes, who made up 90 percent of the Faculty of Advocates.

Opportunities existed in medicine, although the growing reputation of the Scottish universities in this field meant that competition was strong. To rely on one's pen for a career was extremely risky and involved finding a reliable and helpful mentor.[10]

Whether Callender was ever in the position to pay the £15 to £20 sterling in fees for a six-month term at university is not known. He certainly attended some classes given by William Cullen, the famous chemist, at the University of Edinburgh; but as lectures were frequently open to the public, his presence did not necessarily signify a desire for a career in medicine. What can be surmised is his early fascination with books and with their authors and his ambitions of a literary career. In his first pamphlet, published in 1782, he wrote: "When a boy peruses a book with pleasure, his admiration riseth immediately from the work to its author. His fancy fondly ranks his favorite with the wise, and the virtuous. He glows with a lover's impatience, to reach the presence of this *superior being*, to drink of science at the fountain-head, to complete his ideas at once, and riot in all the luxuries of learning."[11]

But a love of books and a desire for literary fame could not be the foundation of a financially rewarding career for a man of Callender's marginal social position. An aspiring author required alternative means of support, and in 1782 Callender became a subclerk in the Edinburgh Sasine Office. He demonstrated great tenacity by remaining for nearly eight years in what was a menial and poorly paid occupation which offered few opportunities for advancement.[12]

A sasine is a registration of a change in land or property ownership, and Callender's job entailed transcribing individual transactions into a central register. Working in the Sasine Office must have been a mind-numbing experience. Between 1617 and 1868 subclerks such as Callender and his friend William Gillan filled 3,779 volumes of the Old General Register. Callender claimed personally to have covered, in best copperplate script, 40,000 pages during his tenure, being paid fourpence for each page. Omitting from calculation the fines that he suffered for unacceptable work practices, he earned on average about £80 sterling a year, a sum that he rightly believed to be lower than the salaries of clerks in other establishments.[13]

II

The dreary routine of the Sasine Office failed to diminish Callender's ambition to enter the world of letters. In 1782 and 1783 he published anonymously his first two pamphlets, which he doubtless hoped would become the foundation of a literary career. His subject in both pamphlets was the famous Dr. Samuel Johnson. In some ways this was a shrewd choice, guaranteed to attract the attention of all Scotsmen, for

Johnson was unpopular north of the border. Johnson had been scathing about the Scottish renaissance, telling James Boswell in 1768 that the Scots "have learnt a little from [the English], and you think yourselves great men." His toryism, his dislike of religious dissenters, his British government pension, and his caustic comments on Scottish civilization following his well-publicized trip through the North in 1773 further compounded the Scots' low opinion of Johnson. He was a perfect target for Callender, who at the very outset of his literary career demonstrated many of those characteristics which were to become hallmarks of his style.[14]

Callender's *Deformities of Samuel Johnson* (1782) was not great literature or a work of judicious criticism but a slashing attack on Johnson's literary reputation and his fame as a lexicographer. His approach was to combine personal with literary criticism of his subject, a style which he was to perfect in the United States in the 1790s. "In almost every department of learning, from astronomy down to the first principles of grammar," he wrote, Johnson's ignorance "seems amazing. . . . his personal appearance cannot much recommend him; his conversation would shock the rudest savage. . . . I . . . have attempted to illustrate his . . . entire want of general learning; his antipathy to rival merit; his paralytic reasoning; his solemn trifling pedantry." As for his literary creations, Johnson's volumes "are of no great value. . . . His ignorance, his misconduct, and his success, are a striking proof that the race is not always to the swift, nor the battle to the strong."[15]

Callender's critique covered most of Johnson's writings but concentrated on *Lives of the Poets*, which he criticized for its pedantry and lack of subtlety, and Johnson's most celebrated work, the *Dictionary*. Most of the definitions in the *Dictionary*, claimed Callender, could be divided into three classes: "the erroneous, œnigmatical, [and] superfluous." Many of the words were of Johnson's own coining, "with roots and authorities often ridiculous, and always useless." The *Dictionary* "is prodigiously defective. . . . It has no force of thought." Much of the impact of *Deformities* rested on Callender's ability to use Johnson's more arcane words as a satirical device. Thus, on Johnson's critique of Dryden he commented: "some *narcotic* seems to have *refrigerated* the red liquor which circulates in the Doctor's veins, and to have *hebetated* and *obtunded* his powers of *excogitation*." Similarly, referring to Johnson's supposed inability to say anything sensible about the professions, Callender stated that the doctor's position could be regarded as "a turbid ebullition of amphibological inanity." As a critical device both to attack Johnson and to defend the purity of the English language, Callender used satire effectively and unscrupulously.[16]

To be fair to Callender, the *Deformities* was not a mere catalogue of

abuse. He quoted innumerable examples of possible neologisms, pleo-
nasms, archaisms, and tautologies, as well as examples of Johnson's
prurient tendency to dwell on indecent words. Without doubt Callender
had studied the *Dictionary* and Johnson's other writings with great
assiduity, and by sheer weight of examples he must have compromised
Johnson's reputation in some quarters. His criticisms may have been
harsh and vehement, but many were based on arguably strong authority, and Johnson, well known for a tongue and a pen equally as sharp as
Callender's, was only receiving in kind what he had previously given.

Callender's choice of subject for his first pamphlets, although appealing to the insular element in Scottish life, did not mean that he
sought public recognition at the expense of principle, for in his texts he
quietly incorporated political views that were antithetical to majority
opinion in Scotland and that placed Callender firmly among a small
minority who represented the first stirrings of Scottish political awareness. The audience he hoped to reach when writing the pamphlets was
of necessity the Scottish literate public in general; to make his mark,
widespread sales were needed. Opinion in Scotland, however, was
overwhelmingly behind the British government in its war with the
American rebels. Most Scottish intellectuals were in favor of the re-
pression of the colonists by force, and Scottish members of Parliament
were virtually unanimous in support of government.[17]

Callender's assault on Johnson was thus a subtle rather than an
overt promotion of patriotic principles and was especially a defense of
American and Irish patriotism. Johnson, of course, was closely associated with British government policy toward the colonists, for he had in
1775 published *Taxation No Tyranny*, a vigorous demolition of the
American patriots' constitutional arguments. Callender's critique of
Johnson and his dwelling on the latter's government pension sought to
appeal to the war-weary who by 1782 might have been amenable to the
prospect of some political or economical reform.[18]

Although most of his political statements in his first two pamphlets
were understandably covert, Callender was undoubtedly a patriot in
the early 1780s. He applauded, for example, the Irish Volunteers, who
were in the process of bluffing their way, by the threat of armed
violence, toward obtaining an independent Parliament. Moreover, at a
time when the English radical John Wilkes remained unpopular for his
anti-Scottish propaganda in the 1760s and there was still a swell of
sympathy for Lord Bute, George III's Scottish favorite, Callender
gleefully used the Wilkites' nickname of "Pomposo" for Samuel Johnson and suggested that Scotsmen should disavow Bute, who had given
Johnson his pension in 1762. Thus, unlike most of his Scottish contemporaries, who seemed incapable of overcoming their political apathy

and who saw their self-interest closely linked to the union with England, Callender's vision was broad, embracing the patriot movements in England, Ireland, and America and acclaiming Adam Smith—to the probable dismay of the Scottish elites—for his "supreme contempt of national prejudice, and a fearless attachment to liberty, to justice, and to truth."[19]

Calvinism, one of the major influences on Callender, is noticeable in his emphasis on Johnson's scatalogical excesses. In addition, the works, opinions, and the satirical techniques of Jonathan Swift had a considerable impact on his early writings. Such was his admiration for the early eighteenth-century pamphleteer that Callender saw himself as the Scottish Swift. Callender was never in the habit of eulogizing individuals (Thomas Jefferson, as we shall see, was an exception), so his comments on Swift are worth quoting at length. In 1782 Callender wrote:

> Swift had the splendid misfortune to be a man of genius. By a very singular felicity, he excelled both in verse and prose. He boasted, that no *new* word was to be found in his volumes. . . . He was no less remarkably clean, than *some* are remarkably dirty. His love of fame never led him into the lowest of all vices; and a sense of his own dignity made him respect the importance and feelings of others. He often went many miles on foot, that he might be able to bestow on the poor, what a coach would have cost him. He raised some hundreds of families from beggary, by lending them five pounds a-piece only. He inspired his footmen with Celtic attachment. Whatever was his pride, he shewed none of it in "the venerable presence of misery." Though a poet he was free from vanity; though an author and a divine, his example did not fall behind his precepts; though a courtier, he disdained to fawn on his superiors; though a patriot, he never, like our successive generations of blasted orators, sacrificed his principles to his passions. "His meanest talent was his wit." His learning had no pedantry, his piety no superstition; his benevolence almost no parallel.[20]

At first glance it may appear incongruous that Callender viewed Swift in this light and used him as a role model. After all, the Anglo-Irish pamphleteer adhered to many of the same opinions as Samuel Johnson. He was a High Church Anglican, a critic (in *A Tale of a Tub*) of Calvinist theology. Politically he was a Tory, although he did not accept the doctrine of the divine right of kings. And he disliked Scotsmen! But in Callender's eyes Swift had political and personal virtues that far outweighed these particular vices. He was, for example, virulently anti-Whig, hostile to the corrupt practices of the Whig grandees of Walpole's regime and to the union between England and Scotland, which, he claimed in 1707, would result in a ship of state "with a double Keel," an ungovernable "crazy double-bottom'd Realm" wide open to the evils of faction. Above all, Swift was both a patriot and a pacifist, strongly opposed to British rule in Ireland. "His intrepid eloquence," wrote Callender of Swift in 1782, "first pointed out to his oppressed countrymen, that path to Independence, to happiness, and to glory, which their posterity, at this moment, so nobly pursue." In addition, Swift's *The Late Conduct of the Allies* (1711) was instrumental, thought Callender, in bringing the wasteful war against Louis XIV to an end: "He taught the English nation the dangers of a continental war, dispelled their delusive dreams of conquest, and stopt them in the career to ruin."[21]

Swift was, moreover, notorious for his misanthropy. In a famous letter to Alexander Pope in 1725 he wrote:

> The chief end I propose to myself in all my labours is to vex the world rather than divert it. . . . I have ever hated all nations, professions, and communities, and all my love is towards individuals. For instance, I hate the tribe of lawyers, but I love Counsellor such a one, Judge such a one; for so with physicians . . . , soldiers, English, Scots, French and the rest. But principally I hate and detest that animal called man, although I heartily love John, Peter, Thomas and so forth. This is the system upon which I have governed myself many years . . . and so I shall go on till I have done with them. . . . And I will not have peace of mind till all honest men are of my opinion.[22]

All of Swift's works, but especially *Gulliver's Travels* which Callender had read, are suffused with this morose view of man and reflect his extreme distaste for the pretensions, greed, and pride inherent in human nature. It was a cynical, pessimistic view to which Callender felt strongly drawn, even when he was a young man. What had soured Callender so early in life cannot be ascertained. His Calvinist upbringing may have contributed to his misanthropy, and possibly some personal disappointment of which we know nothing may have given him a jaundiced view of the world. Either or both—as well as Swift's influence—may have been the source of Callender's contempt for the famous and of his desire to cut them down to size, a point of view that would not, of course, have appealed to the Scottish literati. The famous, he decided, all too frequently failed to live up to expectations. "The laurels which human praise confers are withered and blasted by the unworthiness of those who wear them." Their reputations were accepted too uncritically. "The novice unhappily presumes that men who command the passions of others cannot be slaves of their own; That a historian must feel the worth of justice and tenderness; . . . That an assertor of public freedom will never become the dupe of flattery, and the pimp of oppression: That the founder of a system cannot want words to explain it; . . . That a preacher of morality will blush to persist in vindictive, deliberate, and detected falsehoods." Even when a notable figure manifestly prostituted his position—as Johnson had done by becoming a hireling—mankind was normally too deferential to complain. Someone, however, even someone who "is without interest or connection," must intervene: "He is unfit to be the friend of virtue who cannot defend her dignity; who dares not execute her vengeance." We can only speculate why Callender felt that "the world is buried in prejudice," but the supposed wrong ran deep and was to color his life to its bitter end.[23]

Notwithstanding his patriotism and his contempt for the great, Callender's first pamphlet was sufficiently successful to go into a second edition, published in London. According to Callender, it was received on both sides of the border with some degree of notice by "men of learning," including the influential Lord Kames.[24] Perhaps Callender envisioned Kames offering him an entrance to literary society. If so, he was to be disappointed, for Kames died that same year, although he may have been instrumental in Callender's appointment as clerk in the Sasine Office. With little positive response to his pamphlet and certainly with no literary patronage in view, in 1783 Callender attempted to revive interest in his writings by publishing a second volume on the same theme. It was not a success, for it was repetitive and unoriginal, sinking quickly into a morass of minor, irrelevant detail. Taking a good idea beyond its limits was an error that Callender was to repeat later in his career; at this point it brought his literary advancement to an abrupt halt.

Callender had to fall back on his subclerkship at the Sasine Office in order to make a living. His experiences in that office in the next few years were to give him firsthand knowledge of the corruption and influence within the British political system, which previously he had known of only through the writings of pamphleteers such as Swift. The Sasine Office was to further Callender's political and social education and would turn him into a political pamphleteer.

III

In eighteenth-century Britain the state functioned through the judicious distribution of patronage by influential landed aristocrats and gentry who either were in government themselves or were closely associated with those in power. "Government offices were obtained through the intervention of a great man, a man of influence, and a job-seeker without such connections had virtually no chance of success in his quest." Positions in the established churches (the Anglican in England, the Presbyterian in Scotland), the armed forces, the law, the court, the East India Company, and the bureaucracy were all available as patronage, from the highest positions, such as the keeper of the great seal in Scotland, to the very lowly, such as landwaiters and tidesmen in the customs service. By manipulating the system of patronage, influential men created networks of friends, thereby building up for themselves an interest in their local region, as well as a fund of support for the government of the day. Toward the end of the century the patronage system, which had worked very effectively in Scotland, faced increasing opposition from those who felt it enabled the influential to engross power and to become parasitic on the state. In his attacks on patronage, William Cobbett was to call it "Old Corruption."[25]

One of the more valuable public appointments in the gift of the government in Scotland was that of keeper of the General Register of Sasines and the Particular Register for the Lothians. The Edinburgh Sasine Office in the 1780s was just one of a number of departments that were concerned with the creation and keeping of official records in Scotland. Its province was the registration of sasines, conveyancing writs recording a change in the ownership of land and property. In a society that naturally laid great stress on property ownership, the Sasine Office performed an extremely important task, for unlike in England, where there have never been written instruments of sasine, proof of ownership in Scotland depended on the accurate recording, in a specified time and in a specified manner, of the sasine.[26]

The Sasine Office's role was also important in another way, for its staff was responsible for registering what were known as taillies, which could be of assistance to wealthy landowners wishing to create fictitious or nominal votes for parliamentary elections. Unreformed Scottish electoral law enfranchised those in the counties who either possessed property or superiority land, held of the crown, valued at forty shillings in the "auld extent" or, where the extent was no longer known, who held land valued at £400 Scots (£1 Scots was worth 1s. 8d. sterling). The franchise, however, was vested not in the land but in the superiority, and this encouraged wealthy landowners, by a complicated series of legal maneuvers, to separate their property from its superiority in order to create additional voters. By 1790 nearly one-half of the 2,665 county electors in Scotland were "parchment barons," whose right to the franchise was based on land still legally owned by someone else.[27]

In the eighteenth century the vote was generally seen as a form of property, which could be given to a parliamentary candidate in return for favors or money. Legal holders of the franchise naturally disliked the devaluation of their property by the creation of additional votes and frequently contested the qualifications of nominal voters. Because an elector had to prove that his qualifying sasine had been registered more than a year and a day before the meeting of freeholders that drew up the electoral roll, freeholders closely scrutinized the sasine registers in the hope of finding mistakes or anomalies to invalidate the claims of parchment barons. It is clear, therefore, that for Scottish property owners the Sasine Office fulfilled particularly important functions, even more so than the Office of Hornings and Inhibitions, which dealt with debts, or the Court of the Lord Lyon, which as part of its duties regulated the activities of Scotland's bailiffs, the messengers-at-arms. As the substitute keeper of the sasines wrote in 1821, the role of the office "is one of the greatest responsibility, and of the utmost importance to the security of proprietors, as well as mortgagees."[28]

The person ultimately responsible in theory for the efficiency of the Sasine Office in Edinburgh was the keeper of the General Register of Sasines. The position in practice, however, was a lifetime sinecure in the gift of the government in London. Two other positions in the Sasine Office were filled at the wish of the keeper: his deputy, who also was inactive, although unlike his superior he lived in Edinburgh; and a substitute who, while no stranger to the Sasine Office, still delegated most of his duties to a sub-substitute (in effect a chief clerk). These duties included overseeing the daily workings of the office, signing each page in the registers, and keeping the financial accounts.

At the bottom of the Sasine Office hierarchy were the engrossing clerks, who actually transcribed the sasines into the General Register. They were "kept in daily and laborious employment during the whole year." How large the clerical establishment was in the 1780s is not known, but in 1821 there were seven or eight clerks and by 1837 eleven. Their numbers increased roughly in proportion to the volume of work. Using as a guide the keeper's emoluments—which were determined by the number of pages filled in the registers—it would appear that between the 1780s and 1837 the volume of work increased more than threefold. In the earlier period, therefore, probably four clerks worked in the Sasine Office.[29]

The keeper of the sasines from August 1781 was Andrew Stuart (d.1801), M.P. for Lanarkshire 1777–84 and for Weymouth 1790–1801. His deputy was the lawyer Alexander Robertson, who had been principal clerk of session since June 1776. On his death in 1788 he was replaced by John Davidson, writer to the signet (d.1797). Davidson was for many years crown agent in Scotland and agent for many leading Scottish landowners, including, from at least 1779, Andrew Stuart. Receiving the deputyship of the Sasine Office was undoubtedly a reward for Davidson's past services, and possibly also an encouragement to continue his distinguished researches into Scottish history and antiquities. In accordance with tradition, he played little role in the running of the Sasine Office. Stuart's substitute was William Leslie, "an honest, intelligent, and accurate a man as ever filled a public office," who had, however, by the early 1780s "given up everything but a nominal connection with the Sasine Office"; that is, he was rarely seen but continued to collect his fees.[30]

In the 1780s the sub-substitute's or chief clerk's position was held successively by David McPherson and Andrew Steele (1759–1832). The latter's career exemplifies the ways, both legally and illegitimately, in which ambitious men sometimes were able to achieve financial security and upward social mobility through their connections with "Old Corruption." The son of an Edinburgh merchant, Steele possibly studied chemistry under William Cullan and law at the University of Edinburgh. In 1786 he joined the Speculative Society, whose membership included many other socially aspiring students and lawyers such as the future radical Thomas Muir and, later, Henry Cockburn. At about the same time he entered the Sasine Office and began to advertise as a writer (attorney) in the Edinburgh trade directories. In 1788 he became a writer to the signet. After many years of assiduous service to Stuart, Steele eventually was to be appointed deputy keeper of the sasines.[31]

IV

Before his successful upward mobility, however, Steele found his position in the Sasine Office threatened by the complaints and protests of Callender, who sought to bring to official attention the chief clerk's corrupt activities. Although envy cannot be discounted as one source of his animosity, there were other reasons, of a public nature, that also stimulated Callender's wrath, as an examination of the financial structure of the Sasine Office makes clear. The system of distributing emoluments primarily determined the administrative methods used in the office and the ways in which the management and the office clerks interacted. First pig at the trough was Andrew Stuart, who received an annual salary of £200 sterling from the Scottish civil list, the only source of funds not generated by the office's own services to the public. The public paid for a number of services: for the registering of sasines, searches of the register, and the registering of taillies. In addition to his salary, Stuart also received the largest proportion of these fees, obtaining £1.13.4 Scots for every leaf filled in the General Register and £2 Scots for every leaf filled in the Edinburgh district Particular Register. In the 1780s these combined sources of revenue annually brought him, on average, the considerable sum of nearly £800 sterling, which he received in Edinburgh and spent in London and various spa towns.[32]

The deputy had three sources of revenue: a fee proportional to the length of each sasine, the fees from "broken" or unfinished pages, and search fees. A proportion of these fees was transferred to the substitute as his slice of the cake. The chief clerk's salary came largely from the keeper's emoluments, with some "topping up" from the deputy. While these fees were being accumulated and distributed among the officers, the clerks were being paid at piece rates, fourpence for each page they transcribed. Few clerks in Edinburgh at that time would have been so poorly paid: "No Agent's Clerk would leave his Master's Desk to write it [a sasine] at less than sixpence."[33]

The self-financing aspect of the Sasine Office (it never contributed a penny to government revenue) ensured that "lurks and perks" abounded, with the whole office hierarchy involved. It was not only the officers who stood to profit from manipulating the system: piecework and the low rate of pay ensured that the clerks too had a stake in defrauding or overcharging the public. Thus the Sasine Office was a classic example of how "Old Corruption" both oiled the wheels of state—Lord North's patronage guaranteed Stuart's vote in the House of Commons—and, a point usually missed, also drew people inexorably into the spoils system.

This was done in a number of ways. To favor the deputy's interests, for instance, the clerks were encouraged deliberately to end on a new page. According to Callender, the first lesson he had learned on being employed in the office was: "Never end at the bottom of the page—bring it over—or stop two lines above it, that the Depute may have a broken page." Extending the document was obviously the best tactic, for it gave the keeper a full page, the deputy a broken page, and the clerk an extra fourpence. The customer was swindled, but everyone in the office gained.[34]

Another way of augmenting fees was to reduce the number of lines on the register's pages and increase the size of the clerks' writing, thus making the customer pay for more completed pages. Although the number of words and lines on a page were determined by law, by the 1780s the average number of words on a page was only two-thirds of the legal minimum. Again, everyone in the office profited from this practice.[35]

Such stratagems to increase the size of fees were not, within government administration, regarded as reprehensible in the eighteenth century, for they were the norms by which the system of patronage was sustained. Admittedly, there was never enough patronage to satisfy demand in Scotland, but manipulating that which was available enabled it to trickle down the social scale. As the largesse spread, deference grew in strength and effectiveness. From an economic standpoint this patronage society perhaps was inefficient, but it had other, more important functions: through the mechanism of friendship it reinforced social ties, strengthened the spirit of hierarchy and the status quo, and, of course, was a welcome source of financial resources. Custom, which defined acceptable practices and licit perquisites, legitimized patronage and stopped it from degenerating into anarchy. There were ground rules to which those who played the game adhered, and while they did so the system worked smoothly (and silently).[36]

In the 1780s, however, the security and stability of the Sasine Office were disturbed by the actions of staff prepared to breach convention and to overmanipulate the system. The innovations that created unrest went beyond the usual sharp practices to outright fraud by successive sub-substitutes. David McPherson had for five or six years charged the public for fictitious pages, using a double bookkeeping system and pocketing the extra fees. An affable man, McPherson charmed the legal agents into acquiescence. His successor, Steele, continued the practice, but his abrasive character soon caused disquiet. He responded to charges concerning the high cost of sasines by publicly blaming the clerks, whom he accused of writing in too large a hand. Steele thus broke convention in two ways: his manipulations were to his advantage alone, and he caused dissension within the office itself.[37]

At some point in 1785 Callender, representing all the clerks, in very oblique terms complained to Keeper Stuart about Steele's behavior. An investigation by Robertson and Leslie, because they had no knowledge of the double bookkeeping, failed to uncover any malpractice. Steele thereupon repaid the clerks by surveying their writing habits and persuading Robertson to raise the number of words per page by 20 percent. Effectively this was a wage cut of the same percentage for the clerks, and it left Steele free to create fictitious pages at will. In July 1786 Callender alerted Leslie to Steele's high-handed manner with the customers; as a result Steele was threatened with dismissal if his conduct failed to improve.[38]

Steele nevertheless continued to charge for fictitious pages and also discovered other ways of maximizing his profits. The Sasine Act of 1617 insisted that a writ be registered within forty-eight hours of presentment, but as the volume of work increased it became impossible to fulfill this clause. By the late eighteenth century lawyers tried to minimize the inevitable delays by paying the fees in advance. Steele took advantage of this practice to create a new "office rule," by which change from advanced fees would no longer be returned. Furthermore, in 1788 Steele, on his own initiative, again raised the number of words on a page and abandoned the distinction between English and Latin words (the latter, used for registering taillies, were longer and therefore were expected to take up more space). A letter of complaint from a clerk called Hewat was returned unopened by the new deputy, John Davidson. At the same time, Steele was charging clients from his own law firm less than the rest of the public.[39]

Thus by 1789 harmony within the Sasine Office had broken down, with Steele farming the system for personal profit as effectively as he could. He was bilking Stuart and the clerks by crowding the legitimate pages and fining the latter when they transgressed. He was also defrauding the public by charging for fictitious pages. Much of the blame must rest with the officers, who failed to control their overseer. As Callender was to tell Stuart, "Confidence abused, has been for ten years past, the bane of the Sasine Office. Mr. Robertson when Deputy trusted everything to Mr. Leslie, and, he, again, trusted everything . . . to Mr. Steele. The result was such as might have been expected. . . . Mr. Steele's plain design is, by contracting the number of real pages, to prevent the public from grudging at the charge of fictitious ones."[40]

Eventually, because "much noise has been made about the extravagance of the fees in the Sasine Office, and this has been uniformly attributed to the selfishness of the Sub Clerks," Callender took advantage of one of Stuart's very rare visits to Scotland to lay a series of charges against Steele, in which he claimed, in addition to "enormous" peculation—"He politely pilfers 50 pounds a year"—that "there is no species of misconduct, no imaginable method of blundering in private or of giving offence in public of which your present substitute has not been guilty." In collusion with his embittered colleagues, Callender sought a rise in salary for the clerks, to sixpence a page, and threatened to expose Steele's activities in a pamphlet which would guarantee "the annihilation of the General Register."[41]

Hearing of Callender's complaints, Steele "instantly came over with pistols and a bludgeon in order to murder" him, greatly alarming Callender's family. For several days thereafter Steele conspicuously flaunted his pistols in the Sasine Office. There was not, claimed Callender, "an assistant Clerk about the Sasine Office who has not heard him solemnly vow my destruction." Such a display of naked hostility was unnecessary, for Stuart ignored Callender's charges. Increasingly frustrated, he addressed the keeper twice more, in one letter seeking "very moderate" personal compensation for the insults he had received. Rather naively, he assumed that Stuart, whom Steele was cheating as well as the clerks, would intervene. "Truth," he told Stuart, "requires no tenderness of investigation and disdains all subterfuges." Perhaps so, but in the world of patronage, when consensus over the distribution of the spoils system broke down and those at the bottom of the hierarchy began to protest, the truth was easily ignored.

The officers closed ranks against the new threat of the clerks acting in unison. Within a matter of months Callender was dismissed from the Sasine Office.[42]

V

His years in the Sasine Office were important to Callender, for they brought him into contact with what appeared to be a sink of corruption and an organized form of state asset-stripping. His experiences gave a particular focus to the general insights that he had learned from Swift's writings. He obtained firsthand knowledge of the patronage system at its base and came to realize that "Old Corruption" infected everyone. Even the clerks, on the very lowest rung of the ladder, were dragged into the spoils system through the mechanism of piecework, until they became expendable once they showed signs of an independent train of thought.

Moreover, through the task of registering taillies, Callender gained an insight into the realities of Scottish politics. He became aware of how easy it was for the powerful, by satisfying the self-interest of individuals, to manipulate the political system. Thereafter he would rarely feel confident in the effectiveness of any plans for political reform. Debased human nature would always find a way of profiting from even the purest of political structures. If it remains unclear, therefore, why Callender's outlook on the world had been so gloomy in 1782, his misanthropy in 1790 is much more explicable. The theoretical tenets that he had gleaned from Calvinism and from Swift had been given credence by the injustices he had seen occur in the Sasine Office. His political opinions were now on a far firmer footing.

In one major way, however, Callender's failure to persuade Stuart to intervene in the affairs of the Sasine Office was potentially disastrous. In 1787 Callender had passed the examination and paid the necessary fee to the Court of the Lord Lyon to become a registered messenger-at-arms in Edinburgh. This was, and remains so today, a paralegal occupation involving the executing of writs from the Court of Session (for civil cases) and the Court of Justiciary (for criminal cases). Thus this was a relatively prestigious position and would have considerably enhanced Callender's social status and importance in the community. Messengers-at-arms had two badges of office: a silver blazon stamped with the king's arms, which they wore on their coats, and a small wand or rod, which represented their authority to execute their judicial duties. For someone of Callender's apparently menial social background, these badges of office, displayed in the streets of Edinburgh, would have reflected his rise in the world.[43]

To be a messenger-at-arms indicated the possession of certain skills. The examination at the Lyon Court ensured some exclusivity, for applicants had to demonstrate "literature qualifications and good conversation," as well as provide bonds from two respectable individuals "of credit" who were prepared to act as guarantors of one's good character and to accept financial liability for any malversation on a messenger's part in the exercise of his duties. The guarantors for Callender's conduct remain unknown.[44]

There is no evidence that Callender performed the duties of a messenger-at-arms while he was working at the Sasine Office. The long office hours would probably have reduced his opportunities of additional employment. In any case, too many qualified messengers existed for the available work. A significant number of applicants probably qualified just for the status involved, in the same way that many lawyers obtained their qualifications with no intention of practicing.[45]

The messengers' work was distributed by the lawyers involved in the cases for which the writs were issued. Callender was thus in a perfect position in the Sasine Office to bring himself to the attention of future employers, for lawyers brought the property transaction documents to the department for recording. He no doubt felt that he had another occupation to fall back on if he ever decided to leave the Sasine Office. But the circumstances of his dismissal in 1790 put his alternative job at risk, for there can be little doubt that Steele blackened Callender's name with visiting lawyers. It would have been a simple matter to have hinted that Callender was dismissed because he could not be trusted. Within the legal profession Callender was branded as a troublemaker. Whatever advantage Callender may have gained from working in the Sasine Office was quickly lost. His attempts to defeat corruption had cost him both his future prospects and his reputation.

Grub Street, Poetry, and Patronage

I

In 1790 Callender was thirty-two years old, with a wife and family to support. It is not known whom or when he married, but certainly by 1789 his wife had borne at least one, and probably more, children. He and his family lodged in one of the large tenements in Canal Street, situated close to the bridge that linked the Old Town of Edinburgh with the New Town. His landlord was James Webster, second son of the Presbyterian minister Dr. Alexander Webster, who himself owned much property in the High Street area. As in Paris and other major European cities at this time, Edinburgh's housing was socially mixed, with what had once been upper-class town houses subdivided into apartments. These tenements, or "lands" as they were called in Edinburgh, were virtually palimpsests of the structure of society, for each story was inhabited by a particular social group. Tradesmen and artisans lived on the ground floor, wealthy middle-class merchants and professionals occupied the middle floors, and scions of the aristocracy inhabited the top floor. All the apartments were reached from a common staircase. In only one way did these tenements fail to reflect the contemporary social structure. The poorest inhabitants lived not below the rest but in the insalubrious garrets.[1]

In Callender's time this social mix was beginning to break down, as population increase, which between mid-century and the 1790s was nearly 50 percent in Edinburgh, put pressure on available housing stock and encouraged the wealthy to seek a more genteel environment. For Callender, who as a poorly paid clerk almost certainly lived on the ground floor, the prospect of moving up a floor would have seemed attractive, but in 1790 his aspirations would have been replaced by fears that focused on the possibility of shifting to the garrets. With neither job nor good prospects, thanks to Steele, he must have seen the abyss of poverty and degradation opening up before him and his family. His reputation for insubordination and rebelliousness would have reduced further opportunities both as a messenger-at-arms and as a clerk, even if he had been prepared to continue the soul-destroying existence of working in an office. Seemingly totally reliant on his own resources, his pen remained his only possible means of salvation. To assail the citadel of the aristocracy of letters was the obvious next step, although the prospect of Grub Street, where authors "write for bread, and are paid by the sheet," threatened if he failed.[2]

Entry into the world of Scottish letters was difficult to achieve. In the 1780s Edinburgh was in the midst of a printing and publishing boom, as dozens of aspiring authors flocked to take advantage of the capital's reputation as "the Athens of the North." Spawned by the successes of the Scottish Enlightenment and basking in the reflected glory of Adam Smith, David Hume, Lord Kames, and William Cullen, a literary subworld of journalism, science, philosophy, and the arts mushroomed in the wynds, closes, and alleys of Edinburgh Old Town, made up of aspiring literati who had found that talent alone did not ensure fame or fortune. Edinburgh's literary world was effectively controlled by a small group of intellectuals who determined taste and presided over a Scotland which was a cultural province of Hanoverian England. Their patronage defined success or failure, and their presence helped to create an ambivalence in the world of Scottish letters, for a tension existed between an urbane Augustan style of literature, which looked to England for example and before which Scottish social elites genuflected, and a vernacular literature which emphasized aspects of Scotland's historic and independent past. Without the imprimatur of the literati a career as a writer was virtually impossible.[3]

Throughout the 1780s Callender had maintained some links with the Edinburgh literary world, for he claimed to have attended social occasions at which he heard Adam Smith in conversation. But it is clear that he was an onlooker rather than a participant in these intellectual soirees. At this point, Callender was apparently unassuming in the company of his social superiors and displayed no signs of seeking the glare of publicity. In 1792, as a member of the Scottish Friends of the People, he showed no inclination to take a leading part in their public deliberations, being content to act in a supportive role. When in 1798 a group of Federalists were openly harassing him in Richmond, Virginia, Callender told Thomas Jefferson: "Horace brags of being pointed at. My ambition does not run in that way." It was only after his arrest and imprisonment in 1800 that he showed unmistakable evidence of courting public attention for himself rather than for his Republican ideas. That he then took self-publicity to extreme lengths suggests the reaction of someone who was belatedly bursting out of an austere Calvinist straitjacket. Rather prim and puritanical, ever conscious of his marginality, and with a cynical attitude toward his surroundings, Callender in the 1780s remained on the fringes of polite society, an increasingly frustrated outsider looking in on a high-powered intellectual world.[4]

Callender's milieu was thus not that of the Royal Society of Edinburgh or the exclusive Newtonian Club, where elite cultural supremacy was exercised. Rather, his social life revolved around unstructured and informal gatherings and possibly also some of the less exclusive clubs and societies. Late eighteenth-century Edinburgh, as most other urban centers where the ideals of polite Augustan society prevailed, was crammed with places where both men and women could meet to indulge in relaxing and enjoyable conversation and where, in theory, urban and urbane became synonymous. Respectable taverns, coffee shops and eating houses abounded, their rooms used for various clubs and societies. "Edinburgh was celebrated for its social clubs and literary or debating societies. There were institutions existing for all classes. . . . The excitement of debate was the passion of the hour." The Pantheon, for example, was a debating society open to all classes, "where the grand concerns of the nation are debated by a set of juvenile Ciceros"; it had as one of its purposes "to relieve literary merit in distress," and every "liberty of speech, and freedom of debate" were allowed. Although the historian of these clubs has argued that they functioned more to entertain than to educate a growing middle-class public, some of the subjects of debate had strong political overtones. "Whether unlimited toleration in religion would be advantageous to a state?" and "Whether the British legislature could alter the Articles of the Union?" were two serious issues discussed at the Pantheon when James Boswell was in attendance.[5]

But in the tenement cellars a rougher and more twilight world of tavern and eating-house life encouraged informal discussions, possibly of a speculative nature, among artisans, journeymen, small shopkeepers, impoverished students, and those on the fringe of polite society. Similar groups intermingled in bookstores such as Berry and Robertson's in Bridge Street or William Creech's in the High Street. According to the Whig lawyer Henry Cockburn, Creech's bookshop was "the natural resort of lawyers, authors and all sorts of literary idlers. . . . All who wished to see a poet or a stranger, or to hear the public news, the last joke by Erskine, or yesterday's occurrence in the Parliament House, or to get the publication of the day or newspapers— all congregated there." Callender would certainly have been one of those browsing through the new publications in the bookshops or examining John Kay's latest caricature in the window of his small printshop in Parliament Square. In 1794 the Philadelphia bookseller and publisher Mathew Carey accused Callender—who ought to have been composing a new edition of Guthrie's *Geography*—of "listening away your time in bookstores and elsewhere."[6]

According to Nicholas Phillipson, "voluntary societies proliferated [in Edinburgh] throughout the century, creating a complex network of sympathetic relationships which extended from an aristocratic social elite through the professions to the population of young, upwardly mobile men of humbler origins which every centre of government and politics necessarily attracts." Particular examples of the talented being elevated by patronage, however, do not prove them to be the norm, for it is not known what proportion of hopeful social climbers failed to impress. Even Robert Burns considered emigrating to the West Indies before his first successes, and he also ensured that the world knew of the lack of patronage that drove another poet, the clerk Robert Fergusson, to an early grave. James Mill, son of a cobbler and father of a philosopher, by his own abilities and "some timely patronage" received a university education in Edinburgh, but he had to take the highroad to London in 1802 "to earn an arduous living by literature." There he promoted the meritocratic ideal of intellectual powers rather than wealth or birth as prerequisites for leadership.[7]

The careers of the engraver John Kay and of Callender's friend and fellow clerk William Gillan were more typical than either Burns's or Mill's. Kay (1742–1830) was a barber in Edinburgh when one of his customers, Nisbet of Dirleton, took an interest in his sketching ability. Moving to Nisbet's countryseat, Kay neglected his job in favor of his artistic interests. Nisbet financed Kay's wife and eleven children who remained in Edinburgh and promised to leave Kay "a permanent provision for independence" on his death. Kay's patron reneged, however, leaving him "in somewhat awkward circumstances, having, as it were, fallen to the ground between certainty and hope." Nisbet's heir, with an annuity of £20 sterling, saved Kay from penury. Returning to Edinburgh, Kay totally abandoned the hairdressing trade to sell his engraved prints and painted miniatures. The latter were more profitable, but it was engraving that fascinated Kay, much to the disgust of his second wife.[8]

William Gillan was Callender's friend and colleague in the Sasine Office. Their lives followed a similar path until, seeking better prospects, Gillan moved to London, where he again worked as a clerk. Interested in literature, he was involved in at least one of Callender's publishing ventures in Edinburgh and had connections with fellow Scottish literati in London. He is last heard of in 1792 planning to join the East India Company in a final attempt to achieve success. "I have," he wrote to Callender, "met with so many disappointments already in my small progress through the world that I allow my hopes to be as little sanguine as possible."[9]

This would be a suitable epitaph for all those aspiring young men who poured into Edinburgh at the height of its fame, only to find that the world of literature was closed to them, for there is good reason to believe that in the 1780s, as elite society became less flexible, avenues of advancement into the highest circles closed up. In the Scottish incorporated societies established since the 1770s "there was an unmistakable division upwards: aristocrats, intellectuals, and scholars separated themselves and gathered together in societies which were no longer open to those in the middle ranks of society." Landed society was increasingly giving up the Edinburgh season altogether, leaving the capital's social life in the hands of the professional classes and petty gentry, who saw little prestige in patronage.[10]

The French Revolution, causing fears and doubts among the very conservative Scottish elites, accelerated this process of withdrawal, even before a Scottish reform movement established itself. In 1791 the popularity of open debating societies such as the Pantheon declined. University students, always a voluble part of the audience, established their own exclusive societies, where they were able to discuss more daring political topics. It was not accidental that at least four prominent members of the Friends of the People were medical students, two of whom—John Edmonds Stock and Alexander Aitchison—were to be involved in Robert Watt's revolutionary conspiracy of 1794.[11]

II

In 1790, for one of the only times in Callender's life, fortune seemed to smile on him. Some of his poetry caught the attention of one of the few in the Scottish nobility who were both interested in literature and held mildly progressive views. Francis Garden, Lord Gardenstone (1721–1793), was the only member of the Scottish bench to have taken an active part in the burgh reform movement since its inception in 1782. He was also noted for his literary patronage, being the first to recognize and to promote the talents of the poet James Beattie, author of "The Minstrel" and later professor of moral philosophy and logic at Marischal College, Aberdeen. David Loch (d.1780), a writer on Scottish commerce, was also Gardenstone's "Bottle Companion and protégé." Spending part of the year at his countryseat of Morningside, near Edinburgh, Gardenstone attracted a group of aspiring young literary figures: "The young and frolicsome delighted in his society." Unmarried, eccentric—he kept a pig in his bedroom over which he draped his breeches to keep it warm—a poet, and mildly reformist, Gardenstone was predictably frowned upon by his fellow peers both for his behavior and for "the secondary sort of company" he kept. He was, wrote William Forbes, never "very choice in the selection of his convivial associates."[12]

His patronage was a boon to Callender in a number of ways. In August 1790 Gardenstone sent two letters of reference on Callender's behalf to prospective employers, one of which helped him obtain the post of messenger-at-arms to the lawyer James Balfour. No longer would Callender have to free-lance as a messenger; he was now guaranteed the work from Balfour's firm. Balfour would not have been swayed by Steele's whispers against Callender, for he had been one of the few lawyers prepared to complain of Steele's behavior in the Sasine Office. On one occasion in 1788 he had told Steele that "he would pay only what he pleased and actually struck off eight or ten *real* pages" from his account. Steele, blustering, had backed down. Balfour thus regarded Callender's experiences at the Sasine Office with some sympathy. Moreover, Gardenstone informed Callender that, unlike many hard-nosed prospective employers, Balfour would "not like you the worse for being a Good Poet."[13] Gardenstone had temporarily solved Callender's most pressing problem; the threat of garret life receded if it did not totally disappear, for it is unlikely that Balfour's law practice generated sufficient work to keep Callender regularly employed.

The quality of the verse that attracted the eccentric judge is difficult to assess, owing to Callender's preference for anonymity. Gardenstone was impressed by some of Callender's poems in the *Star* and the *Edinburgh Magazine*.[14] Other poems, of variable quality, were published under Callender's pseudonym of "Timothy Thunderproof."[15] These represent only a fraction of the verses Callender wrote. On the basis of internal evidence, it appears that many of the poems first published in *Miscellanies in Prose and Verse* in 1791, and since attributed to Gardenstone, were Callender's. Some of the poems in this volume, which Gardenstone and Callender coedited, were probably the joint production of the young men who met at Morningside. They are in the libertine tradition of the earl of Rochester, Jonathan Swift, and John Wilkes, the sort of mildly erotic and misogynist verse one would expect to emerge from the all-male society surrounding the unmarried judge.[16]

Other poems in the volume are in the satirical style of "the immortal Swift."[17] They are almost certainly Callender's rather than Gardenstone's. They express in verse social and political views that Callender was developing in his prose writings, and they are written from the perspective of a young, marginal cynic. Callender's misanthropy is again evident:

> *Such is the in-born baseness of mankind,*
> *A grateful heart We seldom hope to find.*[18]

In "On the Death of a Friend"—definitely Callender's work—he regreted:

> *That modest Merit rarely meets her due;*
> *That happiness recedes as we pursue.*[19]

The young were naive and believed:

> *That native merit their success insures;*
> *That she they sigh for has a heart like yours.*
> *But soon, by life's calamities opprest,*
> *Conviction, bursting on the tortur'd breast,*
> *Their blasted hopes the bitter truth reveal,*
> *That men may talk of what they do not feel.*[20]

The harking back to the pamphlets of 1782 and 1783 was continued in "The Diversities of Life" and "Sketches of Celebrated Characters, Ancient and Modern," with satirical attacks on Dr. Johnson ("Pomposo") and his friends James Boswell and Joseph Warton.[21]

But the views espoused in some of the poems express the maturing of Callender's political opinions, which by 1791 made him one of the most rebellious men in Scotland. One theme in particular that he was to emphasize in his political writings in 1792 was already developed in his verse published a year earlier. In "Imitations of Horace," which brought to one critic's mind "the force and sentimental dignity of Dryden"—and, it might be added, Swift's poetry in the tradition of Horace—Callender condemned the European desire for imperial expansion with its subsequent atrocities against native populations. To castigate Spanish or French imperialism under the Bourbons was a commonplace, but Callender also specifically censured English expansionism, especially in India.

> *Nor let old England, with absurd disdain,*
> *For deeds like these, insult atrocious Spain;*
> *Since, in the task of scourging human kind,*
> *Calm Truth can hardly rank us far behind.*
>
>   . . . . .
> *See! every tie of faith and mercy broke,*
> *Ill-fated Bengal bleed beneath our yoke.*[22]

Callender disparaged the hypocrisy that enabled British poets and historians to condemn conquests by other countries yet to extol the virtues of British arms and British victories. His contempt for this double standard was to fuel his political opinions in ensuing years.

Callender's verse made no great mark on the contemporary literary world, although the eccentric Gardenstone thought it had "more of the true Spirit of Poetry" than Alexander Pope's. A generation later, however, when Gardenstone was thought to be the author, it was regarded with some respect, one critic suggesting it to be the best Scottish satire of the previous fifty years. By that date, as Shelley was to claim, "poets [were] the unacknowledged legislators of the world," but in the 1790s verse, especially of the Augustan rather than the new romantic style, was perhaps not the most effective medium to express the fears, hatreds, and demands that came in the wake of the French Revolution:

> *For almost nobody has taste, or time,*
> *To feel and cultivate the sweets of rhyme.*

The poetic muse abandoned Callender in 1792; thereafter he expressed his political and social views only in prose, which better suited his corrosive talents.[23]

III

The paradox of the patronage system for all men aspiring to fame and independence in the late eighteenth century was that success became possible only by surrendering to the whims and dictates of a patron. Even Robert Burns, the most successful of the rising literary figures, was to feel the full force of official disapproval of his radical politics in 1793–94 and, publicly at least, had to recant. In some respects Callender was more fortunate, in that Gardenstone possessed liberal sentiments that lightened the burden of his patronage. Not obtaining an entrée into the highest social circles was the price that had to be paid for this loosely fitting yoke, for Gardenstone—although a lord of session and thus at the peak of the Scottish hierarchy, as well as a member of several prestigious clubs and societies—was not sufficiently respected by his peers to have much influence. He was, moreover, reclusive and frequently sick; he spent as much time as possible at his countryseat.[24]

Thus Callender had some of the benefits of patronage; but because his patron was a social maverick, he was unable to scale the walls of the establishment. He remained an outsider, albeit a protected one. On the other hand, the freedom he possessed under Gardenstone enabled him to promote his own views, which were aimed at blowing up, rather than scaling, the establishment's outworks. This explains why Callender, although patronized, could continue to attack the patronage system. In one of his poems he wrote, with some pride:

> *To pomp or pathos I make no pretence,*
> *But range in the broad path of common sense.*
>
> . . . . .
>
> *And if, by turns, contemptuous and severe,*
> *Candour must own the verses are sincere;*
> *Nor at a fool's command politely grieve,*
> *Nor vindicate a system none believe;*
> *Nor whet a pimp, nor serve a tyrant's end,*
> *Nor gain their sire a farthing or a friend.*[25]

The patronage system was abhorrent and independence-sapping; it usually "suffered [the victim] to live poor, and die bankrupt."[26]

Gardenstone's lines of social communication lay with the tiny elite opposition to Henry Dundas's dominance of the Scottish political system. Within this milieu Callender began his political pamphleteering. His first opportunity came with the growing disenchantment of the big Scottish brewers with the Excise Service, which for many years had been corruptly managed in Scotland and threatened to make Scottish beers uncompetitive with English imports. The basic cause of corruption was the practice of augmenting the salaries of both the solicitor of excise and his officers by allowing them portions of the fines exacted from brewers found guilty of smuggling. This practice, which was intended to encourage the efficient implementation of the excise laws, only inspired the officers to force brewers into illegal practices, thereby increasing the volume of fines. Various stratagems were used to this end. The excisemen, for example, were deliberately lax in overseeing the breweries and thus encouraged the production of illicit brews. Then a sudden crackdown brought in a host of fines. Even the most law-abiding brewers were forced into illegal practices to prevent their products being undercut. On other occasions partiality in the amount of fines, with some paying 2.5 percent and others 80 percent of the legal penalty, produced the same effect. All brewers were forced to produce illegal supplies in order to remain competitive.[27]

When in 1789 the big Edinburgh brewers put into operation a new scheme whereby they all agreed faithfully to pay the excise and not to smuggle, Solicitor of Excise Bonar broke the cartel by levying only one-third of the duties on selected brewers. At this point Hugh Bell, a burgh reformer who owned an extensive brewery in Edinburgh, employed Callender to write a pamphlet condemning the Excise Service and its corrupt practices. This pamphlet, the product of Callender's pen rather than, as has been thought, Bell's, was published in the autumn of 1791. With his firsthand knowledge of the workings of "Old Corruption" from his days in the Sasine Office, Callender was the ideal author.[28]

The primary purpose of the pamphlet, wrote Callender, was to warn landholders and farmers who supplied raw materials that the Scottish brewing industry was threatened with collapse, owing "to the oppressive mode of collecting revenue" by the "subordinate agents of excise." Explaining in great detail how corruption pervaded the Excise Service and how the brewers' attempts to self-regulate the industry had been thwarted, Callender displayed a bold willingness to go beyond mere generalities and publicly to name offenders, a reckless approach which most pamphleteers in the eighteenth century were careful to avoid. Bonar was "a devil in a club of witches," at one time illegally siphoning off £1,800 sterling a year by his manipulation of the system. As in his pamphlets on Johnson and in some of his poetry, Callender felt under no obligation to temper his views or to spare personal feelings. There were no gray areas in his perception of the world; individuals were either right or wrong, good or bad. Callender's was an artless and angry view of life which was to cause him endless trouble throughout his career.[29]

An Impartial Account of the Excise was not, however, merely a catalog of specific abuses; it was also Callender's first stealthy attempt to transpose Swift's ideas on Ireland to his own country and to propagate Scottish nationalist opinions. Callender began the pamphlet by ridiculing the convention that the British Constitution of 1688 protected every citizen: "Puffed up by a consciousness of the excellence of the constitution under which we live, and intoxicated with the idea that we are the most free people in the world, we tamely submit to see our constitutional rights invaded, and our liberties daily trampled upon, by a set of designing and interested men." He then suggested that under this constitution the Scots suffered more than the English. In England excise officers had no compelling reason to act corruptly, for they did not receive part of their earnings from fines. But there was an ulterior motive for their Scottish counterparts retaining this privilege: it was part of a conspiracy to destroy Scotland's industries and to bring the country totally under England's heel. Already, claimed Callender, the Scottish starch and soap industries had been undermined and a disaster in the spirits industry only narrowly averted. It was now the turn of the brewers. Without a common excise policy, implemented equally throughout Britain, £200,000 sterling would drain across the border to England each year just to pay for beer. Scotland's would become even more emphatically a client economy.[30]

Callender needed to be circumspect with his nationalist views. Not only did they smack of treason, but they were also unpalatable to his paymasters. Although many of the brewers were to join the reform movement in 1792, they were not politically extreme. They sought only minor changes to the political system, ones that would increase the power of the rising middle classes in Scotland. Accordingly, the bulk of Callender's pamphlet was concerned with the specific corruptions within the Excise Service; Scottish nationalist ideas were mentioned only briefly. The brewers seemed to have been content with Callender's performance, for a year later they proposed his compilation of a second pamphlet. He was to have the pleasure of rejecting a bribe of £5 sterling to refuse the brewers' proposal. Before he could proceed, however, Callender was forced to flee the country. "The freedom of the press was now annihilated in Britain; and the brewers of Edinburgh, along with other dissatisfied people, were condemned to silence."[31]

The pamphlet for the brewers was not Callender's only literary enterprise at this time. For a few months after its establishment in December 1790, he was assistant editor for James Anderson's magazine the *Bee*. He worked with Gardenstone on the *Miscellanies* project, for which he wrote a life of George Buchanan. In 1792 John Kay employed him to write potted biographies for his caricatures of notable figures, which he intended to publish in a collected edition. This would have been a congenial pursuit, for Kay had reformist sympathies and produced likenesses of radical leaders such as David Downie, Thomas Muir, Thomas Paine, and Thomas Hardy of the London Corresponding Society. Paine's print was so popular that it sold at fourteen shillings a copy. Kay's publishing plans foundered, but some of Callender's work was incorporated into an edition of the caricatures which was eventually published in 1877.[32]

Callender's reduction to this sort of hackwork by 1792 suggests that in the longer term Gardenstone's patronage failed to protect him from poverty. Perhaps Gardenstone was too canny with his money. In 1792 Gillan, only half in jest, congratulated Callender on his political writings: "You tell me," he wrote, "that my old master was much pleased with the political strictures on our country, but did he send five or ten guineas to the author?" Perhaps the reality of Gardenstone's marginal position within Scottish elite society was finally being demonstrated; opportunities could not be found for those writers failing to promote the Dundas line. Nevertheless, Callender remained close to his mentor; one government source in late 1792 called him Gardenstone's "Fidus Achates," and another claimed him to be his lordship's "intimate friend and advisor." In the meantime, as the reform movement in Scotland flourished, Callender read copiously and worked feverishly on the pamphlet that ultimately was to be the cause of his outlawry and flight to the United States.[33]

3

The Political Progress of Britain

I

In January 1792 Callender began writing his political testament, the distillation of ten years' deliberation on British society. In its original form it was published, between February and June, as a series of eight letters in the *Bee*.[1] With the rapid progress of the radical movement in Scotland from July he began to revise it in pamphlet form, the first edition of which was published in Edinburgh and London in the autumn of 1792.[2] Almost immediately he started work on a second volume, which was not, however, to be published until 1795.[3]

The Political Progress of Britain was the only lengthy treatise vehemently attacking British political institutions to be published in Scotland during the era of the French Revolution. It was also the only one to promote the virtues of Scottish nationalism and of Scottish independence from England. Although fear of arrest prevented Callender from openly avowing revolution, *The Political Progress of Britain* was one of the most inflammatory, undeferential, and militant texts to be published in the 1790s. As a pungent critique of imperialism, war, and corruption only Thomas Paine's *Rights of Man* could rival it. It is strange that —particularly as it was an early Scottish nationalist tract—its significance has for so long gone unnoticed.

The Political Progress of Britain was also important because it reflected so clearly the revolutionary potential of the Grub Street mentality. Its sources derived from the milieu of the literary mandarins, but it interpreted the world from the very different social perspective of the marginal literary adventurer. A similar perspective became revolutionary in contemporary France, introduced into the Revolution by the hundreds of hack writers, such as Marat, Brissot, Desmoulins, and Collet d'Herbois, who bubbled to the surface after the fall of the Bastille. They, like Callender, had failed to scale the heights of the High Enlightenment in the 1780s. In June 1789 P. J. B. Gerbier wrote of Paris: "Where does so much mad agitation come from? From a crowd of minor clerks and lawyers, from unknown writers, starving scribblers, who go about rabblerousing in clubs and cafés. These are the hotbeds that have forged the weapons with which the masses are armed today." In the careers of these "famished scribblers," "poor hacks," and "riffraff of literature," one can envision what Callender might have accomplished if a Scottish revolution had occurred.[4]

II

It was as a historian that Callender attempted to promote his political views. He claimed that *The Political Progress of Britain* offered "an impartial history of the abuses of government." Truly it was more a work of historical polemic than of contemporary political theory, but, like most "histories" of that era, impartial it was not. Nor was Callender's methodology modern in the style of David Hume, William Robertson, Catherine Macaulay, and Sir John Dalrymple. They, sometimes spasmodically, consulted primary documents; Callender essentially compiled his pamphlet from secondary sources—Swift, Hume, Tobias Smollett, Dalrymple, Sir John Sinclair, Dr. James Anderson, and Adam Smith. This is perhaps understandable, for although he had access to Gardenstone's library at Morningside, his work and family commitments in Edinburgh reduced his opportunities to consult primary materials, even if he had so wished. It is unlikely he owned many books himself; fringe writers of his kind normally had to rely on friends or fellow scribblers for the loan of specific books. This is not to suggest, however, that *The Political Progress* was a typical hack writer's scissors-and-paste account of British history and politics, for it had several well-defined objectives, it was logically organized (in its pamphlet form at least), and it was not padded with extraneous material. Admittedly it ends rather abruptly, but the publishing limitations on pamphlet size explain this; Callender regarded the pamphlet as the first in a series.[5]

Unsurprisingly, Callender had a low opinion of those historians who were part of the established literati and thus without independence. Seemingly unconscious of the irony, he wrote that "in Britain, men of independent fortune will seldom submit to the drudgery of writing history, and little can be expected from an author whose dinner depends on the sale of his book." Historians acted cravenly and without principle by glorifying "the war system" that sustained the Whig interpretation of England's past. "One chief incentive to British wars," he wrote, "hath been the inflammatory and vaunting style of most of our historians. Violations of public faith have been applauded, and acts of barbarity related with exultation. Volumes upon volumes have resounded panegyrical portraits of kings and courtiers, who were in reality the dregs of the human race."[6]

Callender did not castigate all historians. Sir John Dalrymple and James Macpherson of Ruthven were honorable exceptions, for they had demonstrated their independence by publishing evidence inimical to the Whig view of history, even though their own sympathies were

Whiggish. But because they had "laid open an abyss of [Whig] political perfidy," they were persecuted and induced to give up writing.[7]

Callender also praised for their independence of spirit historians attached to groups in opposition to the Whig grandees. He approved, for example, Swift's view that modern history "contains nothing but the very worst effects which avarice, faction, hypocrisy, perfidiousness, cruelty, rage, madness, hatred, envy, lust, malice, or ambition can produce." Hume too should have been another exception. Callender ought to have sympathized with a man who was for much of his life an outsider, who sought to write a truly impartial history of England, and who used history to criticize those having "a stranglehold on places, positions, and literary taste." In fact Hume, whose skepticism naturally appealed to Callender, was—with Swift—a major source of his historical data, but as "in Mr. Hume's history of England doctrines of despotism are almost everywhere inculcated"—although artfully he "occasionally intermixed sentiments that will admit of an opposite construction"—he could not be included in the pantheon of honorable historians.[8]

Callender's criticisms of historians reflect, of course, his own ambitions as well as his desire to destroy the Whig interpretation of history that, by the 1790s, was almost totally dominant. His tactics were deliberately to transpose his and the Whig historians' respective positions and to suggest that because their reputations rested on Establishment approval, they could not afford to be independent, whereas he, an interloper, had nothing to lose and could therefore tell the whole truth. "The first duty of a writer," he replied to a critic in June 1792, "is to be *consistent with himself.*" If well-to-do historians who offered a non-Whig interpretation could be browbeaten into silence, and the literati constrained by their dependence on elite approval, the cause of Truth must be left in the capable hands of the penurious, patronageless, but therefore truly independent pamphleteers. "In Britain, authors of pamphlets have long conducted the van of every revolution. They compose a kind of forlorn hope on the skirts of battle; and though they may often want experience, or influence to marshall the main body, they yet enjoy the honour and the danger of the first rank, in storming the ramparts of oppression." Pamphleteers could use evidence from "Tory" historians as well as Whigs in order to arrive at the "independent" truth. Thus Callender, even though personally disapproving of the historical opinions of Hume and Smollett, could happily draw on their materials to support a partisan onslaught on Whig historiography.[9]

Callender's self-imposed duty was to expose the machinations of the governing classes and to demystify their shibboleths by offering an "impartial" history of British politics since 1688. To achieve this aim he had to destroy the myth of the British Constitution, the totem behind which the propertied had gathered in 1792, as the popular reform societies gathered momentum in Britain and the Revolution in France slipped toward confusion and terror. There was no need for sudden political or social reform, the propertied claimed, because the 1688 Revolution, and the subsequent Act of Settlement and Act of Union, had established a British Constitution that guaranteed everyone's liberties under the rule of law. Change, if it were to occur, should proceed piecemeal, as had always been the case.[10] Nonsense, replied Callender, the British Constitution was a phantom aimed at protecting the wealthy: "What 'our excellent constitution' may be in theory, I neither know nor care. In practice, it is altogether A CONSPIRACY OF THE RICH AGAINST THE POOR."[11]

Nor was the source of the Whig Constitution, the Revolution of 1688, such a glorious event as the propertied and "the idle writers who pester us with fulsome panegyrics on *our present happy establishment*" claimed.

> What *glory* can be annexed to the affair, it is not easy to see. An infatuated old tyrant was deserted by all the world and *fled* from his dominions. His people chose a successor. This was natural enough, but it had no connection with *glory*. . . . The characters of the leaders in the revolution will not justify a violent encomium on the purity of their motives. The selection of William was reprobated very soon after, by themselves, which excludes any pretence to much political foresight. Here then, is a *glorious* event, accomplished without an actual effort of courage, of integrity, or of wisdom.

In the annals of modern history, he continued, real glory could be found only where the Swiss, the Scots, the Americans, and the Corsicans wrestled for national independence "against the superior forces of despotism." Switching dynasties was a mundane affair, for it was merely moving from one despotism to another. "Since the Norman conquest," Callender declared, "England has been governed, including Oliver Cromwell, by thirty-three sovereigns; and of these, two-thirds were, each of them, by a hundred different actions, deserving of the gibbet."[12]

Their chief ministers aided and abetted British monarchs in their conspiracies against the people. Callender castigated Walpole, Lord North, Chatham, and Pitt the Younger. During Walpole's long tenure British history was "nothing but a dull, uniform, and disgusting scene of treachery." The name "Walpole" became synonymous with bribery. The warlike Chatham was even worse: "With a more destructive minister, no nation was ever cursed." Yet, because of the servility of historians, Chatham's reputation was higher than Walpole's. It should not be, claimed Callender, because Walpole had the inestimable quality of detesting war. Even his institutionalization of corruption faded somewhat in significance before his pacifism: "He therefore differed from his successors in office, as a pickpocket differs from an assassin."[13]

Since 1688 British monarchs and their chief ministers had presided over what Callender called "the system of war and conquest," but which we today would call mercantilism. The lust for foreign luxuries stimulated Britain's bellicosity and was at the root of the evils of Britain's political system. Denouncing the wars with Holland (one), France (five), Spain (six), the "civil wars" in Ireland and Scotland in 1688–89, two rebellions in Britain (1715 and 1745), and "the endless massacres in Asia and America," Callender computed that 30 million people had been killed, £380 million sterling wasted by the British government, and between 16,000 and 20,000 merchant ships lost, leaving a national debt of £250 million sterling. The dead, he wrote, "have been sacrificed to the balance of power, and the balance of trade, the honour of the British flag, the rights of the British crown, the 'omnipotence of Parliament', and the security of the Protestant succession."[14]

Imperialism brought out the worst features of the English: "At home Englishmen admire liberty. . . . Abroad they have always been harsh masters." For the sake of "tea and sugar, and tobacco, and a few other despicable luxuries," he continued,

> what quarter of the globe has not been convulsed by our ambition, our avarice, and our baseness? The tribes of the Pacific Ocean are polluted by the most loathsome of diseases. On the shores of Africa, we bribe whole nations by drunkeness, to robbery and murder. . . . Our brandy has brutalized or extirpated the aborigines of the western continent; and we have hired by thousands, the survivors, to the task of bloodshed. On an impartial examination, it will be found, that the guilt and infamy of this practice, exceed, by a considerable degree, that of any other species of crimes recorded in history.[15]

British belligerence had led to an enormous national debt and to a vast extension of corruption among military officers, politicians, and speculators in government securities. Government fundholders "remind us of a band of usurers, embracing every advantage over the necessities of the state; while the ministers of the crown seem like desperate gamesters, who care not by what future expence they secure another cast of the dice." In the War of American Independence, in addition to the cost of financing the army and navy, £50 million sterling was "happily for mankind, expended in jobs, and bubbles of all kinds, and in bribes to the peers, the house of commons, and their *constituents*." Expenditure on corruption was, nevertheless, preferable to expenditure on yet more mercenaries. Taxes of all kinds, including the despised excise, were extorted to pay for these wars. "After such work," wrote Callender of the wars against Louis XIV, "it is not wonderful that we are now harnessed in debts and taxes, like horses in a carriage."[16]

Students of eighteenth-century British (and American) republicanism will have recognized by now the familiar arguments Callender used in *The Political Progress of Britain* against the Whig political system. His critique, using their linguistic arsenal, closely followed the views of the Commonwealthmen, with their opposition to corruption, a public debt, and high taxation and their fear of the concentration of power leading to the demise of British liberties and the rise of despotism. Like Bolingbroke, Burgh, and American revolutionaries such as John and Samuel Adams, Callender was concerned with dissecting the old conundrum, "Quis custodiet ipsos Custodes?"[17]

Where Callender differed from his contemporaries, however, was in his solutions to the problem of the engrossing of power. In Britain, the solutions of the Commonwealthmen were aimed at a continuous scrutiny of the politically powerful and included a wider franchise (the most radical promoting universal manhood suffrage), annual parliaments, and the ballot. In the United States, one solution relied on checks and balances, either between different parts of the political system or between different interest groups. Commonwealthmen on both sides of the Atlantic believed constrictions on power to be more effective in a republic than in a monarchy.

These responses to the problem of power were justified by alternative theories: the theory of the Ancient Constitution and the theory of natural rights. In the 1790s the theory of the Ancient Constitution, which held that a "democratic" constitution had prevailed in Anglo-Saxon England before the Norman Conquest and ought to be revived, retained considerable vitality, even after the historical evidence buttressing it had been convincingly refuted. At the same time, the ahistorical doctrine of natural rights, which could be traced back to a radical interpretation of John Locke's philosophy, received a major boost from Thomas Paine's enormously influential *Rights of Man*, parts one and two. Like the Commonwealthmen, Paine targeted the monarchy, aristocracy, widespread corruption, and the national debt for his assaults and encouraged the spread of republican ideas.[18]

Callender promoted neither the piecemeal solutions nor the specious justifications for change offered by his contemporaries. As a Scottish nationalist, his neglect of the quintessentially English theory of the Anglo-Saxon constitution is understandable. As a historian he knew that no supporting evidence of an ancient and ideal constitution could be found. "At what era this *freedom* and *virtue* existed, nobody could ever tell. . . . British annals . . . [are] full of calamity and disgrace. . . . Some people talk of restoring the constitution to its *primitive* purity. They would do well to inform us what that purity was and where its traces are to be found."[19]

More surprisingly, however, Callender never once mentioned the doctrine of natural rights in his Scottish writings. His position was premised on an ethical conception of justice and of truth and on a Calvinist-inspired picture of man's depraved nature. In contrast, underpinning Paine's natural rights theory was an optimistic understanding that through the use of reason human nature could be improved and eventually perfected. This was a vision that Callender had never accepted, nor would he ever.

One consequence of Callender's dismissal of reason as an effective engine of improvement was his rejection of the usual political solutions to Britain's ills. He would not accept, for instance, the superiority of republicanism over monarchy. Indeed, following Hume, he specifically emphasized the fact that it was "the Republic of Cromwell" that had devastated Ireland in the seventeenth century, whereas James I and Charles II at least had ensured periods of peace. Democracy, or "mob government" as he called it, Callender also rejected. Nor would annual or triennial parliaments be effective.

> The reader will meet with no mournful periods to the memory of *annual* or *triennial* parliaments; for while the members are men such as their predecessors have almost always been, it is of small concern whether they hold their places for life, or but for a single day. Some of our projectors are of opinion, that to shorten the duration of parliament would be an ample remedy for all our grievances. The advantages of a popular election have likewise been much extolled. Yet an acquaintance with Thucydides, or Plutarch, or Guicciardini, or Machiavel, may tend to calm the raptures of a republican apostle.

If the duke of Richmond's plan for universal suffrage had been adopted in 1782, said Callender, "it is possible that we should at this day, have looked back with regret, on the humiliating yet tranquil despotism of a Scots, or a Cornish, borough."[20]

Callender's dismissal of universal suffrage and annual parliaments as mere bagatelles was predicated not only on his thoroughgoing suspicion of human motivation but also on his awareness of how Scotland was dominated by English interests in London. He preceptively realized that Scotland's position within the British Empire was merely that of a subservient colony, no different from that of the American colonies before 1776. To the English, he wrote, "we were for many centuries a hostile, and are still considered by them as a foreign, and in effect a conquered nation." England had conquered Scotland not by force of arms but by the trickery of the 1707 Act of Union. "It is remarkable that though the Scots are constantly talking of their constitution, and their liberties, the whole fabric is entirely founded on one of the grossest and most impudent acts of usurpation ever known. I refer to the celebrated *Union*. The whole negotiation, bears on its face the stamp of iniquity." In reality, Scottish rights and liberties did not exist, for the Scots were represented in Parliament by timeservers, who were "the mere satellites of the minister of the day; and are too often as forward as others, to serve his most oppressive and despotic purposes." Instead of wasting money electing (or rather, selecting) forty-five Scottish M.P.s, he continued, "an equal number of elbow chairs, placed once for all on the ministerial benches, would be less expensive to government, and just about as manageable." In his opinion, even universal suffrage would not change matters; under parliamentary government with massive patronage at its disposal, the same type of greedy, corrupt politician would continue to be elected.[21]

The only solution, thought Callender, was the complete breakup of Britain, with Scotland obtaining "a wise, virtuous, and *independent* government." No longer would "our southern masters" then be able to destroy all Scottish manufactures that threatened English development. No longer would taxes be spent on foolish wars; instead, investment in domestic improvements would convert "the whole country, like the Swiss cantons, into gardens, corn-fields, and pastures." Only a fraction of the cost of "an ordinary French war" would enable the foundation of a colony of fishermen in the Hebrides which would be "worth all our foreign possessions put together." Population increase, unhindered by warfare, would eventually lead to the establishment of manufacturing villages along the west coast and to a totally self-sufficient Scottish nation. No longer would Scotland, Ireland, and Wales be like "three plants of inferior size, whose natural growth has been stunted by the vicinity of an oak." Tinkering with the mechanism of the British Parliament was thus irrelevant; Callender's vision could be fulfilled only by snapping all connections with the warmongering, corrupt machine in London. Separate development, as the Americans had accomplished, and the Irish hoped to, was the only path to follow.[22]

Unclear from Callender's work are what form of government he wanted for Scotland and how the breakup of Britain was to be achieved. He obviously had no love for monarchical systems, and he seemingly thought little of the achievements of past republics. If he did have a model of government in mind, that of the United States appears the most likely. Certainly Callender preferred a written constitution, and in favorably comparing the relatively short time the Americans took to frame their Constitution with "the six or eight hundred years of botching" taken in England to produce a constitution that supported "political anarchy," he placed himself in league with Paine and his radical colleagues who saw the American experiment as exemplary.[23]

Similarly, like Paine, Callender was reticent on how far he was prepared to go to achieve his political goals. To have countenanced revolution openly in the atmosphere of 1792 would have led inevitably to arrest and imprisonment. Of all the political writers of this time, Callender and Paine came closest to advocating revolution. Both ridiculed and denigrated existing political institutions, and by doing so stripped away the aura of sanctity surrounding them. To what extent Callender was prepared actively to promote his revolutionary vision can only be assessed by examining his role in the radical movement that developed in Scotland from July 1792.

III

When news of the French Revolution reached Scotland in 1789, there were only two small associations—the burgh reformers and the county reformers—representing even the slightest opposition to the political and social hegemony of Henry Dundas, Pitt's manager of North Britain. Both organizations, which were constitutionally separate but had some overlap in membership, had arisen in the early 1780s. Although the burgh reform association was concerned primarily with local issues relating to the nature of town corporations, both it and the county reform movement took spasmodic interest in parliamentary reform. The burgh reformers sought to break down the corrupt town council oligarchies that under the royal burgh franchise chose the delegates who in turn elected the fifteen M.P.s from urban Scotland. In Edinburgh, for example, according to one contemporary Whig, the corporation was "omnipotent, corrupt, impenetrable. Nothing was beyond its grasp; no variety of opinion disturbed its unanimity, for the pleasure of Dundas was the sole rule of everyone of them. . . . Silent, powerful, submissive, mysterious, and irresponsible, they might have been sitting in Venice."[24]

In the counties, the use of taillies to create "parchment barons" had slightly extended an extremely narrow franchise. This had, however, only increased the influence of particular landowners, especially the nouveaux riches, leaving most rural dwellers, including many wealthy landlords, smaller and middling gentry, and tenant farmers, with no political influence at all. The county reform movement sought at most to extend the franchise to smaller landowners, while even the most advanced burgh reformers—who did not include Gardenstone in their number—did not want the vote given to those below their own class. Most of the members of these associations, therefore, remained socially conservative, seeking minimal changes on behalf of the propertied. The most "extreme" burgh and county reformers were Foxite Whigs who supported the moderate and tentative demands of the London Friends of the People.[25]

Callender, of course, had no sympathy with what he regarded as the pusillanimous political views of the county and burgh reformers. On the other hand, before mid–1792 no organization existed in Scotland to represent more radical opinions, although pressure for parliamentary reform had begun to grow and small groups of reformers were meeting spasmodically in Edinburgh and Glasgow. There is no evidence that Callender attended any of these meetings, although his presence would not be surprising. He did, however, manage to forge links with reformers in other parts of the country.

In London, expatriate Scotsmen were involved in the reform movement that began to develop in the first months of 1792. Among these were Dr. Charles Webster (1750–1795), Dr. William Thomson (1746–1817), and Thomas Christie (1761–1796). Webster was both a physician and an Episcopalian minister who owned a bookstore in Edinburgh. He was a relative of James Webster, Callender's landlord, and it is possible that Callender first opened correspondence with the Scots in London either through this connection or through Gardenstone.[26]

William Thomson, the son of a carpenter and farmer "of decent circumstances," received the patronage of the earl of Kinnoul when he attended the University of St. Andrews. Presented to the parish of Monzievard in the Presbytery of Auchterarder, Thomson's moderation in religious matters alienated his parishioners, who were "remarkable for religious gloom and fanatical austerity." He resigned his living, and with an annual pension of £50 sterling from Kinnoul he went to London in the 1780s to seek his fortune as a man of letters. Aided by further patronage from prominent Scotsmen, Thomson became "intimately connected with the literature and eminent literati of the age," editing or writing for a number of journals and magazines, as well as publishing a large number of books of history, travel, biography, and memoirs. In the early years of the French Revolution, like so many of his type, "he suffered his mind to be dazzled, for a time by [the Revolution's] splendours." Regarded by the Scottish M.P. George Dempster as "the best pen we now have belonging to our country in the line of a Public Writer," the Dundas connection bought him off in late 1792.[27]

One of Thomson's fellow Scottish literati in London from the 1780s was Thomas Christie, whose uncle, William Christie, was to establish the first Scottish Unitarian congregation, in Montrose, in 1791. Christie too was involved in magazine publishing, but he is best known for *Letters on the French Revolution* (1791), a reasoned refutation of Burke's *Reflections on the French Revolution*. A strong proponent of complete religious liberty for the individual and politically a mild radical, Christie was a member of the London Friends of the People. In April 1792 he helped to write their "Address to the People;" in the summer he joined the more plebeian and more radical London Corresponding Society.[28]

Callender probably came into contact with these reformers through his and Gardenstone's desire to publish *Miscellanies* in London. In May 1792 the London Scottish reformers contacted Callender via William Gillan to suggest that he set up a patriotic bookshop and publishing firm in Bishopgate Street in London. No competition existed in the area, and Christie offered to introduce him to the principal people in the district. It was thought that Lord Gardenstone would finance Callender if he chose to accept the offer. Callender, believing his prospects to be good in the burgeoning Scottish reform movement, declined and continued writing *The Political Progress* in letter form. Thomson, Christie, and Webster looked elsewhere, and soon afterwards another patriotic bookseller, Daniel Isaac Eaton, moved his bookshop from Hoxton to Bishopgate Street. A member of the London Corresponding Society, Eaton was soon in trouble for publishing and selling banned books, including Paine's *Age of Reason*. Like Callender, he eventually had to flee to the United States; he later returned to London and continued his radical career.[29]

If Callender had chosen to go to London it would have been an admission of defeat, for although he might have rationalized it as an opportunity for advancement, it would not have helped him promote his nationalist pretensions. By the spring of 1792 conditions were deteriorating in Scotland and Callender's hopes of political change were rising. Among artisans, laborers, and shopkeepers—who were the bulk of the radical rank and file in the next few years—disaffection grew as a major economic slump began. Among the Scottish middle classes opposition to the government increased owing to Pitt's unpopular policies, which included the passing of a corn law in 1791 and the rejection of Richard Sheridan's burgh reform motion and dissenters' relief bill in 1792.[30]

At the same time, opposition to the excise laws, which Callender had so ably dissected in the previous year, took on a political coloration. It was increasingly recognized that the landed gentry, who dominated Parliament, out of self-interest deliberately kept excise duties high so that the land tax could be kept low. As John Brims has noted: "By the later part of 1792 the age-old popular opposition to high taxation in general and the excise service in particular had become politicized. The exciseman was no longer simply the object of popular vituperation or assault: he was the personification of 'Old Corruption', the symbolic representative of a hateful political system."[31]

The first signs of this politicization came in the week before anti-Dundas riots broke out in Edinburgh on 4 June, the day set aside to celebrate the king's birthday. A number of handbills circulated, including one calling on tradesmen "and all others who wish well of their Country" to gather on the king's birthday to give "a general salute in the way it was given to Captain Porteous of the Town Guard"—a reference to the Porteous Riots of 1736—"to Mr. Maitland, General Supervisor of the Excise who has been a Scourge to this Country for some years past, and unjust and dishonest in the Execution of his Office to the blackest degree."[32]

The author of this placard remains anonymous, and no evidence implicates Callender. On the other hand, the handbill accused Maitland of taking bribes from the wealthy and "skimming" from the poor who could not afford to bribe him. Callender had made just these accusations himself and even gave an example of a poor "tobacco woman" who was victimized because she could afford to buy her wares only in very small quantities. Even if he was not the author, therefore, Callender had helped to publicize the evidence on which the protest was based. He doubtless watched with some satisfaction as a mob, irate at the introduction of dragoons into Edinburgh on 4 June, burned Dundas in effigy and attacked the homes of both Dundas and his nephew, the lord advocate.[33]

In July 1792 the county and burgh reformers held separate meetings in Edinburgh. Parliamentary reformers awaited the results of their deliberations with interest, hoping that both groups might acknowledge the necessity of parliamentary reform. When they failed to do so, the reformers established the Associated Friends of the People, whose objectives were "to attempt by all Constitutional means, the attainment, first, of an equal Representation of the People; and second, of a more limited duration of Parliamentary Delegation." From the outset, therefore, the society mirrored the aims of the Foxite Friends of the People in London, keeping its demands vague but openly stressing its legality and constitutionalism. The prevention of revolution through moderate reform was its primary aim.[34]

So popular was the Edinburgh society in the next few weeks that it had to be subdivided, with each branch supplying delegates to a central committee. Callender became a member of the Canongate No. 1 branch. Elsewhere in Scotland similar societies sprang up, especially in the autumn and early winter of 1792. Writes Brims, "When the Friends of the People met in Edinburgh in convention on 11 December 1792 they had, by any sober calculation, the backing of a sizeable proportion of the population."[35]

As the movement grew and encompassed the aspirations of artisans, clerks, and small shopkeepers, its character and aims became more various and more radical. There were three tendencies discerned within the movement: committed members of the burgh and county reform movements who followed the policies of the London Foxite Whigs; moderate radicals, who sought to use public opinion to force Parliament to grant the franchise to all males possessing even a small amount of property; and the militant radicals, who thought petitioning Parliament a waste of time. The militants demanded universal suffrage and were prepared to use force to gain their ends.[36]

The group of revolutionary militant radicals within the Friends of the People in Scotland were strongly influenced by Paine's *Rights of Man*, which in the autumn was distributed widely throughout the country.[37] Although Callender's role in the society remains unclear, there is no doubt that he was part of the militant group that met weekly at the Canongate house of a baker called Buchanan. Unlike the Foxite members of the society, whose numbers were sufficient to dominate official policy, Buchanan's group had contacts with the radical London Corresponding Society. Callender, through the links he had forged during the spring, may have helped to initiate this connection.

On only one occasion did a spy's report mention Callender by name, when at a meeting of delegates from the Edinburgh branches he seconded a motion to elect Thomas Muir as vice-president. Callender apparently preferred to work behind the scenes, leaving public activities to more extroverted speakers such as Muir. Although Muir was not an avowed militant, he was on the extreme fringe of the moderate radicals, and like other moderates he sided with the militants on certain issues. He and Callender had many political opinions in common, and they obviously enjoyed each other's company. In 1796, after he had escaped from Botany Bay and was in Monterey in California, Muir wrote to the Scottish lawyer John Millar, Jr. (who was to follow Callender to the United States in 1795): "Great God, can I indulge the delicious idea of meeting so soon, with the friends of man in America, with Priestly, with Cooper, with Russel, and many whose names I cannot possibly know. Do you know where Mr. Thomson Callender is— If you do, present him my remembrance, and tell him I hope to spend some other evenings with him once more. The idea of Reunion, with those whom I love, whom I esteem, will animate my vigour." Callender for his part remained proud of his links with the Scottish radical leaders. "I was their intimate friend," he told Jefferson in 1798, "and quite as deep in the unlucky business as they were."[38]

The Canongate No. 1 branch of the Friends of the People elected Callender as a delegate to the national convention that met in Edinburgh from 11 to 13 December 1792. There, although he remained silent, or at least went unreported, Callender was part of a small, but not uninfluential, group of militants. They were a major nuisance and source of concern to the more moderate delegates, for on 1 December Henry Dundas had issued a royal proclamation against seditious writings in Scotland which inspired an immediate loyalist reaction. The Foxite Whigs, who opposed the calling of a convention but who attended in order to control it, tried to pretend that the militants did not exist; the moderate radicals desperately sought to modify the militants' extreme demands. In reality, the militants remained a minority throughout the convention, although they could not be ignored.[39]

Their presence was felt on the second day when Muir introduced an address from the Dublin Society of United Irishmen, signed by William Drennan and Archibald Hamilton Rowan. It referred to Scotland as a separate nation: the United Irish were pleased that the Scottish reformers "do not consider yourselves as merged and melted down into another Country but that in this great national question you are still Scotland—the land where Buchanan [whose biography Callender had written] wrote, and Fletcher spoke, and Wallace fought." Many at the convention were greatly concerned that these references to nationalist sentiment, combined with certain Painite opinions—"It is not the Constitution but the People which ought to be inviolable"—might be construed as a condemnation of the authority of the British Parliament. The Foxites and many of the moderate radicals believed that if the convention acknowledged the Irish address, they would lay themselves open to charges of treason or misprision of treason.[40]

On three occasions, however, the militants supported Muir's motion for a formal reply to the Irish address before they were finally defeated. Their persistence raises the question of how widespread Scottish nationalist sentiment was among the Friends of the People. Two historians have argued that there was "a strong Scottish nationalist aspect . . . in the early 1790s," but they offer no supporting evidence. Certainly, by the middle years of the decade a desire for national independence was growing in Scotland, and Muir—in France after his adventures around the world—plotted to obtain an independent Scottish republic. But in 1792 his nationalism was muted and unformed, and other evidence for widespread nationalist sentiment remains weak. In January 1793 Lord Daer, a member of both the Scottish and London Friends of the People and of the London Corresponding Society, who had been prominent as a moderate radical at the Edinburgh convention, informed Charles Grey—the future Whig prime minister— that anti-union sentiment in Scotland was strong. "Scotland," he wrote, "has long groaned under the chains of England and knows that its connection there has been the cause of its greatest misfortunes." Daer, anguished at the prospect of the London Friends of the People reneging on their plan to petition Parliament, may have been exaggerating nationalist sentiment in order to influence the Foxites' policies, but what is certain is that he was using Callender's writings to support his point. "We have existed as a conquered province these two centuries," he wrote, echoing *The Political Progress*.[41]

It thus appears that the few nationalist ideas that did exist in Scotland in 1792 and early 1793 stemmed primarily from Callender's work and from his personal influence. His writings underpin the only written evidence supporting nationalist sentiment, and the militants in the Edinburgh convention who supported the Irish address included those who met with Callender at Buchanan's house. Scottish nationalism was not a prominent doctrine in the early stages of Scottish radicalism; but what there was may plausibly be attributed to Callender.

Although the Convention of the Friends of the People rejected the nationalism implicit in the address of the United Irishmen, reports of the debates nevertheless made their way to the lord advocate, Robert Dundas, and to his uncle, Henry Dundas. On 13 December Robert Dundas decided, if he could obtain a copy of the United Irish address, to charge Muir with treason; a copy became available within a few days. He also cast around for suitable ways of implementing the king's proclamation against seditious writings. Inflammatory documents, preferably published in Scotland, were required, whose authors could be prosecuted in order to intimidate the Friends of the People. Two possibilities were found in Scotland: one was the anonymous broadside *To the People and Their Friends*, written by James Tytler and distributed in Edinburgh toward the end of November. Tytler, like Callender, urged his readers to ignore Parliament, which was controlled by "a vile junto of aristocrats," and to petition the king directly to dissolve Parliament and allow the people to elect representatives "of good understanding and character." If the king refused: "Keep your money in your pockets [i.e, refuse to pay taxes], and frame your own laws, and the minority must submit to the majority."[42]

The other literature suitable for prosecution was Callender's *Political Progress of Britain*. The combination of political radicalism and nationalism made it a particularly dangerous document. It was also undoubtedly influential. According to Callender, sales of the pamphlet, both in London and in Edinburgh, had been lively, with five times the original price being offered for copies in the Scottish capital. The 1,000 copies of the Edinburgh edition were quickly sold, and there were requests for 500 more copies in London before the end of the year.[43] Although less obviously seditious than Tytler's, Callender's work reached a much wider audience in 1792 and was of longer-term interest and significance. As well as being reprinted in the United States in its second and third editions in 1794 and 1795, the third edition was also republished in London by Daniel Isaac Eaton in 1795. Deciding that examples must be made, Dundas and John Pringle, the deputy sheriff of Edinburgh, put out feelers to discover the authors of these incendiary documents.

IV

In the later 1790s Callender's enemies used a particular interpretation of events in Edinburgh during the last few weeks before his flight to America to discredit him. Their accusations have colored every subsequent interpretation of his career. Historians have been unanimous in accepting, or at least in not questioning, the contemporary view that Callender, faced with the prospect of arrest for writing *The Political Progress*, saved his own neck by accusing Gardenstone of being the author of both the letters in the *Bee* and the ensuing pamphlet. Biographers of major political figures whom Callender assailed have regarded contemporary opinion maligning Callender's character as useful confirmation of his role as an amoral, hired character assassin, prepared to calumniate individuals of all political persuasions provided the price was right. Thus contemporary libels of Callender are used to discredit Callender's supposed libels of other people, the truthfulness—untested—of the former helping to confirm the falsity of the latter.[44]

It is, however, possible to trace the origins of the allegation that Callender incriminated Gardenstone during his interrogation by deputy sheriff Pringle in 1793. The evidence clearly exonerates Callender and in fact condemns Gardenstone himself, who, anxious to safeguard his position as a lord of session and to protect his social standing, incriminated Callender. The only way he could account for being under suspicion without incriminating himself was to accuse Callender—who had by then fled and was thus unable to refute him—of treacherously implicating him in a project of which he was totally unaware. Gardenstone, and possibly Dr. James Anderson, whom Pringle also interviewed, later assiduously spread this report throughout Edinburgh.[45] A generation later Robert Chambers, in a biographical sketch of Anderson, claimed that the editor of the *Bee* had refused to give the authorities any information, but that "The real author, a worthless person named Callender, being afterwards about to quit his country for America, waited upon the authorities, and insinuated that the papers were written by Lord Gardenstone, a man to whom he owed many obligations. Immediately on hearing of this infamous conduct, Anderson came forward, and refuted the charge by avowing Callender himself to be the real author." Henry Meikle, who in 1912 wrote the most thorough account of Scotland in the period of the French Revolution, accepted this interpretation. To this day the innocence of Gardenstone and Anderson and the treachery of Callender have remained the received opinion in Scotland.[46]

News of Callender's purported treachery reached the United States in 1795, brought there by Rowena Millar, née Cullen, the wife of the lawyer John Millar, Jr. According to Callender, she spread the canard to repay him for having once called her father, the famous doctor and chemist William Cullen, a quack.[47] Her source was probably James Anderson, her father's friend and devotee.[48] Callender's enemies thereafter frequently used this information. Federalist writers, enraged at his treatment of Alexander Hamilton, did so from 1797, combining the accusation with their belief in Gardenstone's authorship of *Political Progress*. Callender's "conduct, with respect to the real author of the Political Progress, is almost too bad to be credited, and is said to have precipitated that imprudent, unfortunate man [Gardenstone] into an untimely grave."[49]

After Callender's defection from the Republican party in 1802, Jeffersonian newspaper editors took up their opponents' theme. William Duane, for example, himself an émigré and at one time Callender's close colleague in Philadelphia, used the story of Callender's treatment of Gardenstone to discredit the Scotsman's attacks on Thomas Jefferson. Callender had treacherously turned on a mentor once before; his accusations against the president should therefore be attributed to the failure of his attempt to blackmail Jefferson and consequently should be ignored. "The benevolence of Lord Gardenstone raised you from extreme indigence. He saw in you . . . the rude materials of genius. He encouraged and sought to advance you in society. . . . The first act of your life was an attempt to destroy your benefactor. You had the baseness to threaten him with an information for the share which he had in the *Political Progress*, in order to extort money from him."[50] Although Duane's accusations were part of a vicious and partisan newspaper war, since 1802 no one has questioned the validity of his remarks. Historians have closely examined Callender's accusations against his political foes; they have always accepted uncritically the reciprocal charges against him, the truth or falsity of which ought to have some relevance to Callender's trustworthiness on other issues.

Far from Callender incriminating Gardenstone, however, the original transcripts of government interrogations make abundantly clear that it was Gardenstone who incriminated Callender. In the days following the Scottish convention in Edinburgh, Robert Dundas and John Pringle sought the author of *The Political Progress* by the obvious expedient of questioning those involved in its printing. James Anderson and his journeymen became primary targets, as did John Robertson, the printer of the pamphlet, his journeymen and apprentices, and his bookselling partner, Walter Berry.

On 29 December Pringle interviewed Robertson, Berry, and their employees. Questioned separately, the apprentices were commendably unanimous, all refusing to divulge the secrets of their master. Only one, John Lamb, was tricked into agreeing that part of the pamphlet was set in type in Robertson's printshop. Robertson admitted publishing *The Political Progress*, but refused to identify the author, and claimed to have destroyed the original manuscript and corrected proofs in November. Berry, however, cracked under questioning. Claiming to have been in London when the pamphlet was being prepared, he refused to name the authors—he spoke in the plural—but conceded that many customers asked for "Lord Gardenstone's" or "Mr. Thunderproof's" pamphlet. Both Robertson and Berry were charged, the former with publishing, the latter with selling, a seditious libel. Robertson later received a six months', and Berry a three months', jail sentence.[51]

Dundas and Pringle then turned to the printers of the *Bee*. James Anderson was evasive in his first interview, although he offered to ask the author for permission to reveal his name. At his second interview, on 31 December, he was given twenty-four hours to identify the author and was threatened with committal proceedings. Immediately Anderson wrote to Gardenstone, asking him to stand bail. The reply was swift and most disconcerting; owing to ill health, Gardenstone had decided "to take no concern in the affair you mention in your letter." Anderson then asked Callender to convince Gardenstone of the need to help. If he failed to persuade him and did not come to his shop by 11 A.M. the next day, Anderson said he would be forced to reveal Callender's identity.[52]

The next day Anderson again refused to implicate Callender, but his journeyman printer was less strong-willed. He informed Pringle that the original manuscript letters were in Callender's hand and that he had also revised the proofs, although some of the corrections were in another hand. Callender was then brought in for an interview. He agreed that he had visited Morningside the previous evening, but at the request of Gardenstone, not of Anderson. No sooner had he got there than Gardenstone had suffered a coughing fit, preventing anything of note being discussed. Callender, somehow hearing of the sheriff's wish to interview him, did not stay for dinner but returned immediately to Edinburgh. As to the authorship of *The Political Progress*, Callender refused to comment "because of private friendship" and "would not answer [the] question of Gardenstone's involvement" (he could hardly say otherwise, without incriminating himself). He denied being "Timothy Thunderproof" and suggested the pamphlet may have been written by more than one person.[53]

Pringle thus received no confirmation from Callender of Gardenstone's involvement. On 2 January he visited Morningside, where Gardenstone, asked if he knew the author of *The Political Progress*, replied that "the young man whose name is James Thomson Callender and who is a messenger to employment is the author both of the letters and of the pamphlet." Admitting that he had occasionally helped Callender, Gardenstone claimed never to have read the pamphlet. Immediately Pringle ordered Callender's Canal Street lodgings to be searched. Two letters from Gillan in London were found, which slightly compromised both Callender and Gardenstone with regard to the *Bee* letters. But of Callender there was no sign. Prudently he had fled, only hours before his home was raided. His visit to Morningside had convinced him of his vulnerability.[54]

Dundas remained certain of Gardenstone's guilt—rightly so, for Gardenstone had helped correct Callender's work—but without evidence from Callender he could not charge him. He did, however, issue a warrant for Callender's arrest. When Callender failed to attend court on 28 January, he was outlawed. Outlaws were "put to his highness's horn, and all . . . moveable good and gear [were] escheat and inbought to his majesty's use." Ironically, it was the responsibility of messengers-at-arms to implement this policy. Callender, as an outlaw, was formally suspended from his position as a messenger in March 1793. It was an empty gesture; by that time Callender was en route to the United States. Four months later Gardenstone died at Morningside. If the cause of death was a broken heart, Callender should not be blamed.[55]

V

When Thomas Paine emigrated to the American colonies in 1774 he was thirty-seven years of age and had "lost two wives, a home, and every job he had held." He was "a born loser."[56] Callender too, as he went into hiding in January 1793, could reflect on thirty-five years of disappointment and frustration. His life seemed to have consisted of short periods of hope and expectation, dramatically exploded by sudden disasters, and rather longer periods of concentrated effort to overcome failure and to earn a decent living. Particularly galling would have been the recognition that in the late 1780s, before his final confrontation with Steele and Stuart in the Sasine Office, his prospects had seemed bright. He had three strings to his bow: his clerkship in the Sasine Office, his position as messenger-at-arms, and his talent for writing. He was sufficiently confident of his future to marry at about this time and to embark on a family. Between December 1789 and December 1792, however, his world collapsed, and from a position of quiet respectability he had descended to outlawry.

Whereas others less self-righteous, less encumbered with the moralism of orthodox Calvinism, and more aware of their own self-interest may have grudgingly submitted when faced with injustice, Callender was fueled by an inner rage which impelled him to risk all in vain attempts to cleanse society of what he perceived to be blatant wrongs. His pent-up frustrations molded his radicalism, making it more an emotional than an intellectual commitment. Although there is no evidence that he was a practicing member of a church, Callender was an avenging angel, always protecting a Calvinist Truth and Justice, rather than a political philosopher, rationally dissecting society's ills. His emotional defense of abstract values reflected a paradoxical and essentially destructive character, making him particularly dangerous to those around him when his aims were frustrated.

It also gave him a contempt for humanity which his personal experiences only strengthened. For all his political extremism, he was not "one of the people"; indeed, his personal strategy was to rise above them, to lift himself into a social milieu where independence, self-respect, and peer esteem were admired values. In this regard Callender was no different from a great many other radicals of his era, whose political opinions were predicated on a demand for an open, meritocratic society. But whereas Paine's belief in progress and in the ultimate perfectibility of mankind influenced many radicals, Callender's inability to throw off the shackles of his Calvinist upbringing prevented him from accepting this essentially positive and optimistic worldview.[57]

His contempt for human nature did not, as it might be thought, offer consolation for the disaster of his outlawry, for although he could rationalize his predicament partly in terms of a corrupt society overwhelming the righteous and the pure, his misanthropy could not dissipate the despair ensuing from a recognition that Gardenstone had forsaken him. The depth of feeling between Callender and his mentor remains obscure, but Gardenstone seemingly acted as a father figure for Callender, whose natural father apparently disappeared early in his life. Harking back to the views of Jonathan Swift, Callender's intellectual preceptor, who wrote that "I have ever hated all nations . . . and all my love is towards individuals," one can perhaps envision the impact on Callender of Gardenstone's apostasy. It was akin to parental rejection.

In addition, of course, the actions of both Gardenstone and Anderson, as ultimately craven representatives of advanced political opinions, greatly weakened any faith Callender may have had in the probity and integrity of his fellow social critics. His opinion in 1782 that "the laurels which human praise confers are withered and blasted by the unworthiness of those who wear them" was confirmed by the events in Edinburgh a decade later. Although Callender fled to America still a committed radical, he was to view the New World through the jaundiced eyes of a disappointed cynic. This combination of vituperative misanthropy and extreme political values would be a dangerous brew in an environment where political warfare was at a high pitch.

Part Two

Philadelphia

4

Asylum of Liberty

I

Callender was among more than one hundred British radicals who were obliged to emigrate to the United States in the 1790s. Most refugees were either Irish or English; only fifteen Scotsmen are known to have fled to the United States on account of their political opinions and activities. Some, like Callender, were outlawed; others, with their livelihoods destroyed by their political beliefs, perceived the new American republic to be the best place to resurrect their careers.[1]

Those outlawed were hard-pressed to avoid the authorities before slipping across the Atlantic. Mathew Carey was dressed in lady's attire when he escaped from Dublin; James Cheetham was carried onto a ship at Liverpool in a chest marked "dry goods." From Scotland, Callender's fellow ultraradical James Tytler managed to flee in January 1793 to Belfast, where he remained for several years before sailing to Boston. In 1794 the Paisley poet James Kennedy escaped into the heather surrounding Edinburgh, where he pined for his wife and son—patriotically named Citizen—and wrote romantic antigovernment verse. He too eventually escaped to the United States.[2]

According to one Edinburgh source in February 1793, Callender had fled to France where he was editing and publishing a newspaper.[3] In fact, however, he had made his way to Dublin, where he was to remain for two months. He probably chose the Irish capital as a temporary refuge because of the close links that Muir and other members of the Scottish Friends of the People had forged with the Dublin Society of United Irishmen in the fall of 1792. There, trading on his friendship with Muir, Callender was able to seek assistance from prominent radicals such as Dr. William Drennan and Archibald Hamilton Rowan, respectively chairman and secretary of the Dublin United Irishmen.[4]

During his short sojourn in Dublin, Callender carefully considered his future options, finally deciding to start afresh in the New World.

The choice of future residence would have been relatively easy to make even if the United States had not possessed the reputation of accepting the oppressed from Europe. As a proclaimed outlaw Callender remained permanently in danger of arrest if he stayed in the British Isles. Moreover, with Britain and France now at war, the European continent offered few attractions. Accordingly, in March or April 1793 Callender boarded the snow *Ann and Mary John*, bound for the Delaware River. One of twenty-seven passengers, he was forced to travel without his wife and children. He arrived in America on 21 May 1793.[5]

Callender immediately made his way to Philadelphia, then the capital of the state of Pennsylvania and the temporary capital of the United States. Like most other cities on the eastern seaboard south of New England, Philadelphia—including its suburbs—was expanding rapidly, its population in the process of rising from 44,000 in 1790 to nearly 62,000 in 1800. Many inhabitants were of Scottish extraction. In Pennsylvania as a whole, about 8.6 percent of the population was of Scottish descent, a slightly higher proportion than that for the entire United States.[6]

Laid out in a grid pattern between the Delaware and Schuylkill rivers, with red brick and white marble-trimmed houses and a growing number of impressive public buildings, the central core of Philadelphia attracted the admiration of visitors, who magnanimously ignored the smells and noise associated with the finest markets in the United States and the less salubrious sections of the suburbs. For the duc de La Rochefoucauld-Liancourt, Philadelphia was the finest city in America and one of the most beautiful in the world.[7]

Philadelphia was big, "noisier, richer, and busier than any other urban area in North America." It was the nation's leading banking and commerical center and the major entrepôt for a vast hinterland, offering considerable economic opportunity for merchants, lawyers, and the many artisans and craftsmen who plied their trades, mainly in the traditionally personal "bespoke" manner. Those involved in the luxury trades had a limited clientele, except during the sittings of Congress when the political leaders of all the states converged on the city and the representatives of foreign nations hovered around the government offices. The richest part of Philadelphia's society comprised no more than two hundred old, established families, their wealth deriving primarily from mercantile activity. They effectively dominated the social and political life of the city. At the time Callender first arrived, Philadelphian society remained essentially hierarchical, although cracks in the facade of elite hegemony were beginning to appear.[8]

In the 1790s Philadelphia became the first urban melting pot in North America, "one great hotel or place of shelter for strangers."

Although the United Irishman John Daly Burk wrote that "from the moment the stranger puts his foot on the soil of *America*, his fetters are rent in pieces, and the scales of servitude which he had contracted under *European* tyranny fall off, [and] he becomes a FREEMAN," not all emigrants found themselves welcome in their new surroundings. The growing cosmopolitanism of the capital was beginning to stimulate nativist sentiment, and some newly arrived immigrants felt its first sullen impact. Only a year after Callender arrived, for example, the Scottish poet Alexander Wilson, trudging with his nephew between Newcastle and Wilmington, Delaware, en route to Philadelphia, found that "we made free to go into a good many farm-houses on the road, but saw none of that kindness and hospitality so often told of them." Both the United Irishman Wolfe Tone and the imperious English lawyer Charles Janson commented on the ordinary American tradesman's propensity to bilk his new countrymen. In addition, of course, the new immigrants themselves, if they were to settle relatively painlessly, had adjustments in outlook and manners to make in a country "where the language, the customs, and every thing that they had so long been accustomed to think right, would be laughed at, and they themselves would be looked on as unknown, and perhaps suspected strangers."[9]

Callender had the advantage over many other immigrants of having firm ambitions for his future. Not for him the arid prospect of teaching in a school, the highest expectation of so many of his fellow Scottish immigrants. The long journey across the Atlantic had failed to disperse the sweet smell of printer's ink in his nostrils and the hope of fame and fortune that it conjured up. The world of the printer, the publisher, and the man of letters continued to hold him in thrall. Within a fortnight of arriving in Philadelphia, Callender had obtained work from two Philadelphia publishers.[10]

Armed with letters of introduction from his friends in Dublin, Callender first made his way to the South Market Street bookshop of the former Dublin radical Mathew Carey. At this time Carey was embarking on a long career which was to culminate, after many vicissitudes, in his becoming the major publisher and bookseller in North America. Having been forced to flee Dublin on account of his political activities a decade earlier, Carey was sympathetic to Callender's plight, but at first he could offer only part-time editorial work on the Old World sections of Guthrie's *Geography*, which he was publishing in installments in a new edition. In October, however, after the death of the man writing the American section of the book, Carey offered Callender $12 a week to "begin an account of America generally, taking up its history from the first discovery to the present time."[11]

In the meantime Callender also had obtained a temporary position as assistant to John Dunlap on the *American Daily Advertiser*. He took advantage of this to puff himself by writing a fulsome review of Carey's edition of Guthrie. He also published his first political article in America. Calling himself "A Correspondent just arrived from Europe," Callender wrote half a column promoting his pacifist opinions and warning the United States against becoming embroiled in the European conflict. "War," he wrote, "may be of advantage to a race of barbarians, who have nothing to do, and nothing to lose; but, for a commercial nation, it can be nothing better than a farmer deserting his harvest to bet at a horse race. . . . In an infant government like ours, to hazard a foreign war, unless from the very last necessity, would be the height of madness."[12]

Thus Callender, in his first political statement in the United States, reiterated his long-held belief in the totally destructive nature of war. But he was now professing his old ideas in a new context, and certain decisions, even accommodations, had to be made if he was to succeed in his plan to become politically involved, for from the American political process in 1793 were emerging two political parties, to one of which Callender would have to pledge allegiance. The rapturous welcome given in Philadelphia to Edmond Genêt, the new French minister to the United States, only a few days before Callender's arrival; the growth of the popular democratic societies; and Thomas Jefferson's decision in July to resign as secretary of state at the end of the year, all pointed to the breakdown of consensus politics and the eventual formation of a party system.[13]

The choice that Callender had to make was not quite so inevitable as hindsight might suggest. Although Jefferson called the Federalists "Monocrats" and "Placemen" and the Federalists called their opponents "Jacobins" and "mobocrats," both parties adhered to republican ideology and traced the origins of their principles to the same body of Real Whig and Lockean ideas that sustained the oppositionist groupings to which Callender had belonged in Edinburgh. In addition the Federalists, at least the majority from New England, were also heirs to a Calvinism similar to Callender's, which stressed the innate depravity of man and emphasized the need to retain the past as a source of exemplary guidance. One period from which lessons could be gleaned, moreover, was the English Augustan Age, in which Swift's antidemocratic satire and imagery loomed large for many Federalists anxious to discredit the populist pretensions and utopianism of the Republicans.[14]

Embedded within Federalist ideology, therefore, were sources of influence similar to those that motivated Callender. But the solutions that the Federalists embraced were not those of Callender, who struggled against the conservative implications of his intellectual inheritance. The Federalists' suspicion of human nature and fear of innovation led them to cling to a conception of civil order in which an elite of wealth and learning acted on behalf of a passive, deferential "democracy." In contrast, Callender's misanthropy was so thoroughgoing as to be egalitarian. Neither wealth, nor learning, nor family background could create an elite superior to the mass of mankind. His was the egalitarianism of a common depravity, premised on the belief that no social group had the moral requirements to exercise authority. With Callender as with Swift, only a few individuals could display moral qualities worthy of respect. Callender's was thus an intensely negative conception of equality, a perversion of the ideal which ensured his permanent opposition to whoever controlled government. In 1793 it brought him, by a very singular route, into the orbit of the Republican opposition, whose egalitarianism by contrast was established on "faith in the virtue of republican peoples." The seeds of future tensions, therefore, were present from this very early stage.[15]

In the meantime, practical political issues cemented his connections with the slowly forming Republican party. If pacifism, hatred of corruption, and Scottish nationalism colored his political perspective, then notwithstanding his deep-seated similarities with the Federalists, Callender had to side with the Republicans, who interpreted Alexander Hamilton's financial and fiscal programs as the first step toward the corrupt "placeman" system that Callender had vilified in *The Political Progress of Britain*. Moreover, in the new social context in which Callender found himself, his Scottish nationalism was easily stripped down to an intense Anglophobia, similar to that of such ardent Republicans as James Monroe, Tench Coxe, John Beckley, and the many British radical émigrés who were making their way to the United States.[16]

Finally, personal ambition ensured that in the 1790s Callender put his pen at the disposal of the Republican party. Throughout his life Callender, perhaps paradoxically, pursued two objectives: independence of mind and of condition and a father figure, whom he could revere as the source of the virtue that he felt was so lacking among mankind in general. Several years were to pass before Callender found a new mentor, but the search for independence began immediately. He, like most émigrés to the United States in the 1790s, was to discover that perseverance and effort were necessary before personal independence became possible, but the Republican party at least promoted the ideal of careers open to the talented, whereas the Federalists' ideal vision, although not totally hostile to upward mobility, envisioned a hierarchical, deferential, socially restricted society, particularly for new immigrants, of whom they were suspicious even in 1794.[17]

II

If several offers of employment quickly raised Callender's enthusiasm for his new country, the outbreak of yellow fever that devastated Philadelphia in late summer and early fall 1793 must have given him second thoughts. From 19 August to 15 November between 10 and 15 percent of the city's population died, while another 20,000 fled to the comparative safety of the countryside. The enormous impact of the disease can be seen from the fact that even as late as December, fewer than 10 percent of the electorate voted in a special election to replace state senator Samuel Powel, himself a victim of the pestilence.[18]

One of Callender's jobs disappeared, for Dunlap discontinued the *Advertiser* between 15 September and 30 November. Indeed, only Andrew Brown's *Federal Gazette* continued in Philadelphia throughout the epidemic, and Philip Freneau's *National Gazette* disappeared forever.[19] Presumably Callender continued his part-time work for Carey, but there must have been a few awkward weeks for him to negotiate between the shutting down of the *Advertiser* and Carey's offer of permanent employment in October. Fresh opportunities arose, however, when in December 1793 Andrew Brown offered him a job on the *Federal Gazette* (it became the *Philadelphia Gazette* in January 1794). Brown required an expert shorthand writer to report congressional debates for his newspaper. This was a golden opportunity for Callender, as the job was well paid, brought him to the very center of American political life, and enabled him to view and to comment on America's political heroes from close range.

He may not have fully appreciated that the role of congressional reporter had been controversial since Congress had first met in 1789. One of the more paradoxical features of the new republican system established under the Constitution was that "the Sovereign People" had to rely for political information on the willingness of newspaper editors to pay reporters with stenographical skills to record congressional debates and speeches. From its inaugural meeting in New York, the House of Representatives had failed to appoint an official stenographer. Moreover, by meeting behind closed doors the Senate excluded the public from even hearing its deliberations. Reporters, however, were permitted access to the floor of the House of Representatives. Soon, a number of newspapers were publishing verbatim reports of its debates.[20]

Not all congressmen welcomed the reporters' presence in the chamber. As early as September 1789 Aedanus Burke of South Carolina complained of inaccurate reporting, and he was supported by Elbridge Gerry of Massachusetts, who, fearing that reporters might become the tools of a political faction, in vain suggested the appointment of an official stenographer. In the next session reporters at first prudently sat in the gallery, where they found it difficult to hear the speeches, but after a debate initiated by Jefferson's friend John Page, they were readmitted to the floor on an informal basis. Rumbles of discontent, however, continued, and in April 1792 Gerry again complained of inaccurate information being deliberately published; once more no action was taken.[21]

When in December 1793 Callender took his place at one of the four narrow desks set aside for stenographers in the overcrowded chamber, the position of newspaper reporters remained politically sensitive, with their probity already having been questioned. There were good reasons—without resorting to charges of partisanship—why reporters frequently found it difficult to record accurate accounts of the debates. Distractions were common: "From the silence which prevailed . . . on coming to order, after prayers . . . , [there arose] an occasional whisper, increasing to a buzz, after the manner of boys in school, in the seats, in the lobby, and around the fires, swelling, at last, to loud conversations, wholly inimicable to debate." When Callender came to publish his notes of debates in book form in June 1795, he gave further reasons in mitigation of inaccuracies. Some debaters, he wrote, spoke too softly; the loss of a few words frequently made a whole section of a speech unintelligible. Other speakers, having misunderstood what was previously said, made inconsequential comments, difficult to report in any sensible way.[22] Finally, it might be added, with no possibility of relief and constantly having to dip one's pen into an inkpot, it was well-nigh impossible for a reporter to record accurate and verbatim speeches, especially those delivered extempore. As contemporary newspaper reports show, shorthand writers were obliged to omit some speeches altogether, to mention others only briefly, and at best to paraphrase the larger effusions of garrulous congressmen. Inevitably, politicians on both sides of the House were to find fault with the way in which their speeches were reported in the newspapers.

Opposition to Callender's reporting of events in the House of Representatives began with the debates in January 1794 on James Madison's "Commercial Propositions," by which, in response to the implementation of the British order-in-council of November 1793, he sought to introduce retaliatory duties on British ships and merchandise. According to Callender's own later account of events:

In this wilderness of scribbling, many particulars transpired, which members were ashamed to confess and afraid to deny. Four members were especially irritated, viz. Theodore Sedgwick, Dr. William Smith,

Samuel Dexter and Robert Goodloe Harper. . . . Dr. Smith was by far more rancorous than the other gentlemen collectively. During the debate on Madison's resolutions, Mr. Abraham Clarke of New— Jersey said, turning round to his right hand, and *looking at Mr. William Smith*, that a stranger in the gallery might suppose there was a British agent in the house. The nickname of *British agent* became general. Mr. Smith was burnt in effigy in Charleston. On the rising of the session, he found it convenient to shun a meeting with his constituents by a tour for the ensuing summer, into the eastern states. The blame of this whole scandal was imputed to the pen of the guilty taker of minutes for the Philadelphia Gazette. Influence was employed, but in vain, to procure his dismission. This occurred in January 1794.[23]

It cannot now be ascertained whether Callender accurately reported Clarke's comments on Smith. The exhaustive reports of the debates in the *Gazette of the United States* and in the *Aurora* fail to allude to Clarke's accusation. It is mentioned in the *Annals of Congress*, but this was compiled many years later from newspaper reports and may only be quoting Callender himself. Callender was certainly wrong to suggest that fear of unpopularity in South Carolina kept Smith in the eastern states in the summer of 1794; for several years previously he had rarely spent time in his home state. Even his friends thought he ought to return more often. But Callender was more accurate in his view of Smith as, if not a British agent, at least a stalwart defender of British interests, representing in Charleston a High Federalist Anglo-American commercial phalanx in which there were many old Tories.[24]

To the Republicans, therefore, Smith was a worthy subject of attack, especially as rumor suggested that Alexander Hamilton had been the author of Smith's first speech in the debate. Jefferson told Madison in April 1794:

> I am at no loss to ascribe Smith's speech to it's father, every tittle of it is Hamilton's except the introduction. There is scarcely anything there which I have not heard from him in our various private tho' official discussions. The very turn of the arguments is the same and others will see as well as myself that the style is Hamilton's. The sophistry is too fine, too ingenious even to have been comprehended by Smith, much less devised by him. His reply shows he did not understand his first speech, as its general inferiority proves its legitimacy as evidently as it does the bastardy of the original.[25]

Madison's resolutions put the Federalists in an awkward position. By seeking to retaliate against the British for seizing American shipping, the Republicans were able to accuse the Federalists, who opposed the resolutions, of putting their support for the British before the interests of America's own merchant marine. At times the debates became overheated, and personal relations between congressmen deteriorated. Tench Coxe informed Jefferson in February: "I do not think there is more moderation in our parties than when you left us. Personalities, which lessen the pleasures of society, or prevent their being sought, have accused in private and at Tables." Callender's first service to the Republicans, therefore, seemingly was to help stir the pot of discord in Congress.[26]

The second session of the Third Congress opened in November 1794, and Callender was at his desk with his pen newly sharpened. In the following four months he gained the personal enmity of Federalists Theodore Sedgwick, Samuel Dexter, and Robert Goodloe Harper. But he was also the source of irritation to many others, on both sides of the House. He attended every day throughout the session, doing "whatever was in my power to give a candid account of what passed in that place." He would have done better to have followed his fellow reporters and absented himself for much of the time. As his rival scribbler William Cobbett wrote when the House finally adjourned in March 1795, Congress had "spent four months in wrangling about trifles."[27]

During this session two major debates took place in the House of Representatives, one on the reply to Washington's Address to Congress and one on amendments to the Naturalization Act. In both, partisan spirit reached a high pitch, and tempers were frequently lost. During the debate on Washington's address, clashes occurred over the propriety of agreeing with the president that the "self-created societies"—by which he meant the democratic societies—were implicated in the recent Whiskey Rebellion in western Pennsylvania. During the Naturalization Act debate, tempers became frayed over a Republican amendment forcing aliens seeking citizenship to give up any titles to nobility and a subsequent Federalist amendment to this amendment forcing aliens to surrender their rights to any slaves they might possess. Both amendments were partisan attempts to embarrass the opposing political party.

Neither party would have desired the publication of full reports of these debates. The Republican plan to smear the Federalists as closet aristocrats had been partially successful, as the Massachusetts Federalists Fisher Ames and Theodore Sedgwick admitted. But Samuel Dexter's counterattack aimed at southern Republican slaveowners had also struck home, forcing Republican deputy House leader William B. Giles and his fellow Virginia representative John Nicholas into lame protestations in defense of slave society. In addition, the debate on the address in reply to the president had degenerated into farce. One amendment, for example, wasted four whole days of debate, and no final division took place because the frequently amended resolution ultimately made no sense. Congressmen, impelled by partisanship, seemed temporarily to have lost their sense of proportion. Abraham Baldwin of Georgia spoke for many bemused representatives when he stated that "he felt a very mortifying impression at having been this week a witness to such trifling as had taken place in the House." By January 1795 a rather embarrassed and contrite House finally managed to move on to more germane affairs.[28]

But not only did party tactics require a decent veil of obscurity. The personal reputations of many congressmen were also at risk as misunderstandings, misapprehensions, and ambiguities punctuated their increasingly belligerent speeches. To the debaters' chagrin, Callender dutifully reported every tittle of the proceedings in the *Philadelphia Gazette*. Even Giles found his confusions and uncertainties circulating around the capital. On balance, however, the Federalists suffered more from Callender's perhaps mischievous zeal for absolute precision. Sedgwick, for example, was quoted as saying that morality had "no particular reference whatever to religion, or [to] whether a man believes *any* thing or *nothing*," an opinion hardly likely to be popular among his New England constituents.[29]

Callender directed his animus particularly toward Samuel Dexter, who was prominent in both the "self-created societies" and the naturalization debates. Undoubtedly, Dexter appeared a personal threat to Callender. In November 1794 he hinted that when free speech and a free press "were so abused as to become hostile to liberty and theaten her destruction, the abuses ought to be corrected." A month later he warned the House of the party violence likely to arise from the unrestricted immigration of "vagabonds, fugitives from justice, etc, etc, [who] may deluge this land." In response, Callender gleefully brought some of Dexter's more impromptu comments to his readers' attention. The congressman's definition of *republican* as a "hackneyed," overused word, which embraced "anarchists" as well as lovers of a restrained liberty, and Giles's reply that Dexter seemingly viewed republicanism as meaning *"anything or nothing,"* were duly paraphrased, probably in a garbled fashion. When Dexter, a few days later, "entered at some length into the ridicule of certain tenets in the Roman Catholic religion," Callender felt obliged to editorialize, pointing out in parentheses that "a great number of points of faith ascribed to the Roman Catholics are utterly unfounded."[30]

Callender rarely intervened with his own comments in his newspaper copy. Normally he used subtler, more artful means of spreading his opinions. He favored two particular techniques. One was to observe in parentheses that the orator looked at, or pointed toward, a named individual—usually a Federalist—when making general but controversial statements. Another technique was to italicize certain words in the text. Forced by puzzled readers to explain his motives, Callender claimed that "they are used when an expression is uncommonly forcible, or conveys an idea on which the argument hinges. The public may rest assured that they have always been the exact words of the speaker, with the variation perhaps of a particle. Where the smallest doubt could take place, as to the meaning of the member, and this happens every day, even among the gentlemen themselves, italics never have been employed." One may doubt that Callender kept invariably to these rules, especially when he reported the speeches of the major Federalists.[31]

Toward the end of the session in February 1795, when Callender was publishing the debates on the Indian frontier that dented the pride of Robert Goodloe Harper, the new Federalist member from South Carolina, the House established a committee to report on a petition from Edmund Hogan, a Philadelphia printer, seeking support as the official publisher of congressional laws and debates. Thus arose again the question of appointing an official stenographer. The committee, consisting of William L. Smith, Theodore Sedgwick, and the Republican John Page, made suggestions consistent with Federalist disapproval of the current unregulated mode of reporting debates. The Federalist *Gazette of the United States* fueled the fire. "Without paying the least attention to consistency," intoned *Gazette* editor John Fenno, the Republicans " blunder over stories, which cannot deceive the most illiterate—and appear to constantly practice the principle, that a falsehood well stuck to is as good as the truth; and repeat, and re-repeat sentences which never had existence but in their own brains." The committee's report, calling for skilled stenographers seeking the position to present themselves for examination at the beginning of the next session, was accepted by 28 votes to 26, after both Smith and Dexter "complained bitterly of the minutes of the *Philadelphia Gazette*."[32]

The Fourth Congress, which convened at the end of 1795, had a Republican majority, and not until January 1796 was the issue of an official stenographer debated. Callender, in the meantime, had continued reporting for the *Philadelphia Gazette*, but he must have been furious when, after William Smith had informed the House of the famed Scottish stenographer David Robertson's willingness to take the job for $4,000 per session, Andrew Brown offered Congress $1,100 for the manuscript copy of the debates. Callender's anger rose to a towering passion when Republicans Giles and Nicholas both strongly criticized the current standard of reporting. Giles spoke of the disgraceful manner in which speeches were recorded: "Not only misrepresentations, but falsehoods, absurdities and contradictions, are published, so that the design of publishing is frustrated and the people disappointed of receiving that information to which they are entitled." Nicholas claimed that speeches had been published which members had never uttered. One such had been attributed to him. It was, he admitted self-deprecatingly, a good one, "and written in a handsome stile—better than he was master of."[33]

The Federalists joined in with gusto. Both Harper and William Lyman picked out Callender for particular condemnation. According to Lyman: "The debates, or what are so called in one of the Philadelphia papers, had been altogether exceptionable, and he was sorry to learn that these debates had been collected and published in a book entitled *The Political Register*, by which means they would be preserved in existence and descend perhaps to posterity. He had not seen the book, but if the speeches were the same with those published in the newspaper . . . they were a libel on the House of Representatives." In response, Giles pointedly refused to defend Callender, merely expressing the opinion that some reports were correct and accurate.[34]

The House finally decided not to appoint an official stenographer but to allow the current unsatisfactory state of affairs to continue. Neither party was eager to see a stenographer made an official officer of the House and thus become susceptible—in Sedgwick's words—to "an unprincipled majority" who might use their influence "to overawe and lay prostrate a virtuous minority."[35]

But as far as Callender was concerned, the damage was done, for Andrew Brown took advantage of the controversy to dismiss him. Their relations had been deteriorating since Edmund Hogan had sought to become the House's official printer in February 1795. In attempting to rebut Hogan's claims, Brown had, perhaps unwittingly, offended Callender by giving himself the credit for the congressional reports in his newspaper. The ever-prickly Scotsman, convinced that his reporting had raised circulation figures, characteristically responded by publicly ridiculing his employer in the rival *Aurora*.[36] Although this dispute died down and Callender continued reporting in the ensuing session, Brown determined to rid himself of his controversial reporter when he discovered Callender's regular, if unpaid and anonymous, political writings for Benjamin Franklin Bache's *Aurora*. The debate in Congress in February 1796 gave Brown his opportunity.

Callender may have been expecting Brown's action, but he would have been surprised by the Republicans' failure to defend him in the House. Although he was not in the pay of the Republican party, he was clearly a partisan. He could hardly have expected to be abandoned so completely. The blame for this Callender, and others, laid squarely at the feet of William B. Giles. Callender gave two different explanations of Giles's behavior. Publicly, he claimed that the Virginian had denounced congressional reporters as a way of escaping from the confused position into which he had blundered during the stenographer debate. Privately, he informed Jefferson that Giles had deliberately conspired with William Smith to ease him out of his job with Brown.[37]

Callender's new rival commentator on federal politics accepted the conspiracy theory. William Cobbett, a violent Francophobe and antidemocrat, whose *A Prospect from the Congress-Gallery* signaled the appearance of a major journalistic talent, also blamed the Virginia delegation in Congress. With exuberant relish he wrote of the stenography debate:

> I cannot conclude this article without reminding gentlemen of their cruelty to my poor Caledonian friend, Callender. How was he mauled! How was his *Register* torn to pieces! One took him by the wig, another by the ear; he writhed and winced and jumped about, as the French say, like a Frog upon a gridiron. I much question if he were in greater torture when the constables of sweet Edinburgh were at his heels. Oh gentlemen of Virginia, how could you belabour this imported patriot? A man that has not only foresworn his country, but has written, or rather transcribed, two whole "Political Progresses" purely to curry favour with you. . . . If this be the way you treat your friends, I hope I shall never be numbered amongst them; at least until your manners and principles change.[38]

It is perhaps surprising, albeit ironic, that Callender's dismissal occurred partly as a result of the Republican deputy House leader's personal dislike of him. Giles, like many Virginians of his day, was proud, quick-tempered, and vain. As a politician he lacked the self-control to reach the heights of power, although, according to an enemy, he was "a man famous for his low cunning." "An often uncharitable debater," he rarely failed to say what he thought, regardless of the consequences. "Few men," writes his biographer, "have made more bitter enemies." He and Callender had, therefore, several character traits in common, although Giles's superior social and political position and his Virginian hauteur ensured his disdain for this rather disreputable Scottish newcomer. From his vantage point Callender, with a high opinion of his own abilities and the burden of a heavy chip on his shoulder, viewed Giles as a second-rate politician, with pretensions to aristocracy, who was in a position too exalted for his talents.[39]

Giles in his calmer moments ought to have had ambiguous feelings about Callender. Disreputable he might be, but he was also potentially dangerous. In the 1790s anyone with an ability to write and whose livelihood depended on his pen had to be carefully handled. Pride could too easily be pricked by the wounding blow in print. Giles may not have recognized this truth, at least to the extent that it applied to himself. He was certainly not averse to enjoying his political enemies' discomfiture. In January 1794 he sent to Jefferson at Monticello newspaper accounts of the congressional debates in which William Smith was ridiculed. Admitting that "the debates are very incorrectly taken," Giles nevertheless thought they would afford Jefferson "some amusement."[40] The boot was on the other foot a few months later when Giles's own inadequacies were similarly publicized to the world. When the opportunity arose during the stenographer debate, therefore, Giles refused to come to Callender's defense. Rightly perhaps, he thought Callender would not be in a position to respond. But the Scotsman was equally unlikely to forget a grudge. He was to seek his revenge in entirely different circumstances a few years later after Giles had again abandoned him to his fate. In the meantime, Callender once more nursed the bitterness of betrayal.

III

Callender's sense of betrayal was heightened by his knowledge that, irrespective of his role as congressional reporter in the previous two years, he had effectively and independently served the interests of the Republicans. He had also begun to stabilize his personal life. The regular fee he earned from the *Philadelphia Gazette*—probably about $800 a session—was sufficient to pay the fares of his wife and three children to Philadelphia. In 1796 another child, Thomas, was born. The family took up residence at 64 Dock Street, between Second and Front streets close to the Delaware River, from where Callender daily set out to work as a "corrector of the press."[41]

Callender's contract with Mathew Carey for revising Guthrie's *Geography* did not long survive the Scotsman's first period of reporting the congressional debates. Angry at Callender's dilatoriness, Carey voiced his displeasure to "8 or 10 people," receiving in return a barrage of complaints from Callender, in his "usual polite and decent style of threatening." He denied tarnishing Callender's reputation, claiming with an hauteur guaranteed to enrage the Scotsman that "I have never judged you of sufficient import to make your ill usage a subject of conversation, except with a few, whom I had every reason to suppose you had, with the address I know you master of, endeavoured to impress with a false idea of the origin of the dispute between us." Carey sought a replacement; Callender continued with his political work.[42]

Until his dismissal by Brown, this work consisted partly of pamphleteering, including a revision and extension of *The Political Progress of Britain* for American publication. A second edition of part one was published in Philadelphia in November 1794, and a third edition in March 1795. In the same year Callender published a disappointingly repetitive second volume. Both parts were reprinted in Mathew Carey's *Select Pamphlets*, volume two, in 1796. As well, Callender compiled his *Political Register* and published, in December 1795, *A Short History of the Nature and Consequences of Excise Laws*.

Apart from his congressional debates, therefore, most of his pamphleteering in 1794 and 1795 concerned issues with which Callender had been involved in Scotland. At the same time, however, he was gaining experience by regularly contributing anonymous paragraphs of political comment to Benjamin Franklin Bache's Republican *Aurora*.[43] Because in the 1790s most newspaper correspondents used pseudonyms, it is very difficult to determine with precision who wrote particular letters and paragraphs. Callender, at this juncture, preferred anonymity, but a close study of the *Aurora* from January 1794 to July 1798 has shown that Bache invariably placed Callender's contributions in his Philadelphia news columns under the heading "From a Correspondent." That Callender wrote all of such denominated paragraphs seems highly probable. The occasional references to his life in Scotland and to his pamphlets, his distinctive idiolect and style—hard-hitting, sarcastic, heavily satirical, and only infrequently and deliberately scurrilous—and his habit of eventually transforming his newspaper writings into books, all convincingly support the contention that Bache kept the title "From a Correspondent" purely for Callender's contributions.

On this basis, Callender had become a regular free-lance commentator on political issues by January 1794. By the end of the year he had dropped sixty-one paragraphs into Bache's letter box placed at the front of his printshop and a further sixty followed in 1795. None of these articles were specifically commissioned, nor did Bache pay Callender for his efforts, although the editor, who would have met the Scotsman regularly when they were both recording congressional debates, knew the identity of the author.[44] The subjects of Callender's writings were wide-ranging, covering most contemporary issues, but the most significant can be placed in five overlapping categories: relations with Britain, the Jay mission and the ensuing treaty, Federalist domestic policy, the Whiskey Rebellion, and the introduction of excise taxes.

In the first months of 1794 relations with Britain were strained almost to breaking point, on account of measures taken by Britain in its war with France. Three major points were at issue: the threat from Algerine corsairs in the Mediterranean, British orders-in-council that ignored America's neutrality, and British involvement in stirring up the Indians on the western frontier. In order to free the Portuguese navy for use against France, in 1793 the British had helped to conclude a treaty between Portugal and Algiers. One subsequent and unfortunate side effect was the freedom allowed to Algerian pirates to roam the Mediterranean and the Atlantic, where they plundered unprotected American vessels with impunity. In America this was viewed, erroneously, as part of a deliberate British plot to drive rival American shipping out of the Mediterranean. Of even greater importance in generating Anglo-American ill will was the order-in-council of November 1793 that permitted British warships to seize all neutral vessels conveying goods to enemy-held islands or carrying enemy-owned goods. Hundreds of American ships trading with the West Indian islands were seized, and many were condemned in British admiralty courts. Finally, the British were accused of keeping troops on American soil, in contravention of the Treaty of Paris, and of encouraging Indian raids on American settlements in the West, in order to keep control of the fur trade.[45]

These issues raised howls of protest in America, particularly from the southern states, and for a period strident calls for war were heard. Callender, who had listened in Congress to the debates on Madison's commercial resolutions, did not add his voice to the demands of the warhawks. Although he never hid his hatred of Britain and its monarchy, he remained consistent in his long-held pacifism. The United States, he declared, undoubtedly had reasons enough for waging war with Britain: "It seems now to be universally admitted that the conduct of the British towards the United States . . . has violated every principle of the law of nations, common justice, and morality." Nevertheless, he counseled caution: "It behoves every man to count the cost dispassionately, before he consents to engage in a war with nations who follow it as a trade. Let him think seriously what, and how much, the great body of the people are to gain or lose by the contest. In deliberating on measures that may involve the fate of millions, he ought to consider what are the true interests of his own country, independent of those of every other nation."[46]

As this passage, with its emphasis on individual decision making, suggests, Callender's views were partly determined by a recognition that before declaring war a republic, based on popular sovereignty, had to consider principles of little significance to monarchies. In a monarchical country, he claimed, national honor and dignity were normally closely associated with the king's personal ambitions and frivolous dynastic considerations. When these were infringed, even cursorily, war was declared, without the people's interests being considered. In a republic, however, national honor was inextricably bound up with the rights of the sovereign citizens. War was warranted only when their rights were affected to an insufferable degree.[47]

It was true, Callender continued, that Britain, in seeking to sustain "her bloated importance, by the virtues of a pedlar, and the vices of a monopolist," had severely compromised America's neutral stance and insulted American rights. Indeed, the policy of neutrality had been a total failure. It had resulted in "contempt, insult, and injury." America had been shown to be "bereft of its vigour, . . . enervated in its honour, [and] emasculated in [its] republicanism." Britain would thus have to pay for its effrontery. But the solution was not to wage war, however gross British infractions of America's neutrality. Rather, all goods to the British West Indies and, if necessary, to Britain itself should be embargoed. The British in the West Indies would starve, and in the British Isles one hundred thousand people would be thrown out of work, with hundreds of merchants rendered bankrupt. If Britain failed to give satisfaction to America within six months, all British assets in the United States should be sequestered. From the sale of these assets the American government could recoup the cost of fighting the Algerine corsairs, compensate merchants and shipowners for the loss of shipping and goods in the Mediterranean and in the West Indies, and give pensions to the widows and families of those killed in the backcountry fighting "George III's Indians." The executive immediately ought to "dispatch a person of respectability, cloathed with authority to make a representation to the British, ask for an explanation of their late conduct, and demand reparation." The only terms consistent with American honor would be the redemption of Algerine captives, payment for the vessels seized by Britain's "allies," the delivery of the western forts, and complete indemnification for "all the robberies in the West Indies." In the meantime, "let Congress prepare for the worst" by organizing the militia and strengthening America's defenses.[48]

The opinions Callender put forward in March 1794 were not uncommon, although he must have been startled when war fever so gripped Federalist Jonathan Dayton that, only a few days after the publication of Callender's paragraph, he too proposed the sequestration of British property. Many Republicans toyed with the idea of confiscation and certainly pushed hard for economic sanctions against Great Britain. Ultimately, however, cooler heads among the Federalists prevailed, economic measures were drastically watered down, and the president decided to send Chief Justice John Jay to England, not to demand reparations, as Callender wished, but to negotiate a commercial treaty. As usual Callender, although promoting policies in general conformity with those of the Republicans, had, short of demanding war, taken the most extreme position on an issue. Even after news of the supersession of the November order-in-council by a more reasonable one in January, Callender remained outraged. "Why should that perfidious and insolent tyrant," he thundered, "presume to arrogate to himself the right of prescribing limits to, or modifying at his will, that commerce which the United States has an unquestionable right to exercise?"[49]

Callender was immediately suspicious of the motives behind the decision to send an extraordinary envoy to Britain. The mission had been deliberately announced, he thought, while the embargo was still under discussion in Congress; it was a cunning ploy to ensure the rejection of economic measures. Callender did not have to seek far for the miscreants in government who were so desperate to prevent sanctions. To blame was "the British faction," a combination of "apostate Whigs, old tories, toad eaters of government, British riders and runners, speculators, stockjobbers, bank-directors, [and] mushroom merchants," who were strongly represented in Congress by, among others, Callender's bêtes noires, Smith, Dexter, and Sedgwick. Seven-eighths of the Federalists, he exaggeratedly claimed, "have been in British pay, and are now under British influence."[50]

Although settled in the United States for less than a year, Callender had, to his own satisfaction, already uncovered a conspiracy threatening his new country's republican institutions. The key to his discovery lay with Alexander Hamilton's economic programs, on which the British faction was parasitic. America's funding system, the national debt, the emphasis on indirect taxation were all copied from British examples. Obviously, they had been introduced as a means of surreptitiously promoting monarchical institutions in America. In Callender's opinion: "The funding system is to the United States what a nobility is to a monarchy. It has a separate representation; for as it forms a phalanx of support, so it has the countenance and sympathy of government. It is a machine which sustains administration at all times, and under all circumstances; and like action and re-action administration sustains it. The funding system is . . . the cause of our imbecility, the means of a submission to the most degrading and humiliating situation, that freemen ever endured."[51]

Similarly, experience had shown that "a national debt is a national curse; that a national debt has created an interest distinct from that of the people; that a national debt has paralyzed our government; that it has banished patriotism from many of those who administer our government; and that it has been the source of all our evils, and the polluted fount from which our disgraces flow." To understand these facts of life was to understand why, unlike in 1776, servile negotiation with Britain was preferred in 1794. The British "plan of debt is an idol that some men have set up to worship, and if untoward events should arise, the example of Britain would cease to have its operation, in producing a general worship, and her influence would no longer assist in assimilating this government to hers."[52]

Callender was not alone in developing a conspiracy theory of politics in the 1790s. The belief that one's political opponents had ulterior and threatening intentions pervaded the thinking of both Republicans and Federalists.[53] Some historians have seen this as mass paranoia, but Gordon S. Wood has brilliantly analyzed the late eighteenth-century frame of mind within the parameters of Augustan thought, Enlightenment philosophy, and the growing preeminence of secular over religious values. "The conspiratorial interpretations of the age," he writes, "were a generalized application to the world of politics of the pervasive duplicity assumed to exist in all human affairs. Only by positing secret plots and hidden machinations by governments was it possible, it seemed, to close the bewildering gaps between what rulers professed and what they brought forth. . . . The belief in plots was not a symptom of disturbed minds but a rational attempt to explain human phenomena in terms of human intentions and to maintain moral coherence in the affairs of men."[54]

Those most affected by this conspiratorial mentality tended to be traditionalists still steeped in eighteenth-century forms that emphasized the individual's total responsibility for his activities and denied that unintended consequences could result from purposive action. Nothing demonstrates more clearly the fundamental ambiguity in Callender's worldview than his simultaneous combination of this mentality with the progressive ideas of Painite, and Jeffersonian, republicanism, which tended to break the connection between cause and effect, between action and consequence. His Augustan inheritance, which he shared with the Federalist satirists, and the conflict between his Calvinist upbringing and his secular values led Callender inexorably into a twilight world where his opponents were not just misinformed but wickedly and morally wrong.

In addition to this particular psychology, much of the vigor and forcefulness of Callender's critique of Federalism stems from his understandable horror at seeing the corrupt institutions he had assailed in Edinburgh seemingly take root in republican America. Even more than the most suspicious Republicans of native birth, Callender could clearly envision the long-term consequences of Federalist policies if they remained unchallenged; he had seen them in their maturity at first hand. Whether Callender's analysis was grossly exaggerated is less important than recognizing that his ferocious political activities in America were driven by a sincerely held perception that the American republic was in danger. No measure was too extreme to prevent the collapse of republicanism. In Callender's perhaps distorted opinion, the ends were always to justify the means.

IV

With Jay en route to Britain and for the next few months incommunicado, the Whiskey Rebellion of June 1794 and the malign influence of the democratic societies became the main features of political disputation. Here Callender was on less favorable ground than in the quarrels over foreign policy, for the rebellious activities in western Pennsylvania gave the initiative, and the high moral ground, to the Federalists, who proceeded to wring as much political capital from them as possible. In particular, they used the rebellion as propaganda to smear the activities of the democratic societies that, according to Fisher Ames, "were born in sin, the impure off-spring of Genêt."[55]

No evidence exists to confirm Callender's membership of the Democratic Society of Pennsylvania, but several of his acquaintances were prominent in its activities.[56] Strongly Francophile and committed to keeping alive "the Spirit of '76," the democratic societies viewed themselves as the public watchdogs of elected officials, promoters of the rights of man, and guardians of free speech and a free press. If not a member, Callender strongly espoused their principles. In reply to a correspondent in the Federalist *Gazette of the United States* who objected to the celebration of French victories by the societies as contrary to America's neutral stance, Callender ridiculed the Federalists' infection by "club-phobia." What have the "courtly" gentlemen to hide, he asked? "Nothing can point out more clearly the utility of the political societies than the terror which they inspire in the minds of a certain description of characters among us; for if their views are upright why dread any enquiry into them [?] If they are not, no wonder an analysis of them should create such alarm." The Federalists, he concluded, viewed good government as one which extended its powers "even to the suppression of free enquiry and debate." A year later, in noting the closure of the Jacobin clubs in France, Callender reiterated his views on free speech. Under a republican government, he wrote, "the right exists of discussing and expressing an opinion on public men or measures—of influencing by arguments—by words, as many of our fellow-citizens, whether rulers or ruled, over to our opinions. This is the right of every citizen in his individual or in an aggregate capacity. It is subject to abuse, and so are the greatest blessings we enjoy; but the line between use and abuse must be drawn on each particular case by a jury of citizens."[57]

It became more difficult to justify such doctrines when the Federalists tarred the democratic societies with the brush of sedition. William

Cobbett, for example, blamed the rebellion on "ambitious Scottish demagogues," who seized every opportunity to revile the government, "representing every tax as an oppression, and exciting the ignorant to insurrection." Callender, however, did not retreat from controversy. With a mixture of satire, controlled invective, and sensible, mollifying suggestions, he attempted to circumvent Federalist accusations by blaming them for the western insurrection and by branding them as pitiless avengers intent on punishing poor, deluded farmers. Like all members of the democratic societies, he readily conceded that the rebels had violated the laws of the country and that government had the right to protect itself. But he claimed the cause of the insurrection lay in the funding system. Intent on creating a body of men devoted to government and to monarchy, the government had introduced "corrupt" forms of taxation, such as the excise, so that speculative money could remain tax-exempt. It would not be surprising, claimed Callender, if everyone "rose up" against the inequalities of the funding system. Neatly associating Alexander Hamilton with the stigma of bastardy, he argued that "the excise is [Hamilton's] child, and a bastard in the American soil, and a bastard indeed of the constitution. The Secretary [of the Treasury] certainly originated it." It was a great pity, continued Callender, as he highlighted the more ludicrous aspects of Hamilton leading 15,000 armed men toward a handful of backcountry farmers, that the poor, embodied in the militia, would be compelled to spill the blood of fellow citizens. "Let stockholders, bank-directors, speculators and revenue officers arrange themselves immediately under the banner of the treasury, and try their prowess in arms as they have in calculation." After all, he concluded in more serious fashion, "the man who has most to expect from government ought to be the first to defend it." In a final fling at the Federalists, he accused certain of their newspapers of inciting hatred against the farmers of the western counties. Remember, he counseled, that they are our fellow citizens and will eventually return to the fold. Magnanimity rather than revenge would be the true republican way of resolving the issue.[58]

As order was being restored in the western counties, John Jay was completing his negotiations with the British government. Callender, like many Americans, had waited impatiently for information on the mission. News filtered through that Jay had waited six weeks between arriving and opening negotiations with Lord Grenville. No doubt, wrote Callender sarcastically, this time had been used effectively, with "many a bow, many a civil word and many a dinner." In reality the British, flushed with their naval successes in the West Indies, were in no hurry to complete the negotiations. "If the present progress in the business is a just criterion," remarked Callender caustically, "this country will for a dozen years at least want its chief justice, and our merchants their property." He was convinced that the negotiations would not take long; the Anglophile Jay was certain to act "sensibly" and to leave the problems outstanding from the Treaty of Paris "for a more peaceable season" when Britain was not at war.[59]

The treaty that Jay provisionally signed in November 1794 would probably have been unacceptable to Callender and the extreme Republicans even if the whole of Canada had been ceded to the United States! As it was, the treaty provisions remained unknown during the first half of 1795, for the Senate discussed them in secret session. Callender, ever quick to interpret the Constitution, claimed that "there is no *authorized* secrecy in our government, and to infer the right from the practices of other nations, is a prostitution of republican principles. As well might we say the President should wear a crown because the king of Great Britain wears one, there being nothing in the constitution forbidding to him this ornament." The French, he pointed out, openly discussed their treaty with Prussia in the Convention. "How very different is the conduct of our government, and yet it is said that 'We the People' are the Sovereign." Why, if the people were to be prevented from judging the treaty's merits before ratification, need its provisions become public thereafter? As popular opinions were shamefully ignored, "better that the expression of contempt for them should be made as strong as possible."[60]

Callender's sarcasm on secrecy ended abruptly when Bache, with the first scoop in American newspaper history, published a rough synopsis of the treaty on 29 June 1795. Only two days before, Callender had suggested that any one of the ten senators who had opposed ratification would, if he leaked the document, perform "an act of patriotism and virtue." In fact, Bache obtained his information from the French ambassador, Adet, who probably had purchased a copy of the treaty from Virginia senator Stevens Thomson Mason. Mason then gave a full copy of the treaty to Bache, who proceeded to print it in large numbers.[61]

A wave of anger, delighting Callender, swept the United States when the details of the treaty became known, for it was widely believed that Jay had failed to protect his country's fundamental interests. In Boston one citizen daubed his reaction on Federalist Robert Treat Paine's fence: "Damn John Jay! Damn everyone that won't damn John Jay! Damn everyone that won't put lights in his windows and sit up all night damning John Jay!" Jay himself, now governor of New York, observed that he could have found his way across the country by the light of his flaming effigies. In Delaware the citizens were split in their opinions: some wished to burn Jay and the treaty-ratifying senators in effigy; others wanted to do it in person![62]

Government supporters initially had great difficulty selling the treaty's benefits to the public. As "Camillus," Hamilton—who was shouted down and pelted with stones at a New York meeting—and Rufus King—who had been guilty of leaking the treaty to George Hammond, the British ambassador—did their utmost to sway public opinion. They pointed to the favorable response to the treaty of most respectable and influential Americans, including the old patriots of 1776. Callender, taking up this "aristocratic" theme, reminded "Camillus" that both Benedict Arnold and the French general Dumouriez were once regarded as old patriots. Such arguments were, in any case, irrelevant. "There is but one touchstone by which to try the treaty—JUSTICE. If it is incompatible with this, no collateral considerations ought to give a gloss to it—no influence distinct from its merits, ought to be a pretext for its acceptance."[63]

By August 1795 the tide of opposition to the treaty began to turn, as emotional responses faded and the virtues of the treaty were considered more rationally and sympathetically. The Federalists had relied on the president's enormous prestige to sway opinion in their favor, and after several weeks of hesitation Washington officially approved the treaty. There followed almost immediately the first of Callender's spectacular outbursts for which he was to become notorious. Until August 1795 Callender, although capable of generalized harsh language interspersed with specific attacks on certain individuals, had relied primarily on reasoned argument, sarcasm, and satire to influence his audience. Now, however, he formally declared war on the president of the United States. Claiming that by signing the treaty Washington had ignored public opinion and descended to the level of a party leader, Callender informed the president that "he must expect to be no longer viewed as a saint; as he has spoken daggers to [the people's] feelings, he must no longer expect a blind devotion to his will. His conduct has impaired their obligations to him, and instead of being viewed as the father of his country, we behold him as a master. The new character he has disclosed ought to awaken us to our situation, and teach us to shake off the fetters that his name has hitherto imposed upon the minds of freemen."[64]

Callender's war plan was thus to undermine Washington's image as the impartial father of his people. Far from listening to the voices of ordinary citizens, Washington felt himself too superior to notice them. Alluding to Edmund Burke's characterization of the people as the swinish multitude, Callender wrote: "Ye swinish creatures dare not approach the presidential sanctuary with your gruntings. Is he to be pestered with your impertinent opinions, and to have his delicate nerves unstrung, by your advice! Is he not your *sovereign*, is he not *paramount* to you and your *constitution*, is he not *infallible, immaculate, omnis-*

cient? . . . Ye hardened and presumptuous wretches, ye deserve not so good a monarch, for thus profaning his hallowed name." Callender appreciated the futility of concentrating criticism only on Washington's decision to ratify the treaty; he needed also to pierce the veil of the Constitution that surrounded and sanctified the president. He had to confront, and destroy, the Federalist strategy "that the President is the constitution, and the constitution the President." Only then could the Republicans, true representatives of the sovereign people, permanently bury the canard, first associated with Washington after his "self-created societies" statement, that opposition to government measures reflected conspiratorial designs on the Constitution itself.[65]

Callender was only one of a number of Republican penmen to attack Washington in the last months of 1795. In the *Aurora*, "Hancock," "Valerius," "Belisarius," "Atticus," "Pittachus," and "A Calm Observer" (John Beckley) made strenuous efforts to undermine Washington's popularity and reputation for impartiality. Their arguments, losing their initial shock value through repetition, became sterile, although as representative of the first phase in a long campaign against the president, they ultimately played some part in Washington's decision not to stand for reelection in 1796.[66]

During Callender's first two years as an independent political commentator, he helped to set the Republican agenda by drawing out the implications of Hamilton's economic programs and by bringing to his readers' attention the dangers that "the British phalanx" represented to republicanism. His masterly control of the English language, from which he extracted new forms of invective; his effective use of sarcasm, irony, and satire; and his ability to interpret political events as part of a larger conspiracy reflect the emergence of a new and mature talent upon which the Republicans could expect to rely. Only his splenetic attack on Washington, which, however, at this point remained under control, suggested problems for the future.[67]

5

"The Foreign Tool of Domestic Faction"?

I

Callender's fortunes spiraled rapidly downwards following his break with Brown's *Gazette*. The prospects of finding regular work in Philadelphia were poor, and Bache was in no position to employ permanent assistance. Accordingly, Callender had to look farther afield, as whatever savings he had accumulated rapidly dwindled. In the spring of 1796 he set out on the hundred-mile trip to Baltimore, along roads Judge Joseph Story of Boston believed were "as execrable . . . as [any that] can be found in Christendom." A printer in Baltimore had offered Callender a job, but although his employer was "a sober honest character," by the end of May Callender felt that the printer was "incapable of fulfilling his engagements."[1]

Callender appears at this time to have wanted to break away from his dependence on writing and to find some financial security, even in a menial job. In a letter to James Madison from Baltimore, he wrote that "my wishes in life are of the humblest kind. It is very long since I envied the independence of a journeyman carpenter. But I am now in my thirty-ninth year, with a wife and four young children; and it is too late to think of anything of that sort by at least a dozen years." Even the prospect of schoolteaching seemed attractive, for he asked Madison about the possibility of obtaining a post as a Latin master in Virginia. "Of the little moral worth to be found," he wrote, "youth possesses the greater part, and is therefore the least offensive society." An anonymous, peaceful life had become his aim. "The *jocunda oblivia vitae* are the only things for which I consider life as worth a wish."[2]

Nothing resulted from his plea to Madison; Callender was forced to return to Philadelphia. It is even possible that he was driven from Baltimore as a vagabond, "who has been whipped and kicked out of one of our capital cities." Back in familiar territory, he reverted inevitably to hackwork, writing introductions to editions of Shakespeare, possibly again revising Guthrie's *Geography*, and ghostwriting congressmen's letters to their constituents. He also continued writing paragraphs for the *Aurora*. No evidence exists to suggest that Bache, always himself strapped for money, paid for the Scotsman's copy in 1796, although Callender possibly began accepting small loans from local Republican leaders. His contract with John Swanwick for *British Honour and Humanity*, published in October 1796, would have kept him from falling precipitously into the debt culture that characterized Philadelphia's printing world. Callender was temperamentally unsuited to cope with the strained social relations that inevitably resulted from this network of small debts. The prospects of peace and independence retreated as he once again became embroiled in partisan controversy.[3]

By the summer of 1796 Callender was firmly enmeshed in the Republican party's Grub Street. His closest associates tended to come from the most radical wing of the party, although he had links with the more moderate, especially those who controlled the local Republican organization. It should be emphasized that, at the national level, the Republican party was not a homogeneous body; it was essentially a coalition of different interests and ideas. It included a group of established elite reformers—centered on the Virginia planter class—commercial farmers, and increasingly from mid-decade, urban tradesmen and artisans, upwardly mobile professional men, and nouveau riche merchants and manufacturers. Many of these groups had supported the Constitution in 1787–88, but now they united with Antifederalists to form an opposition phalanx to Hamilton's taxation and foreign policies and to the Federalists' conception of an hierarchical society.[4]

In Philadelphia, however, the local party was led by men who "tended to be political newcomers, outsiders, ambitious economic types, and influential men tied to the state government." As ambitious arrivistes seeking social eminence in Pennsylvania, they were blocked by the established Federalist elite of old families and old money. In their political maneuverings to achieve their social and economic goals, they—sometimes opportunistically—adopted the doctrines of the Rights of Man, an open society, and the liberation of the human spirit. Although not thoroughgoing egalitarians, they nevertheless appealed to an increasingly politicized artisan class and to the mass of immigrants who poured into Philadelphia and other seaport towns in the 1790s.[5]

In order to succeed in their aim of unleashing a Republican populism, they needed the support of pamphleteers and publicists, those whom Senator William Maclay of Pennsylvania called "gladiators of the quill." Callender was obviously a suitable *tirailleur*, experienced with his pen and, more importantly, ideologically committed to Republicanism. His writings for the *Aurora* in 1794 and 1795, his frequently astringent reports in the *Philadelphia Gazette*, and the reputation of his Edinburgh writings testified to his impeccable credentials.[6]

Among those determined to foster Callender's talents was John Beckley (1757–1807), who had first met Callender through his duties as clerk of the House of Representatives, which included overseeing the congressional reporters in the chamber. Beckley was the Republican party's political manager, its major national organizer as well as an intriguer in Pennsylvania state politics. An incorrigible collector and disseminator of political information, gossip, and rumor, Beckley "had extremely strong and dedicated Republican convictions, verging on fanaticism at times. He was very bold in his political approach, much too bold in the opinion of some more conservative Republicans."[7]

At about this time Callender also became acquainted with Tench Coxe (1755–1824), whom he assisted with printing matters relating to the publication of *A View of the United States* and from whom he borrowed books. Coxe in 1796 was commissioner of the revenue. Originally appointed to the Treasury—claimed Senator Maclay—to act as Alexander Hamilton's propagandist, Coxe held an equivocal political position, working for Hamilton yet corresponding with and assisting Thomas Jefferson, until in 1794 he was overlooked for the position of secretary of the treasury in favor of his rival, Oliver Wolcott. Thereafter, although Hamilton appointed him to another post, Coxe was a disappointed man. He drifted closer to the Republicans, becoming intimate with the militants Beckley and Bache, whose intense Anglophobia he shared.[8]

Coxe, from an old established American family although effectively an arriviste himself, probably was not a regular bottle companion of Bache, Beckley, and Callender, but another who was, and who became part of the Republican literary world in Philadelphia in the mid–1790s, was Mathew Carey's younger brother, James (fl.1782–1801). A cheerful, genially roguish Irishman, James Carey had arrived in Philadelphia in 1792, having previously been editor and joint owner of the Dublin newspaper *Rights of Irishmen*. For several years he traversed the American states, failing in attempts to establish a number of newspapers, borrowing money from his brother, and chasing actresses from theater to theater, until he finally settled in Philadelphia. There he set up a printing press, wrote anonymous Republican pamphlets, and again failed with several newspaper ventures. He and Callender became drinking companions, firm friends, and fellow debtors. In Callender's view, James Carey was the most honest and creative Republican writer in Philadelphia.[9]

Two other Irish colleagues of Callender, both of whom wrote paragraphs and articles for the *Aurora* on a regular basis, were William Duane (1760–1835) and Dr. James Reynolds (fl.1782–1807). Duane, later to be a leading radical Republican newspaper editor, had first come to prominence when deported from India for expressing unwelcome political opinions in his newspaper, the *World*. Back in England in 1795, he had joined the London Corresponding Society, was prominent in their monster meetings toward the end of that year, and with the British authorities breathing down his neck, had escaped to America, where he arrived in July 1796. For a time editor of Thomas Bradford's Philadelphia *Merchant's Daily Advertiser,* he soon achieved notoriety, as "Jasper Dwight," for his attack on George Washington and for his connections with the Bache faction. One of his friends was Dr. James Reynolds, who had arrived in the United States from Ireland in 1794. A leading Freemason in the 1780s and a member of the United Irishmen, Reynolds had been imprisoned in Dublin in 1793. In Philadelphia he was to become passionately involved in partisan politics in the late 1790s.[10]

Bache, Carey, Coxe, Beckley, Duane, and Reynolds formed with Callender a group of militant hard-line Republican propagandists in Philadelphia. Through their activities, Callender became acquainted with several local Republican leaders. In 1798 he could call Alexander J. Dallas (1759–1817), secretary of the Commonwealth of Pennsylvania, his "particular friend." He was also on good terms with the "merchant-Republican" John Swanwick (1759–1798). The son of a Loyalist wagon master, Swanwick began his rise to wealth as financial assistant to Robert Morris, eventually becoming a partner in the mercantile house of Willing, Morris, and Swanwick. In 1794 he defeated Thomas Fitzsimmons for a Philadelphia seat in the House of Representatives. Diminutive, modish, with a penchant for writing light verse, Swanwick was a natural target for Federalist pamphleteers who—enraged by his electoral successes that represented the first clear threat to the old elite's political and social hegemony—ridiculed him for his effeminacy, his foppishness, and his willingness to disport himself at young ladies' boarding schools.[11]

Callender's association with the Philadelphia politician began in 1794, when he became involved in the electioneering that culminated in Swanwick's victory over Fitzsimmons. In 1796, in reponse to the increasingly bitter attacks by Cobbett, Swanwick employed Callender to write a defense of his life, entitled *British Honour and Humanity.* The literary warfare between Cobbett and Swanwick tottered toward stalemate in 1796; Cobbett, too, had to write an autobiography in defense of his career and character. Even after Swanwick suffered financial disaster in 1797, Callender remained faithful to him, and to his reputation after his death in 1798.[12]

Swanwick was only one of a number of wealthy merchants and manufacturers to attain a leading position in Philadelphia Republican circles. Another was Thomas Leiper (1745–1825), one of the city's largest manufacturers of tobacco products and the owner of considerable urban real estate. He had played a significant role in the Revolutionary War; and in the 1788 Grand Federal Procession in Philadelphia, celebrating the new Constitution, Leiper had carried the tobacconists' standard. Like Swanwick, he was a noted philanthropist, serving for many years on the board of St. Andrew's Society, an organization established to give aid to new Scottish immigrants. Of all the people with whom Callender was acquainted in the United States, Leiper was the most helpful and persistently loyal. Following Callender's flight from Philadelphia in 1798, Leiper took in and brought up his children, even though he had thirteen of his own. Callender never spoke of Leiper with anything but gratitude: "The friendship of Mr. Leiper was of one hundred times more consequence to [me], than that of the whole tribe of democrats and republicans put together." He was, for more than two years, a perfect father figure for Callender.[13]

In Philadelphia, therefore, Callender lived his life at three levels: among his family, in increasing poverty from mid–1796; among his fellow scribblers, alternating between printshops, bookshops, and taverns; and, more infrequently, among the society of some of the leaders of the Philadelphia Republican party. His acquaintances had several common characteristics that brought them closer together. Apart from Bache, Coxe, and possibly Duane (who although considered Irish had been born on the Canadian border), all had been born abroad. Dallas had been born in the West Indies, Leiper in Scotland, Swanwick in Liverpool, Beckley in London, Reynolds in County Tyrone, and the Careys in Dublin. Except for Leiper, most of them were of a similar age to Callender, in their mid to late thirties in 1796. All, even Tench Coxe, needed to make their own way in life, which they had done with varying degrees of success. Like Callender, therefore, they were upwardly mobile, aspiring newcomers, at the height of their physical powers, and anxious to improve their status in what they thought ought to have been, but was not, an open society.

By 1794–95 their political views were tending to converge. All of Callender's acquaintances living in the United States in 1789 had supported the establishment of a strong central government. But as Alexander Hamilton's domestic policies emerged, Leiper, Swanwick, Mathew Carey, Cox, and Dallas shifted their ground toward Republicanism. Leiper, Swanwick, Bache, and Dallas became members of the Democratic Society of Pennsylvania. All were strongly Anglophobic. Perhaps their most important common characteristic, however, was their representativeness, not of the conservative agrarian Republicanism of the Virginia planters and western farmers, but of an egalitarian, economic nationalist Republicanism of the urban seaboard. This wing of the party emerged in the 1790s in opposition to Hamilton's policies and was to be vitally important in diversifying the appeal of Jefferson's party. Swanwick, Leiper, Mathew Carey, and Coxe all held a vision of America's future in which agriculture, commerce, the carrying trade, and domestic manufacturing would develop interdependently. The United States, they felt, should become self-reliant. The Federalists' policy of favoring trade with Britain, at the expense of local manufacturing interests and trade with the French West Indies, and the fiscal measures that underpinned their foreign policy needed to be overturned, in favor of a mercantilist policy of economic reciprocity which put America's interests before those of any foreign power.[14]

II

As part of the development of his republican principles, Callender elaborated on his Philadelphia Republican colleagues' economic nationalist views in several pamphlets published between the end of 1795 and Jefferson's electoral victory in 1800. Together, these writings belie the opinion of many historians that Callender was no more than an amoral party hack, the unprincipled conduit for scandalous gossip and billingsgate. One cannot ignore that side of his career, but there was another dimension—his vision of America's future as a freedom-loving, independent, egalitarian republic—that also needs to be addressed if his career is fully to be appreciated. Unlike his fellow scribblers on both sides of politics, who expended most of their energies on immediate, ephemeral issues, Callender, in addition to his political squibs, also attempted to develop a comprehensive theory of revolutionary republican politics. He was never to achieve his aim: the continual worry of feeding his family; the pressure of producing regular newspaper paragraphs and hackwork for the printers; and his own character defects, which included a lack of perseverence, a certain timidity in the face of sudden adversity, and the lure of the bottle and of bottle companions, help to explain his ultimate failure. But among the more organized of his writings can be found the main outlines of a political philosophy which establishes Callender as a true transatlantic revolutionary.

By aligning himself with the Philadelphia economic nationalists, Callender was not rejecting the economic values that he had promoted in Edinburgh. Admittedly, Leiper, Swanwick, Mathew Carey, and Coxe were mercantilists who desired government intervention in the economy, and Callender had violently attacked British mercantilism in 1791 and 1792. But, like the economic nationalists, Callender had always accepted the desirability of a commercial society and had recognized the reliance of America's continued independence on a government-inspired economic policy which protected the nation's interests. For Callender, whether he was thinking of Scotland or of America, the real threat to independence came from British mercantilist policies, which had kept the Scots in subordination and now threatened to do the same to Americans. Hamilton's political economy had to be discredited, not because it was mercantilist, but because it was designed deliberately to dovetail with British trade policies and to recognize America's subordination to British interests.

One feature of Hamilton's program that particularly irritated Republican economic nationalists was the preference for raising revenue by excise duties, rather than by a land tax or a tax on stock or bank transactions. Nothing showed more clearly the British bias of Hamilton's program than his decision to tax American manufactured goods. Protective tariffs, not a tax on manufactures, the economic nationalists asserted, were necessary if America was ever to compete with Britain.

Although the excise laws as a political issue first emerged as part of Hamilton's program in 1791, they only became of major concern in Philadelphia in 1794 when extended to cover a new range of products, including snuff, refined sugar, and carriages. Opposition to this new revenue legislation, which ironically was necessary to pay for war preparations against Britain, was partly channeled through the Democratic Society and was used as an electioneering issue. By campaigning in support of antiexcise candidates, says Roland Baumann, the protesters "left behind the deferential politics of an earlier age as the manufacturers of Philadelphia sought to participate in society and government as equals of the gentry."[15]

This protest campaign was tailor-made for Callender. His background of writing for the Edinburgh brewers probably gave him a more intimate knowledge of the history and workings of the British excise system than anyone else in the United States. In particular, Callender was able to demonstrate that the 1794 Revenue Act was mostly a paraphrasing of British legislation. He had used this knowledge to attack excise policy in anonymous articles and paragraphs in the *Aurora* throughout 1794 and 1795 and thus could claim some credit for Swanwick's election to the House of Representatives and for adding to congressional and popular pressure that eventually led to a revised revenue law in March 1795 and its regular suspension until 1800.[16]

Callender's major role in the antiexcise campaign was to write, on commission from Philadelphia's tobacco manufacturers, *A Short History of the Nature and Consequences of Excise Laws*, published in Philadelphia in December 1795. One of Callender's better works, it was a well-argued, lucid, and effective critique of the inequities, weaknesses, and inefficiencies of the excise system of taxation, as well as a comprehensive account of the antiexcise campaign in Philadelphia. *A Short History* is significant in two ways: as a piece of propaganda and as a work in which egalitarian doctrines were used to support an economic nationalist policy. It was effective propaganda primarily because of its concentration on the insidious nature of excise. Excise, wrote Callender, "may fairly be classed with that noted trio, *famine, pestilence,* and the *sword.* Its effects are less sudden and terrible, but, *like the worm that never dies,* they are constantly acting; and acting not only to destroy the industry, but likewise to subvert the morals of those who are subject to them." Moral degeneration was inevitable, for the high taxes virtually forced manufacturers to give false production figures under oath and offered opportunities for official corruption. Do not be fooled, continued Callender, into believing that only snuff producers, sugar refiners, and carriage makers would suffer. Inevitably, if the British experience was any guide, everyone would eventually be drawn into the excise system, either as other manufacturers became excisable or as the full political and social ramifications of the system unfolded. In a rousing, if exaggerated, conclusion, Callender wrote:

> If these Acts of Congress are not repealed, the mischief will not end with the extinction of sugar refiners, and snuff makers. The *sacra fames* of gauging, disappointed of its prey, will from necessity burst into new channels. The nation that, for eight years, bled in every vein to buy its freedom, will gaze on with criminal apathy while the brewer, the tanner, the tallow chandler, the soapboiler, the paper maker, the nailer, the hatter, and the newsprinter ascend the scaffold of excise. Smugglers and watchers, with the whole gang of spies and informers, will multiply like the leeches of Britain, and spread over the continent faster and farther than the Hessian fly. Bribery and perjury will, as in England, cease to be infamous. A standing army will soon become requisite for supporting a system universally detested. A riot act will be transcribed like our excise laws, from the British original, and . . . will hold out in ghastly characters, an epitaph on departed liberty. Public debt, instead of being diminished, will ulcerate into a magnitude that Potosi could not redeem; while British agents and imports entomb the manufactures of America in the grave of her independence.[17]

This rhetoric, involving an image of Americans losing by government policy what they had gained by a revolutionary war, had a powerful impact. What gave it additional significance for the artisan and domestic manufacturer—for whom the pamphlet was primarily written—was its egalitarian foundations, for Callender demanded the replacement of the regressive excise tax with a progressive land tax. His theoretical justification for this emerged from his consideration of Adam Smith's *Wealth of Nations,* which he used very selectively to buttress his promoters' interests.

Callender began by accepting Smith's proposition, with its Lockean overtones, that "government is in reality nothing but *An association to protect the rich against the poor*," for its primary purpose was to secure the liberty and property of its citizens. But Callender also took up and gave a twist to Smith's point that liberty for the poor—"those who subsist only by their efforts of industry"—was really just another form of property, indeed, their only form of property. With no assets but their labor capacity, the poor must use their liberty (or personal freedom) productively in order to provide their basic necessities. The "profit" or wage ensuing "constitutes their whole riches." Having thus subsumed liberty into property (he ignored the wealthy's liberty), Callender was able to reduce Smith's definition of the role of government to "an association for the protection of property."[18]

Once he had demonstrated, on the basis of Smith's authority, that "property" included the poor's labor power, Callender argued for the state's duty to protect their interests as well as those of the rich. One way of doing this was for government to accept the egalitarian notion that the wealthy, deriving more benefit than the poor from its protection, ought to pay more to support its infrastructure. Again, following Smith (as well as Francis Hutcheson and Sir James Steuart), Callender argued that taxation should conform to the four principles of equity, certainty, convenience, and administrative efficiency. "All taxes," wrote Callender, "ought to be raised, as nearly as possible, in proportion to the quantity of property possessed by individuals under the protection of the state." With simple examples reminiscent of those such as the pinmakers used by Smith in *Wealth of Nations* to explain the division of labor, Callender asked why, if it is natural to expect a man drinking two bottles of wine in a tavern to pay more than a man drinking one bottle, the rich should not be expected to pay more than the poor in taxes, if they were gaining greater advantages? That in reality governments preferred to ignore such arguments and to impose regressive rather than progressive taxes, i.e, an excise rather than a land tax, was simply explained: the wealthy controlled government and ensured the protection of their own interests.[19]

Whether Adam Smith would have agreed with Callender's reasoning is a moot point, although he certainly would have approved of the emphasis on progressive taxation. What is indisputable, however, is Callender's determination to invoke egalitarian principles to discredit both the excise system and the ruling elites. He must have gained considerable satisfaction when the Philadelphia manufacturers, led by Leiper, sent copies of his pamphlet to every senator, congressman, and principal officer in the federal government.[20]

The excise was, however, only one feature of Hamilton's economic program. In the next few years Callender strove to discredit Federalist economic doctrine in its entirety, substituting for it a political economy on which, although in general conformity to the parameters of Republican economic thought, he stamped his own personal opinions. The key to America's long-term future, he felt, was to break free of Europe's malign influence. Callender agreed with Adam Smith that "to prohibit a great people from making all they can of every part of their own produce, or from employing their stock and industry in the way that they judge most advantageous to themselves, is a manifest violation of the most sacred rights of mankind." Although Smith deduced from this that government should pursue a laissez-faire policy, intervening in the economy as little as possible, Callender realized that in current circumstances America's economy would remain lopsided unless there was positive discrimination in favor of home manufactures.[21]

Callender repeatedly hammered home the need to promote domestic manufactures. Until America no longer needed to import manufactured goods, he wrote, its independence would never be secure. "It is ridiculous and humiliating, that we should so frequently send 4,000 miles for a pair of blankets, a pen-knife, a psalm-book, and a quire of paper. This situation, so unnatural and absurd, cannot last long, and, the sooner that we put an end to it, the better." Home manufactures should be encouraged, for they were "a more safe and durable acquisition than foreign commerce. They can involve no external quarrel, and they are beyond the reach of external piracy. The tanner, at Lancaster, has nothing to fear from the corsairs of Barbary; and a potter, or cutler, on the Susquehanna, may smile at the menaces of the British navy."[22]

Manufacturers, moreover, were a more useful class of citizens than the sailor, on whom international commerce depended. "Of the various classes of American citizens," wrote Callender in 1798, "almost none is so truly valuable as an industrious and intelligent manufacturer. The labours of no one tend so directly to establish the independence of the Union." By buying abroad, one supported a tradesman who was not a fellow citizen. "A mechanic, residing in America, forms a part of the nation. His earnings are expended among us. His family are blended with, and augment the general mass of population; whereas a sailor is often but slightly connected with his native country, in which he is indeed a stranger."[23]

Domestic manufactures, however, would not take their rightful place in America's economy—side by side with agriculture—until the Federalists' economic and fiscal programs were overturned. Above all, the Bank of the United States, which "is not merely a nuisance, but a monster,"[24] had to be destroyed. Unconstitutional from the outset, because, as James Madison had claimed in 1790, the Federal Convention had meant to veto Congress's right to create chartered bodies,[25] the Bank of the United States was at the root of many of America's problems. Callender was not, like many Republicans, opposed to banks in general, nor was he opposed to the issuing, in moderation, of paper money.[26] But the Bank of the United States had printed far too much paper money. Partly on account of subsequent inflation, which had doubled the price of labor, the bank had "filled Philadelphia with insolvencies" and had "materially impeded the maturity, or rather infancy, of American manufactures." More directly, however, it had also been the bank's policy to promote foreign trade, through its lending strategy, at the expense of domestic manufacturing. What encouragement it had given the latter was "as but by proxy, through the medium of that wealth which commerce tended to produce."[27]

In general a bank, wrote Callender, "is, or ought to be, designed for the good of society at large. Individuality of discouragement, or of favour, is excluded from the scheme." This was particularly the case for the Bank of the United States, because every citizen, through taxation, was part owner of the capital stock vested in the federal government under the terms of the charter. But "it is notorious that this bank has been employed as an engine of government, to serve the views of the British interest. Discounts have often been refused . . . to men of undoubted opulence, merely on account of the republican principles of those who drew or accepted of the bill. The despotism of paper money pervades every muscle and vein of Philadelphian society. *The domination of British custom-house officers has been exchanged for that of American stockjobbers.*"[28]

The only way permanently to destroy the domination of this British connection was to break the commerical nexus by encouraging home manufactures: "To promote all kinds of domestic industry, is the most effectual method to explode the schemes of foreign monopoly, and the conspiracies of European despotism, to invigorate THE POLITICAL PROGRESS OF THE UNITED STATES, to extend the basis of their prosperity, and ensure their independence."[29]

Callender's heavy emphasis on home manufactures in his political economy put him to some extent outside the Republican mainstream in the 1790s. Although most Republicans—including Callender's fellow radical emigrants from Britain—accepted the reality of America being a commercial society and did not hanker for a static, communal, agrarian society, they tended to follow Adam Smith, Thomas Paine, and Thomas Jefferson in advocating only the bare minimum of government interference. Jefferson's policy, for instance, was "to let things take their natural course without help or impediment." Callender's proposals, in contrast, required government action on a greater scale, in the form of protective trade barriers to allow fledgling industries to flourish.[30]

Moreover, although most Republicans, like Callender, opposed the preferential treatment given by the Hamiltonian system to merchants trading with Britain, they nevertheless positively encouraged the extension of American commerce throughout the world. Paine's vision was of a world living in peace and harmony through unfettered commercial exchange; Jefferson saw an increasingly commercialized American agriculture producing large surpluses for export as a means of ensuring America's future prosperity. Callender, however, held ambivalent views on the wisdom of overseas trade at all. At times he recognized the usefulness of commerce; to it "we are obliged for many of the amusements, of the luxuries, the elegances and even of the conveniences of life." Nevertheless, "without foreign trade, this country may be very happy." If overseas commerce were discontinued, "America would continue to be what she is; for she would still possess the greatest and most inexhaustible sources of all the necessaries and substantial enjoyments of life." Tea would be the only article for which some might grieve. Callender's vacillations resulted from his pacifism; trade had always been at the forefront of the causes of wars, as *The Political Progress of Britain* had so clearly demonstrated. In 1798, when war with France was expected at any time, he even suggested an isolationist policy: "America should, like the armidilla, withdraw within her shell."[31]

Thus, consistent with his earlier vision of Scotland achieving genuine independence with the help of manufacturing villages dotted across the countryside, Callender proposed the same solution to America's problem of growing dependency on Britain. In this instance, based on his Scottish experiences, Callender was more farsighted than most of his Republican colleagues, for world political events after 1800 were to force the Republicans, when in power, to move away from a laissez-faire philosophy toward the mercantilist political economy that Callender had been advocating since the mid–1790s.

One should not, perhaps, take Callender's prescience too far. He was indebted, as were most of his generation, to the ideas of others, both in Scotland and in Philadelphia. Nor did Callender envision the future of America as an urbanized, industrialized nation. He held the common opinion that "such immense capitals as London, Paris, or even Amsterdam, cannot subsist in America, for centuries to come." Thousands of immigrants might swarm across the Atlantic, but there would be ample room for them to avoid "for the sake of subsistence . . . [burying] themselves forever in mines, or unwholesome manufactories, or [rushing] into mercenary regiments." Callender's future America was to be self-sufficient and peaceful, and its people were to be either farmers or independent small tradesmen who "with a moderate portion of industry [could] hardly fail to supply a plentiful competence."[32]

III

Callender's future Americans were also to be democratic republicans. Unlike his economic views, which remained virtually unchanged from his days in Scotland, Callender's political theories in the United States underwent modification, usually along radically democratic lines conforming with the egalitarian Antifederalism of 1787–88. In Edinburgh he had evolved an extended critique of government which, with its emphasis on the ubiquity of corruption and on the unceasing concentration of power in the hands of the rich, he considered still applicable to government under the Federalists in the 1790s. But before his flight across the Atlantic, the positive aspects of his politics had not been developed. As he had recognized in 1782, "it is more easy to demolish a palace than to erect a cottage." His ideal form of government had been left unclear: his views on republicanism were ambiguous; he seemingly had little faith in the political wisdom of the masses; and he questioned the value of elections, frequent or otherwise. Events in America were to change his opinions on all these aspects of politics, although his retreat from misanthropy was to be temporary.[33]

The success of John Swanwick in his contest with Thomas Fitzsimmons for one of the federal seats of Philadelphia in 1794 opened Callender's eyes to the possibilities inherent in a representative system of government. A sitting congressman had been ousted by an electorate which disapproved of his antiexcise stance. In Scotland, the opinions of the population had counted for little at election time; in Philadelphia, public opinion was reflected at the polls. With sudden understanding Callender wrote of the consequences of Swanwick's electoral victory: "It requires nothing more than a change in their representation to produce a change of measures. If those to whom they have entrusted the power of legislation, should be unmindful of their interests and neglectful of the public weal, they can redress themselves on an election day by withholding their suffrages from them in favour of better men. The vigilant and careful exercise of the right of election is certainly the greatest security of freedom and ought never to be neglected." Leading on logically from his conviction of the value of voting was Callender's conversion to annual elections. "One year is long enough" between elections, he wrote. "The nation cannot hold its legislators by too short a bridle."[34]

By the end of 1796 Callender was expressing a fervent commitment to democracy. "Democrat in future shall be my political name," he wrote rather excitedly. Just what he meant by this is not entirely clear, although there is an element of defiance in his statement, a militant response to Cobbett's recent *History of the American Jacobins Commonly Called Democrats* and to other Federalists' increasingly pejorative use of the term to malign their opponents. Nor did Callender have any objection to being called a Jacobin, as long as its definition was confined to the principles of early members of the Parisian club, who were friends "to rational and pacific freedom."[35]

Like many of his contemporaries, however, Callender defined *democracy* in an idiosyncratic manner. With some commentators the term retained its classical meaning as the popular part of a mixed government (monarchy, aristocracy, democracy). At other times, usually in conjunction with the modifier "pure," democracy represented a system of government in a small state where all decisions were made by the citizens as a body. It was this definition of democracy that Madison, in *Federalist* No. 10, set against a "republic," the form of government based on popular sovereignty and the system of representation. By distinguishing a democracy from a republic, Madison was rejecting the definitions of Montesquieu, who of all eighteenth-century political writers did most to popularize the concept of pure democracy. Montesquieu distinguished between two types of republic: a democratic one, where the citizens ruled directly, and an "aristocratic" one, where only a section of the people ruled. When Callender denominated himself a democrat, he used the ideas of both Montesquieu and Madison. Following the former, he claimed that democracy existed when the whole body of citizens held power; when only part of the people hold power, an aristocratic republic existed. But, like Madison and unlike Montesquieu, Callender did not envision a democracy as one form of a republic; it was a system of government in its own right. To be a republican was to be an aristocrat; to be called a democrat was honorable.[36]

If a pure democracy was Callender's ideal, in practice he knew that most of the states were too large and too populous for such a system to be politically practicable. Nevertheless, he continued to fight for a system of government as close as possible to his ideal, as his views on the Federal Constitution demonstrate. Callender's position was straightforward, even simplistic. He totally rejected all forms of mixed government and mechanistic checks and balances, even when they were justified by an appeal to popular sovereignty. Any provision in the Constitution that widened the gap between the sovereign people and the institutions of government was reprehensible and should be abandoned. He queried the need for a federation of states. Unlike James Madison, who believed that a large republic was politically feasible, Callender favored Montesquieu's more traditional dictum that only small republics could survive without eventually succumbing to tyranny. Far from bringing stability and security to the people, a large republic merely increased opportunities for corruption, bringing the tyranny of a minority ever closer. According to Callender:

> The reproach of peculation, is not peculiar to any political system, or to any country. More, or less, this kind of theft must always take place. The larger the territory, the more numerous are the chances and opportunities for plunder. When simpletons or sycophants prattle about a virtuous and uncorrupted administration, it is not easy to resist from smiling. . . . If it is impracticable, for a single man, with the best possible assistance, to manage an hundred farms, it is vastly more so, for a king, or president, to govern with propriety a territory 1500 miles wide.[37]

There were, claimed Callender, "fathomless pitfalls and stupendous contradictions" in the Federal Constitution, including the division of government into four spheres—an executive, two legislative branches, and a judiciary. Whereas the Federalists and moderate Republicans regarded the Constitution's system of checks and balances as a useful way of reducing, by separation and division, the threat of majoritarianism stemming from the doctrine of the people as sovereign, Callender took the opposite tack. The closer the sovereign people came to their government, and the fewer the hindrances to the expression of the popular will, the better. The only branches of government he considered necessary were the House of Representatives and the judiciary, with the latter firmly under the control of the former. The president should never have been allowed to nominate, and the Senate to ratify, federal judges. The power of selection should have been vested in the House of Representatives, with one Supreme Court judge being turned out annually in rotation and not permitted to return for two years. "Thus," he wrote, "the supreme court judges would have been held in a perpetual and formidable check by the representatives of the people."[38]

Callender's opinion on the executive branch of government was determined partly by the absence of direct voting for the presidency and partly by his inability to keep a distinction between the office of president and its incumbents. His personal contempt for Washington and John Adams carried over to the office itself. He denounced the provision in the Constitution enabling a president to seek unlimited consecutive terms of office as the first step toward monarchy. He also accused both Washington and Adams of interfering too much in the domain of the legislature. When in 1798 Congress appeared to be totally subservient to Adams, Callender wrote that it was "no more than the hands and feet of government[;] the executive is the head, and has the sole power to deliberate, to execute means, to originate, deliberate, and conclude on every governmental question, that can possibly arise. [T]o legislate means—to register every edict of the executive. The executive is the actual legislature, the legislature the executive."[39]

Moreover, even if Congress did pass legislation independently, the president could exercise his right of veto. But such power, claimed Callender, presumed the executive to be superior in wisdom, abilities, and knowledge to the combined houses of the legislature. So far, he wrote caustically, the president had displayed only mediocre talents. Again displaying his commitment to extreme democracy, Callender argued that the executive ought to be no more than a figurehead. Apart from signing bills into law, "a trifling or inflammatory speech at the opening of each session of Congress, is almost the only real duty that a president has to perform." The whole job could be done quite competently for $1,000 a year.[40]

The legislature was the branch of government where the popular voice was most clearly heard. But Callender could see no justification for an upper house, whether it was under the Federal Constitution or part of a state constitution. He particularly deprecated the absence of a uniform electoral system for federal senators. Selection by state legislators, an effective muffling of the popular voice, was undemocratic; senators elected in this manner could not be called representatives of the people. Following on logically from this, Callender condemned the idea of senators representing their state, rather than the states' citizens. It was absurd that a chamber in which each state was equally represented whatever its population size and in which the senators numbered only one-third of the House of Representatives had the right to reject any law passed by the lower house. As with the presidency, becoming a senator did not make a man wise or better than a congressman, yet the Constitution assumed this to be the case. The *Gazette of the United States* had even been presumptuous enough to call the Senate and the executive "the two superior branches of government." If this be true, thundered Callender, "it is a usurpation," an attempt "to render the House of Representatives puppets only." In reality, senators had little value. Attending a normal day in the chamber, a senator would "have decently heard prayers, picked his teeth, and paired his nails, till 12 o'clock. He would, then, at the adjournment of the House have lounged for half an hour in the lobby of the representatives, and gone agreeably home to dinner."[41]

In 1800 Callender wrote: "It was the judgement of Patrick Henry, and it is mine, that the federal constitution, as it now stands, is good for almost nothing; that it is as full of imperfections, as a sieve is full of holes; that unless this compact shall meet with numerous and material amendments, it must forever prove a thorn festering in the midriff of

American prosperity." Callender was right to compare himself with Patrick Henry, or at least the Henry of 1788, for his politics, if not his political economy, were Antifederalist. His proposed reforms of the Constitution conformed closely to the unsuccessful program of the Antifederalists during the ratification debates. He was prepared to accept a national government only if it consisted of a unicameral legislature, with a weak executive and a controlled judiciary. He believed in states' rights, including the right unilaterally to withdraw from the Union. He admired several aspects of the old Confederation, which it was currently "fashionable to despise," especially its unicameralism, its focus on annual elections, and the constituents' right to recall their delegates.[42]

Callender's analysis of the Constitution, scattered throughout his writings, confirms his commitment to two basic principles: a long-held fear of the inevitability of corruption and a more recent allegiance to the popular voice being heard frequently, loudly, and unequivocally. The former principle continued to pervade American thought in the 1790s, being held by Federalists as much as by Republicans. But Callender's democratic Antifederalism alienated him from most Republicans, making him the spokesman only for a number of minority groups. This explains why, in the fall of 1798, Callender informed Thomas Jefferson that he was "entirely sick even of the Republicans." He accused them of dishonesty and of disloyalty. "In Europe it is understood," he wrote, "that if a political party does not support their assistant writer, they at least do not crush him, whereas I have been crushed by the very gentry whom I was defending."[43]

Callender appears to have been oblivious to the fact that many of the doctrines he put forward in defense of the Republicans were as unpalatable to most in his party as they were to his enemies. His radical democratic leanings frequently exasperated many moderate Republicans (Callender's "gentry") who held seats in Congress. Their disapproval was partly a consequence of the conflict of his scurrility and bad taste with their rather precious code of conduct and etiquette, but primarily it arose from their distaste for his democratic militancy. Moderate Republicans were content with the existing structure of the Federal Constitution and in principle supported a strong national government. Their opposition to the Federalists stemmed from their conviction of their enemies' misuse of federal authority. The solution, they believed, was not to alter the Constitution but to change the government through the electoral process, with the ultimate intention of converting the Federalists to their version of republicanism. With the moderate Republicans in office, the legitimate powers of the central government would be used wisely and constitutionally.[44]

It is thus hardly surprising that moderate Republicans held ambivalent opinions about their pamphleteer. Calender was, quite simply, too militant, too uncouth, and too independent. In addition, he did little to hide his contempt for what he regarded as the moderates' pusillanimity. He appealed much more to other sections of the Republican party, especially the "Old Republicans" and the urban radicals, as well as to the rougher, less deferential parts of the electorate. The "Old Republicans" and urban radicals were temperamentally Antifederalist, inherently jealous of power and its capacity for misuse, anxious to reassert the doctrine of strict construction, and prepared to amend the Constitution both to simplify and to weaken the central government.[45]

Nevertheless, Callender had, as even his most hostile critics agreed, many qualities that the Republicans desperately needed to tap. He was expert in ridicule, satire, and invective. He could be guaranteed to diminish the public stature of his opponents. He swapped blow for blow in the Philadelphia newspaper war between 1796 and 1798, totally demoralizing John Fenno, editor of the *Gazette of the United States*, and he repeated his victory against the editors of the *Virginia Federalist* and *Virginia Gazette* in 1800. Only Cobbett could compete with Callender as an effective propagandist.

Ultimately, however, Callender was uncontrollable. His pride, vanity, and strong attachment to independence made him extremely difficult to handle. His insistence on attacking the Federalists in his own reckless and often ignorant way frequently startled his less extreme colleagues. He had little tactical awareness and no understanding that the opposition, if they were to gain office, needed to develop a strategy that not only blackened the Federalists but also persuaded voters of the Republicans' suitability to govern. Callender's analysis of the American Revolution is a perfect example of how—in the excitement of harrying specific foes—he could make the most outlandish and politically naive statements. To write, as did Callender in 1798, that the American Revolution was only half a revolution, in that it did not secure equality for all citizens, was perhaps unexceptionable to most Republicans faced with a Federalism which had "now taken the ground and doctrines of George III." But the claim that the Revolution had been unnecessary was met with stunned incredulity. In the *History of 1796* Callender declared:

> A gang of banditti from the town of Boston began the American revolution, by unfurling the standard of villainy. They wantonly destroyed 342 chests of tea, in [the] presence, and with the approbation of an immense crowd of spectators. The act of parliament for shutting up the port of Boston, was the natural and suitable consequence of that shameful transaction. The burning of the Gaspee schooner, at Provi-

dence, in Rhode Island, because it obstructed smuggling, was another
wanton outrage, that must be reprobated by every man who is fit for
living under a civilised government. The whole continent was dragged
prematurely into war, to save the factious townsmen of Boston from a
chastisement that some of them very highly deserved. . . . The wrongs
of America were chiefly in [their] imagination. She was more lightly
taxed than any other country in the world. If the people of New
England had behaved with equal moderation and dignity as those of
Virginia, it is likely enough that we might still have been British
colonies, and in a happy situation, without any revolution at all.[46]

This was an extraordinary statement for a Republican penman to
make. Written in the context of an attack on the Massachusetts Federalist Harrison J. Otis, it presumably was intended to eulogize Virginians (mostly Republicans) by smearing New Englanders (mostly Federalists). The plan clearly backfired in the most embarrassing way. Not
only did Callender irritate all patriotic Americans by belittling the most
decisive and important event of their lives, but he also inadvertently
suggested that Virginians had been timid and lacking in patriotism. It
is hardly surprising that Callender sometimes greatly exasperated his
colleagues and gained a reputation for unreliability.

Nevertheless, the Republicans needed Callender, and although he
desired otherwise, Callender needed the Republicans. They hoped to
manipulate him and to keep his more bizarre opinions under control.
Callender, however, belonged to no man. He remained a runaway
rocket scattering sparks far and wide as he zigzagged through the
political firmament.

IV

Callender appreciated that a democratic society could function only if
its citizens were repeatedly exposed to accurate political information.
"The more that a nation knows about the mode of conducting its business," he wrote, "the better chance has that business of being properly
conducted." But he was also aware that "a representative government
is, from its very nature, liable to embarrassment from *conflicting opinions*." The key to Republican success, therefore, lay in the party's
ability to overwhelm Federalist propaganda by saturating the public
with its own interpretation of political events. Public opinion could best
be swayed through the effective use of newspapers and pamphlets,
particularly the former, for as many of Callender's contemporaries
noted, Americans were avid newspaper readers. Cobbett switched
from pamphlets to a daily newspaper in 1797 because "the thousands
who read [American newspapers] read nothing else." John Ward Fenno
claimed that "more than nine-tenths of the scanty literature of America

is made up of newspaper reading." Pierre Samuel du Pont believed that everybody "assiduously peruses the newspapers. The fathers read them aloud to their children while the mothers are preparing the breakfast." Callender, too, shared this opinion: "It is certain that the citizens of America derive their information almost exclusively from newspapers. Very few political pamphlets are published. . . . It is [the newspapers'] weakness, or ability, that must decide the fate of every administration."[47]

The usefulness of newspapers, however, depended on the sanctity of civil liberties, especially freedom of speech and of the press. Callender's whole career, from his first writings in Edinburgh, was premised on his right, and duty, to impart his versions of Truth and Justice to the world. Callender's only objective was "the discovery and publication of truth, without the smallest concern what nation, or what individual may chance to appear in an unfavourable light." In his new country he found that "it was the happy privilege of an American that he may prattle and print in what way he pleases, and without anyone to make him afraid." In 1800, after many vicissitudes occasioned by his pamphleteering, he remained intransigent: "I believe now, as I have always believed, that there ought to be no restraint upon the liberty of the press, so far as it concerns government, but public opinion."[48]

William Cobbett began his career as a propagandist in America by claiming:

> No man has a right to pry into his neighbour's private concerns; and the opinions of every man are his private concerns, while he keeps them so; that is to say, while they are confined to himself, his family and particular friends; but, when he makes these opinions public; when he once attempts to make converts; whether it be in religion, politics, or anything else; when he once comes forward as a candidate for public admiration, esteem or compassion, his opinions, his principles, his motives, every action of his life, public or private, become the fair subject of public discussion.

Callender agreed. "The conduct of men in public stations," he wrote, "is fair game." In an age when virtue had both a conventional moral meaning and a specific republican one, private vices could not be divorced from public actions. Only virtuous leaders could ensure the continued vitality of the Republic, and only by incessantly watching them could their virtue be assured. By appointing himself a watchdog on behalf of the public interest, Callender justified circulating the private foibles and public misdemeanors of prominent figures.[49]

Some evidence exists—at least for the period before he broke with the Republicans in 1801—to support Callender's claim that "I write truth, and am not a commonplace railer." First, attacks on individuals form only a part of his writings, most of which are concerned with political events and political principles. Second, the subjects of his vitriolic pen were always men in the public eye, either politicians or their adherents. Federalist propagandists such as Cobbett, Fenno, Noah Webster, and William Rind were legitimate targets, as were second-rank Federalist politicians such as Dayton, Smith, Sedgwick, and Harper. In the 1790s Callender did not gratuitously malign innocent or nonpolitical citizens. His victims may have objected to his strictures, but they all conformed to Cobbett's criteria of seeking public admiration, esteem, or compassion. All were subjected occasionally to name-calling, which seemed to be obligatory among propagandists of all persuasions, but Callender generally only accused them of faults and sins of a public nature. When, for example, William Duane accused Robert Goodloe Harper of miscegenation, Callender argued that "the world has no business with that part of a public character, unless . . . it shall be connected with some interesting political truth."[50]

Nevertheless, Callender did, to some degree, deserve his reputation for scurrility. In his political writings he always named names, scorning the contemporary conceit whereby only the first and last letters of a person's name were printed. His style of writing was frequently crude, harsh, and vindictive, a vulgarity of style that, he suggested, "is too well suited to the American character." Refined writing was totally unsuitable in a democracy. "It is not by trimming, or trifling, that the liberties of mankind are to be supported. Upon every political subject, it is proper to take the bull by the horns; and to endeavour, if possible, to cast him upon his back." In the process, however, the essence of truth was sometimes mislaid; opinion became fact, and unsupported facts were given the same level of credence as those that could be substantiated. Callender always claimed a willingness publicly to admit mistakes he had made, and he recognized that in the heat of preparing a daily newspaper, details were sometimes "imperfect, prejudiced, and contradictory." But all too often reasonable standards of evidence were ignored; proof of a fact, an interpretation, or an opinion was taken for granted, if Callender's own version of truth was thereby buttressed. As he had written of his comments on Samuel Johnson in 1783: "If it shall be insisted, that I aver what I have not proved, I answer, that for many averments regular proof is not required. Common report is sufficient."[51]

Callender's notoriety rests primarily on his personal attacks on some of America's greatest heroes: Washington, Adams, Hamilton, and later, Jefferson. Historians' contempt for Callender is thus perhaps understandable. America's Founding Fathers eventually went their own ways in the 1790s, and historians have followed those with whom they most empathize. Most have found, however, a suitable common scapegoat, on whom they could heap blame for bringing to public notice their heroes' limitations and frailties. Washington's partisanship, Hamilton's corruption and/or his adultery, Adams's intolerance of political opposition and "murder" of a supposed British mutineer from the frigate *Hermione*, and Jefferson's seduction of his slave—all either matters of opinion or incapable of proof—came to prominence primarily through the exposés of James Thomson Callender. None of these characteristics, real or imagined, of the Founding Fathers has undermined their essential greatness, but whenever their renown, eminence, virtue, and statecraft are considered, Callender's claims have to be faced. The price of the Founding Fathers' induction into an American Pantheon has been paid repeatedly in the coin of Callender's notoriety.

Washington was Callender's first major target. His attacks continued throughout 1796, as the Republicans vainly sought to destroy Jay's treaty by rejecting its funding, and halted only when Adams became president in 1797. Callender incessantly hammered at what he perceived to be Washington's weak point, his descent from the high moral ground of the impartial Father of his People to the position of a partisan. In what James D. Tagg has called "one of the most famous diatribes ever written against Washington," Callender excoriated the president for his apostasy:

> If ever a nation was debauched by a man, the American nation has been debauched by WASHINGTON. If ever a nation has suffered from the improper influence of a man, the American nation has been deceived by WASHINGTON. Let his conduct then be an example to future ages. Let it serve to be a warning that no man may be an idol, and that a people may confide in themselves rather than in an individual. Let the history of the federal government instruct mankind, that the marque of patriotism may be worn to conceal the foulest designs against the liberties of the people.

On the day of Adams's inauguration Callender rejoiced: "Every heart, in unison with the freedom and happiness of the people ought to beat high with exultation, that the name of WASHINGTON from this day ceases to give a currency to political iniquity, and to legalized corruption." In a key statement explaining why he had for so long assailed the president, Callender concluded: "Nefarious projects can no longer be supported by a name."[52]

Adams's accession to the presidency in 1797 began with a curious interlude. He had undergone a barrage of criticism from Republican writers in the months preceding the election (to which Callender, who had recently published his defense of Swanwick and was working on a new pamphlet, contributed little). But once Adams was known to have defeated Jefferson, the penmen were called to heel. Jefferson, who feared the prospect of Hamilton becoming president in the future, viewed Adams, suitably molded "to administer the government on its true principles," as a bulwark against the former treasurer's ambitions. News of Jefferson's attitude to the new president quickly circulated, and Bache, according to Callender, informed his writers: "Let us give him a fair trial and then, if he actually does wrong, our censures will fall with greater weight."[53]

An uneasy honeymoon period followed, during which the Republican press gently massaged the president's ego. If, wrote Callender later, Adams had "attempted to steer a middle course between the two parties, and to make a moderate use of his immense official patronage in securing funds, his interest must infallibly have been supported by an overwhelming majority of citizens. Without competition, or disturbance, he might have enjoyed his beloved salary, to the end of his life." Adams was not, however, fooled by the Republicans' soft words. According to Abigail Adams, "Their praise for a few weeks mortified him, much more, than all their impudent abuse." By the end of April 1797 Adams was warning his wife that "I shall soon be acquitted of the crime of *Chronicle, Argus,* and *Aurora* praise."[54]

Although John Adams abhorred party spirit and considered himself an impartial president serving the national interest, he recognized the impossibility of implementing a foreign policy capable of uniting the warring factions in Congress. Relations with France had steadily deteriorated in the second half of 1796, and war became a distinct possibility. In May 1797, following news of the French Directory's refusal to receive Charles Cotesworth Pinckney as American ambassador to replace the Francophile James Monroe, Adams made an aggressive speech to Congress in which he defended American honor and called for defensive measures, including a naval establishment. The Republican press turned on him. Callender, who for months had been claiming that America's pro-British policy would inevitably lead to war, was in the forefront of the attack. Adams, he wrote, had only pretended to be impartial; his May speech showed him to be a cold-blooded dissimulator, prepared to defend American honor when France was the aggressor but quiescent when Britain had acted likewise. With his customary blend of personal abuse—the president, that "poor old man" who was "in his dotage"—and sarcasm—"What a friend to the Rights of Man, to the Republic of France and to the peace of the United States is not John Adams"—Callender embarked on a campaign against the president that was not to end until Jefferson's electoral victory in 1800.[55]

V

The way in which Callender's writings on the new president conformed to the wishes expressed by Jefferson at the end of 1796 demonstrates his close involvement in a concerted Republican newspaper campaign, organized through a chain of command which stretched from the Virginia leadership—Jefferson, Madison, and Giles—to the Philadelphia penmen, including Callender, Duane, and Dr. James Reynolds. General strategy was determined at the top and filtered down through party manager John Beckley and Tench Coxe to Bache, who let loose the propaganda hounds. The existence of this chain linking Jefferson to "the gladiators of the quill" in 1797 raises some interesting questions concerning Callender's publication in June of the evidence of Alexander Hamilton's connections with the New York speculator James Reynolds in 1791 and 1792.

The so-called Reynolds affair has been the source of controversy ever since Callender breached the wall of silence surrounding it. It is amenable to three possible interpretations: that Hamilton had a long-running extramarital affair with James Reynolds's wife, Maria, for which he was blackmailed (Hamilton's own version); that Hamilton fabricated evidence of an affair in order to hide his involvement in illegal speculation (Callender's preferred version); and an interpretation that no one, except perhaps James Monroe, has suggested, that Hamilton had an affair with Maria Reynolds at the same time as indulging in speculation with her husband. Historians sympathetic to Hamilton have leaned toward the first interpretation; Jefferson sympathizers have chosen the second. Neither group has suggested that Callender performed a public service by publishing the evidence in 1797.[56]

The Reynolds affair first surfaced in November 1792 when Oliver Wolcott charged James Reynolds and Jacob Clingman with subornation of perjury "for the purpose of obtaining Letters of Administration on the estate of a person still living." Reynolds, who had been involved in shady deals for a number of years, went to jail to await trial, where he "threatened to make disclosures injurious to the character of some head of a Department." Clingman obtained bail and sought the help of his erstwhile employer, Pennsylvania congressman Frederick A. Muhlenberg, whom he told of Reynolds's threats. On 2 December, Muhlenberg sought the advice of Senator James Monroe and Congressman Abraham B. Venable; they immediately visited Reynolds, who repeated his claims that a high official had been involved in illegal financial dealings. That same day, with the knowledge of Governor Mifflin, Secretary of Pennsylvania Dallas, Wolcott, and Hamilton, it was agreed to drop charges against both Clingman and Reynolds in return for the list of creditors they had been using and the name of the person who had leaked the document from the Treasury. On the evening of the twelfth, Monroe and Muhlenberg visited Reynolds's rooms, where his wife, who was alone, reluctantly corroborated her husband's story.[57]

When Muhlenberg, Venable, and Monroe, as previously arranged, visited Reynolds on the thirteenth, they found "he had absconded, or concealed himself." Deciding against giving an immediate report of their suspicions to the president, the three congressmen presented their documentary evidence to Hamilton on 15 December and sought an explanation. That evening they met again at Hamilton's house in the presence of Wolcott. Hamilton explained his relations with Reynolds by producing other documents showing him to be the victim of blackmail as the result of his illicit affair with Maria Reynolds in 1791 and early 1792. The embarrassed congressmen dropped the investigation, leaving Hamilton with the impression that they had accepted his explanation. Hamilton was not corrupt, merely a philanderer.[58]

The Reynolds affair did not become public knowledge at this time, although a number of people soon became aware of it. Jefferson had been informed within days, recording in his *Anas* the names of others who had become conversant with the story. These included John Beckley and his chief clerk, Bernard Webb, whose involvement arose from the need to make copies of the documents obtained from Clingman for Hamilton. Obviously the story spread by word of mouth, for Callender knew of it in October 1795. On the same day as Beckley published an open letter to Oliver Wolcott in the *Aurora* in which he accused President Washington of overdrawing his salary, Callender raised the question of Wolcott's role in suppressing the Reynolds material.

> Quere—Whether a certain head of a department, was not in the month of December 1792, privy and party in the circumstances of a certain inquiry of a very suspicious aspect, respecting real malconduct on the part of his friend, patron and predecessor in office, which ought to make him extremely circumspect on the subject of investigation and enquiry into supposed guilt? Would a publication of the circumstances of that transaction redound to the honour or reputation of the parties, and why has the subject been so long and carefully covered up?

The questions were rhetorical, for no more was heard of the affair at that time, but in 1796 Bache and Beckley used their knowledge as a political threat against Hamilton. Both were motivated by the desire to thwart Hamilton's presidential ambitions, but in addition Bache, the grandson of Benjamin Franklin, contemplated exposing Hamilton in revenge for the rather crude reports on his grandfather's sexual prowess then being published in the Federalist press.[59]

The use of the Reynolds affair as a sword of Damocles, perpetually hovering over Hamilton's head, might have continued indefinitely, had not the Federalists in the spring of 1797 opened a campaign against Monroe as ambassador to France and at the same time conspired to fire Beckley as clerk to the House of Representatives. The temptation to blacken Hamilton's name became too strong to resist. Monroe's part in the Reynolds affair seemed suitable to demonstrate his magnanimity and upright conduct, a useful corrective to accusations of his corruption and treason that had poured incessantly from the Federalist presses. Beckley, of course, sought personal revenge, being goaded into action by Cobbett, who taunted him for hinting at scandals that he would not disclose.[60]

Historians have been virtually unanimous in stressing that the documents which Callender used to support his accusations against Hamilton in *History of 1796* came from John Beckley. The circumstantial evidence is persuasive. Beckley had a strong personal motive; had demonstrated—in line with his role as party manager—a continuing interest in the episode's ramifications after Monroe, Muhlenberg, and Venable's withdrawal; and had access to many of the relevant documents. When Monroe, Muhlenberg, and Venable visited Hamilton on 15 December, they took with them a number of letters obtained from Clingman, which Hamilton admitted had been written by him to Reynolds. In addition, they had three memoranda setting out the events and the evidence they had obtained since Clingman had first sought Muhlenberg's aid and an affidavit by Clingman dated 13 December 1792. On 17 December, Hamilton had asked for copies of these documents. The originals, held by Monroe, were given to Beckley, who handed them to Webb for transcribing. Webb took the copies to Hamilton on 20 December.[61]

Beckley thus had access to the documents, and he obviously took the opportunity to make an additional copy of each. But he apparently did not have them in his possession in 1797. A recently discovered note from Beckley to Tench Coxe, dated 10 October 1796, states: "Enclosed are Hamilton's precious confessions. Be pleased to preserve every scrap; they are *truly* original and authenticated by himself."[62] By "original" Beckley did not mean that the documents were the prototypes; rather, they were exact copies, for the originals had been returned to Monroe in December 1792. This note does not preclude Beckley from having given the documents to Callender; it would not have been difficult to retrieve them from Coxe when required. But it does strongly suggest that the Philadelphia Republican propagandists were working in concert.

The only alternative source for Callender's documents, apart from the copies given to Hamilton, to which he obviously would not have had access, were the originals held initially by Monroe. On several occasions, Monroe claimed to have sent them for safekeeping to "his Friend in Virgina." Just when he did this is unclear. On one occasion in July 1797 he told Hamilton he had sealed up and sent the documents on the evening of 15 December 1792. A few days later, again to Hamilton, he said they were deposited "when I left my country" for France, that is, in May or June 1793. In yet another statement, made in the period between the first two, Monroe and Muhlenberg together told Hamilton that the original documents were placed "in the hands of a respectable character in Virg[ini]a soon after the transaction took place."[63]

The date at which Monroe parceled up the originals was important, because the documents that Callender used in his *History of 1796* included what he called document No. V, which in fact is a four-page manuscript containing three separate statements written at different times: a statement made by Clingman on 15 December 1792; Monroe's record of the interview with Hamilton on that day; and the testimony of Clingman to Monroe of 2 January 1793 in which he claimed Maria Reynolds had rejected Hamilton's account of an affair between them. In the original prototype Clingman's first statement is in Webb's hand, and the other two are in Monroe's. The second statement suggested that Monroe, Muhlenberg, and Venable remained skeptical of Hamilton's version of events after their meeting with him, and the third statement suggested Monroe's misgivings even more strongly. Together, these parts of No. V were instrumental in persuading Hamilton to embark on the disastrous course of publishing a rebuttal and almost led to a duel with Monroe in July 1797.[64]

Hamilton may have been told of Clingman's 15 December testimony, but he was not given a copy, which indicates that it was not among the batch of documents Webb copied before December 20.[65] Webb may have made further copies, including document No. V, after 2 January 1793, the date on the last of its three parts; but the order for the copying was not recorded. Presumably, any transcribing after 2 January must have been with Monroe's connivance and probably at Beckley's instigation, the purpose being to have spare copies available for any eventuality, including publication. However, Beckley stated to Coxe that all the documents he transferred had been authenticated by Hamilton, and Hamilton did not see document No. V until Callender published it, in separate parts, in number 5 and 6 of the pamphlet version of *History of 1796*. It thus is unclear whether Beckley had access to the full range of documents in Monroe's possession.

The other possibility is that Callender used the originals. Monroe's friend in Virginia is generally considered to have been Thomas Jefferson, and there is at least circumstantial evidence to suggest that he had the opportunity to give Callender the original documents. Jefferson had known of Callender's exile in America since 1793, but the first time they met was at Snowden and McCorkle's printshop in 1797, while Callender was seeing the crucial parts 5 and 6 of the pamphlet version of *History of 1796* through the press. According to Callender's account in 1802: "Mr. Jefferson gave me no sort of countenance upon my arrival in this country. I never spoke to him, nor, to my knowledge, did I ever see him for upwards of four years, after my arrival. Even then I did not introduce myself to him. It was Mr. Jefferson that introduced himself to me. He called at the office of Snowden and McCorkle in Philadelphia, in June, or July 1797, asking for me. I was then printing the History of 1796." As Jefferson's own account books show him paying $15.14 for multiple copies of *History of 1796* on 19 June 1797, it appears highly likely that he first met Callender on, or just before, that date. Parts 5 and 6 of the pamphlet version were published on 26 June and about 7 July, respectively; it is thus feasible that Jefferson gave at least document No. V to Callender.[66]

Julian Boyd has denied this possibility, claiming that because Callender's versions of the pre–15 December documents do not entirely conform to the prototypes or to the copies given to Hamilton, he must have used an unknown alternative source. The differences, however, appear to result from errors and omissions in the process of printing and from Callender's editorial intervention to improve grammar and syntax. Callender's version of document No. V coincides with the original.[67]

Jefferson's role thus remains unresolved. Ironically, the only evidence to absolve him comes from Callender himself, who is usually not regarded as a trustworthy commentator. In his *Sketches of the History of America*, published in 1798, Callender denied Jefferson's involvement. "Mr. Jefferson had received a copy of these documents," he wrote, but "never shewed them, nor ever spoke of them, to any person. In summer, 1797, when the vice-president heard of the intended publication, he advised that the papers be suppressed . . . but his interposition came too late. Mr. Hamilton knew that Mr. Jefferson was master of his secret, but had kept it." Callender, of course, had good reason to assert Jefferson's innocence in 1798. As a Republican pamphleteer, his role included the publication of controversial material without implicating his leaders, together with the absorption of the heat of partisan warfare. But in November 1802, when Callender had broken with the Republicans and had brought to light the scandals of Jefferson's private life, his comments on the genesis of parts 5 and 6 of *History of 1796* referred only to assistance from the Jeffersonians, not from Jefferson himself. Although this was an ideal opportunity for further smearing Jefferson's reputation, Callender failed to implicate him in the disclosure of the documents.[68]

Therefore, although links can be confirmed between Jefferson and Beckley, Coxe and Callender with regard to propaganda tactics in 1797, responsibility for making available the relevant documents against Hamilton and for publishing them must remain with the penmen themselves, working independently of their leader. If Jefferson was innocent, a question mark must still remain over Monroe's role, because of his decision in 1793 to make a copy of what Callender called document No. V. This copy remained in Beckley's hands. Much of the significance of *History of 1796* came from Callender's access to that document.

Whatever their source, Callender made extremely effective use of the documents to point up the difficulties involved in Hamilton's explanation of his relations with Maria and James Reynolds. First in *History of 1796* and then, following Hamilton's pamphlet of August 1797, in *Sketches of the History of America*, Callender argued that Hamilton's adultery and subsequent blackmail were smokescreens aimed at hiding the former treasurer's financial speculations. "So much correspondence could not refer exclusively to wenching," he wrote. "No man of common sense will believe that it did. Hence it must have implicated some connection still more dishonourable, in Mr. Hamilton's eyes, than that of incontinency. Reynolds and his wife affirm that it respected certificate speculations." Callender unerringly picked out two major weaknesses of Hamilton's case, for which adequate explanations were never given. First, Hamilton had persuaded Maria Reynolds to burn all the documents that might be traced back to him (although some survived for Clingman to surrender to Monroe and his fellow investigators). Second, he had advised both Maria and her husband to disappear, promising them "something clever" if they did so. "You will determine whether these fugitive measures look most like innocence, or like something else," wrote Callender.[69]

He suggested that the most effective way for Hamilton to prove his case was to have brought forward Maria Reynolds as a witness to the love affair. That Hamilton did not do so, accused Callender in 1798, even though her whereabouts were known, could only be explained by Hamilton having concocted the letters, purportedly written by her, which he used to prove adultery and blackmail and to deflect accusations of corruption. The letters Hamilton showed the visiting committee have not been seen since that evening, so that their authenticity cannot be verified. The questions that Callender raised in 1797 and 1798 continue to hover unanswered, and Callender's belief "that Mrs. Reynolds was, in reality, guiltless" retains plausibility.[70]

VI

With Hamilton's disgrace, Callender reached the apogee of his career as a political propagandist. He was ecstatic. To Jefferson he wrote of Hamilton's *Observations*: "If you have not seen it, no anticipation can equal the infamy of this piece. It is worth all that fifty of the best pens in America could have said against him." To Mathew Carey he claimed: "All parties agree in thinking Hamilton had done for himself, and that I have done great service in putting an end to him by his own pen." Although neither recipient appears to have replied to Callender, their actions in support of their penman in ensuing months are eloquent testimony of their favorable opinions of his coup de main.[71]

Callender's euphoria was to be short-lived. Within a year of the publication of *History of 1796* he was once more an outcast, after plumbing the depths of misery and degradation, watching his wife slowly die in squalor, and being forced to abandon his children. His troubles began with his loss of anonymity, a product of his immense success. No doubt he had anticipated becoming the object of a surge of Federalist hatred, but even he was eventually worn down by its virulence and longevity. To be the butt of personal comment was not new to Callender, particularly from Cobbett. But Cobbett had mostly poked fun at him, as with his pun, *"Newgate* CALLENDER," or when he had accused the Scotsman of suffering from "mania reformatio," a malady caused by an empty "crumea" (a purse). The personal abuse that followed Hamilton's fall from grace, however, was of a rather different character, more persistent and certainly more venomous. Callender was a liar, a drunkard, a "nasty beast," a "little reptile," and "an abandoned hireling." If Cobbett is to be credited, Callender stood out in a crowd. He was a "little mangy Scotsman," who "has a remarkably shy and suspicious countenance; loves grog; wears a shabby dress, and has no hat on the crown of his head; I am not certain whether he has ears or not." He "leans his head toward one side, as if his neck had a stretch, and goes along working his shoulders up and down with evident signs of anger against the fleas and lice."[72]

Callender absorbed these comments with apparent equanimity. Personal abuse, as he too well knew, was usually the last refuge of the frustrated who had nothing more substantial to throw at an opponent. Less pleasant, however, were innuendoes regarding his conduct toward Lord Gardenstone and the first suggestions of his maltreatment and neglect of his wife and children. Also of concern was the threat of violence. When, he later claimed, "I published the all-blasting correspondence of HAMILTON with REYNOLDS, [my] house was twice entered, and [my] family alarmed, by the intrusion of an assassin." Of a timid disposition and with an abhorrence of violence, Callender reacted badly to physical threat. He was to spend much of the rest of his life nervously looking over his shoulder, the price he had to pay for his success and notoriety.[73]

Callender was by no means the only marked man in Philadelphia in the next few months. The Federalists, aided by the financial crash of 1797, made a concerted effort to destroy the fortunes and the reputations of the Republican coterie to which Callender belonged. Beckley had been dealt with before *History of 1796* was published. He was forced to trawl for customers for his hastily established law practice by advertising in the newspapers. Coxe, under increasing pressure from his superior, Oliver Wolcott, was eventually dismissed from his federal position as controller of revenue in December 1797. Already in deep financial trouble, he faced a bleak future. Dr. James Reynolds, as an independent professional, was more difficult to attack, but in 1798 controversy erupted after his dismissal as physician to the Philadelphia Dispensary. Cobbett did not deny the influence of political motives in this decision. "A man's politics, at this time are everything. I would sooner have my wounds dressed by a dog than by a democrat."[74]

James Carey's newspaper, the *Daily Advertiser*, tottered and then collapsed in September 1797, partly as a result of the reappearance of yellow fever. He reverted to jobbing printing and sought the financial aid of his brother. Mathew, however, had his own problems. He had underwritten the costs incurred when James bought out his partner, David Markland, earlier in the year and had only narrowly escaped bankruptcy after James's failure to meet his commitments. In September one of his notes was protested. The abyss of financial disaster loomed once more early in 1798; the Federalist-dominated Bank of the United States refused to discount his bills for a whole month.[75]

Mathew Carey survived the financial uncertainty; John Swanwick did not. His mercantile firm was one of 150 in Philadelphia either ruined or financially crippled in 1796–97. Many of his difficulties stemmed from the war, which prevented the transfer of his credit from the European mainland to London. In addition, the Philadelphia banks refused to assist him, except at usurious rates, and he never received the money owed to him by "the splendid bankrupts" Robert Morris and John Nicholson. In September 1797 he too went to the wall. Forsaken, although not by Callender, he died of yellow fever in July 1798, "a victim of political persecution . . . [and] a martyr in the cause of civil liberty."[76]

Callender also was increasingly enmeshed in debt. Through James's good offices, he received small loans from Mathew Carey, but he was unable to persuade his own debtors—usually printers and publishers such as Snowden and McCorkle—to pay him. The $16 Jefferson gave him in June was welcome, and Leiper probably owned the newly built house close to 12th Street into which Callender and his family moved at this time. By September 1797, with Philadelphia almost deserted because of the yellow fever, Callender was again financially embarrassed. In what would have been a display of desperate bravado had he not already felt assured of Jefferson's support, he sought an advance on the money the vice-president had promised on the publication of Callender's next political volume. Aware of the dangers if his name was connected too closely with Jefferson's, he suggested a draft for $5 or $10 made out to James Ronaldson, "a particular friend of mine."[77]

Apart from such "loans"—probably by now an euphemism to hide the embarrassment of charity—Callender still depended on his pen for his bread, however optimistically he might write of more lucrative alternatives. *The History of 1796* was only one of a series of "histories" that he wrote at this time. He conceived the idea of an annual review of political events, compiled and organized in a more leisurely fashion than the newspapers, faced with the tyranny of deadlines, could enjoy. The *American Annual Register*, published in January 1797, was the first in the series; and it was followed by the *History of 1796*, *Sketches of the History of America* (February 1798), and *Sedgwick and Co.* (May 1798). Mostly reworkings and extensions of his newspaper articles, leavened with additional material from his voluminous reading, these books and pamphlets approached current affairs with a massive bias toward Republicanism. Unsurprisingly, they failed to become bestsellers. None, not even *History of 1796*, went into a second edition. The *American Annual Register* was a flop; it was still being advertised in the *Aurora* six months after publication. Seven hundred copies of his *Sketches* were purchased in the first five weeks, but Callender remained dissatisfied and accused booksellers, including Bache, of deliberately failing to market his work. He also criticized printers in other states for not republishing his writings under their own imprint. Such influence as Callender had remained confined to Pennsylvania, and perhaps New York.[78]

By February 1798, therefore, with his friends already in dire straits and his own publications unprofitable, Callender had collapsed into abject poverty and possibly was compelled to seek poor relief. With gruesome relish, under the banner "CALLENDER AND CO.," Cobbett published an affidavit from James Lowry which stated:

> I do hereby declare, that on the day of the last election for Senator in this city [22 February 1798], I received from the son of Israel Israel one dollar, to purchase wood for James Thomson Callender, while the said Israel was at Callender's door, being then canvassing for votes.

> And I also declare that, about ten days previous to the said election, I received, for the use of the said Callender, six dollars from Thomas Leiper, the snuffmaker. And I do further declare, that, the next day after the wedding of Mr. Dunlap's daughter, I saw large quantities of broken victuals at . . . Callender's house, and that Callender's wife told me the said broken victuals came from the wedding, through the hand of Thomas Leiper.

Within a few months his wife was dead and Callender faced the demoralizing prospect of supporting four young children on his own. [79]

It was Thomas Jefferson who came to Callender's rescue. He was concerned that the Republican press in Philadelphia might "totter for want of subscriptions. We should really exert ourselves to procure them," he told Madison, "for if these papers fail, republicanism will be entirely brow-beaten." Jefferson proposed raising subscriptions from the leading Republicans, ostensibly to finance an assistant for Bache but in reality to support the beleaguered Republican penmen. Jefferson contributed $16 and a list of possible subscribers, including the recently defeated senatorial candidate Israel Israel, Dr. James Reynolds, Mathew Carey, John Smith (marshal of Pennsylvania), and John Beckley, was drawn up. Beckley, presumably owing to his financial problems, was eventually omitted; Smith pleaded poverty. There were three possible candidates for this largesse: Callender, Duane, and James Carey. Carey was finally assisted by his brother, and Duane kept his head above water by working as a journeyman printer for John Stuart. According to Callender: "Mr. Jefferson spoke to Mr. Leiper of Callender. . . . I was preferred to Duane; and, in consequence of this subscription, I wrote occasionally for Mr. Bache, during a few months." [80]

As on previous occasions, the money was available in the form of loans, the subscribers accepting the fiction that Callender would repay them when his financial situation stabilized. The total subscription was not large, but it offered Callender a lifeline. Complete secrecy was paramount; evidence that Jefferson was supporting from his own purse the notorious defamer of Washington, Adams, and Hamilton would have destroyed his carefully constructed image of being above base party intrigues. Nevertheless, Federalist editors eventually got wind of Jefferson's attempt to raise subscriptions for the *Aurora* in Virginia, which gave them some amusing copy at the Republicans' expense. They also guessed that Callender was working permanently on the *Aurora* but assumed Bache was paying him. [81]

Although Bache was at pains to deny Callender's occasional editorial control of the newspaper, there is little doubt that in the crucial weeks of March 1798, during the editor's absence from Philadelphia, Callender wrote the editorials as well as his usual paragraphs. He was thus probably responsible for openly encouraging a major tactical blunder made by the Republicans. America's foreign policy had remained stalled while the three envoys sent by Adams to negotiate with the French in 1797 received little encouragement from Talleyrand. In March 1798, having received dispatches from the envoys, Adams announced the failure of the mission, although, fearing for the safety of the envoys, he did not send the dispatches to the Senate. The more moderate Republicans were prepared to trust Adams without examining the documents, but the radicals, with the *Aurora* in the van, were sure that Adams was withholding information favorable to the French. In reality, the dispatches told of French belligerence and of Talleyrand's agents' attempts to bribe the American envoys. Trapped by their conviction of Adams's desire for an alliance with Britain against France, the radicals began a newspaper campaign to force disclosure of the dispatches, with Callender taunting the president and Secretary of State Timothy Pickering for "being afraid to tell."[82]

The campaign was an unmitigated disaster. After an unholy alliance was formed between the High Federalists and the Republicans, who passed a resolution in Congress calling for the dispatches, Adams handed them over. A wave of patriotic, anti-French anger swept the country as soon as evidence of French corruption and threats to intervene in America's domestic affairs became known. The Republicans, pinioned by their long-established sympathies for the French republic, were devastated. Even the *Aurora* was temporarily struck dumb, and Callender, who had been calling loudly for Adams's resignation, was obliged to confine himself to halfhearted mutterings on the dangers inherent in annoying the all-powerful French.[83]

The immoderate anti-Gallican feeling generated by the XYZ dispatches offered the High Federalists a perfect opportunity utterly to destroy their political enemies. They whipped up a maelstrom of xenophobia, with the expectation of discrediting Republican leaders through their connections with alien "disorganisers" and "traitors." In Philadelphia, Cobbett, following the lead of Harrison J. Otis in Congress, concentrated on maligning the refugees from Ireland, while Fenno was left to confront Callender. Calling him the "foreign tool of domestic faction," Fenno asked: "In the name of justice and honor, how long are we to tolerate this scum of party filth and beggarly corruption, worked into a form somewhat like a man, to go thus with impunity? Do not the times approach when it must and ought to be dangerous for this wretch, and any other, thus to vilify our country and government, thus to treat with indignity and contempt the whole American people, to teach our enemies to despise us and cast forth unremitting calumny and venom on our constitutional authorities." Callender, ended Fenno, had published "sufficient general slander on our country to entitle him to the benefit of the gallows." Fortunately for the Scotsman, the Federalists did not seek such extreme measures; but the more virulent among them, including such old adversaries as Harper, Sedgwick, and Otis, were determined permanently to silence the Republican penmen. James Carey was exaggerating when he claimed that the alien and sedition bills were "all purportedly aimed at destroying Callender"; nevertheless, the Scotsman was at the very top of the Federalists' hit list.[84]

The threat of imprisonment for sedition or deportation for being an undesirable alien came at the very worst time for Callender. Already under intense domestic pressure, he suffered a further blow by falling from favor with the Republicans, who had become increasingly discontented with his maverick tendencies. His error over the XYZ dispatches was compounded in their eyes when suddenly he appeared to be on the brink of switching his allegiance to the Federalists. Callender actually was following his own independent line, but because it entailed support for Cobbett and criticism of Chief Justice Thomas McKean, then a leading moderate Republican and soon to be governor of Pennsylvania, their feelings are perhaps explicable. The issue arose late in 1797 when Cobbett was brought before a Pennsylvania grand jury, accused of libeling the king of Spain and his ambassador to America, the chevalier de Yrujo. The Spanish minister was McKean's prospective son-in-law, and the Chief Justice both gave evidence against Cobbett before the grand jury and presided over it as a judge. Although the charges were dismissed—voting was along party lines—Cobbett quite rightly wondered why he could be dragged into court accused of libel, when Callender, who had called congressmen thieves, "without any dashes, feigned names, or circumlocution," remained undisturbed and protected by his Republican friends.[85]

Callender's reply in *Sedgwick and Co.*, published in May 1798, surprised everyone. Remaining consistent to his ideas on free speech and a free press, he defended Cobbett and criticized McKean. "If a man is attacked from the press," he wrote," let him reply through the same channel. He fights his antagonist with equal weapons. The doctrine of libels has very frequently been a screen for powerful and profligate men, who, being unable to meet their accuser on the fair ground of argument and detail, had recourse to law, that they might overwhelm him by the expence of litigation. In all countries, those who hold the reins of government are the persons who have most to fear from a disclosure of the truth."

The moderate Republicans, claimed Callender at a later date, never forgave him "for these hard rubs." Although Leiper persuaded him to tone down some passages, Callender found it irresistible "to write truth just as it came in the way, without regard for one party more than another." A superficial scanning of the rest of *Sedgwick and Co.*, in which he assailed Federalist luminaries such as William Smith, ought to have convinced the Republicans of Callender's continued commitment to the cause. Nevertheless, with the notable exceptions of the kindly and understanding Leiper and James Carey, who through fear of prosecution had greatly softened his comments in his new newspaper, Callender found himself shunned by his erstwhile compatriots.[86]

Abandoned, stricken with poverty, probably drinking heavily, and, according to a federal senator's report, threatened once again with "assassination," Callender could not face the threat posed by the Alien and Sedition Acts. On 4 June, with Leiper as witness, he became a naturalized citizen of the United States. His last paragraph for the *Aurora* was published on 22 June, and on 13 July, one day before President Adams signed the Sedition Act into law, Callender, leaving his children in Leiper's capable hands, set off on the long trek to Senator Stevens Thomson Mason's plantation in Virginia. He was never again to set foot in Philadelphia.[87]

Part Three

Virginia

6

"The Blood of the Martyrs Was the Seed of the Church"

I

The long, dusty trek from Philadelphia to Senator Mason's plantation in Loudoun County, Virginia—"the Patriot's Progress" as Cobbett maliciously called it—took Callender several weeks to accomplish. The journey was not without incident. Callender had arranged to meet Mason at Lancaster, from where they planned to travel to Mason's Raspberry Plain by stagecoach. But in Lancaster he was recognized, "and as I was well assured that I would not be sure of safety," Callender swiftly moved on to York. There he received word from Mason of continuing danger, so he immediately set off again on his own.[1]

As he trudged south, he had much time to contemplate the events of the past few months and the prospects for the future. He was dispirited, destitute, deracinated, and still grieving for his wife and the forced abandonment of his children. He inevitably seized on the idea of betrayal to justify his distressed condition. He had been defeated less by the quills of Porcupine and the threat of the Sedition Act than by the pusillanimity of the moderate Republicans, who in crisis had shunned him when he most needed protection. The summer of 1798 marks the point at which Callender reverted to his customary philosophy of suspicion of all groups, conceding his trust only to selected individuals. He was never again to be an unquestioning partisan of the Republican party, if that could ever have been said of him. For the next three years his allegiance was given to one man, Thomas Jefferson.

The security of Raspberry Plain was not achieved without one final humiliation. According to Cobbett, magistrates at Leesburg arrested a drunken Callender outside the local distillery, charging him with vagrancy. "With shaved head and greasy jacket, nankeen pantaloons, and worsted stockings," Callender was assumed to be an escapee from

Baltimore's convict wheelbarrow gang. Stevens Thomson Mason later publicly denied Cobbett's assertion that he had been compelled to ride to Leesburg to vouch for his guest's identity. Nevertheless, Callender needed to produce his naturalization papers before he was finally released. He entered the sanctuary of Raspberry Plain with the laughter and jeering of the Federalists ringing in his ears.[2]

During the next few months his health improved and his shattered nerves slowly mended. By the middle of November he was able to inform Jefferson: "I have got more sound sleep since I came here than I have enjoyed for some years before. I am now master of my own time and rid of the burden of too much society, so that I can write at leisure, and not scrawl myself into headaches." Mason, who "in every way behaved with the utmost kindness," was a sympathetic host, stoutly protecting Callender from "the scenes of printing, and swearing, and flat perjury" stirred up by the arrival of this Republican bugbear in the midst of strongly Federalist Loudoun County.[3]

Fresh air, regular meals, leisure, and access to a good library in which to browse all contributed to Callender's revitalization. But more than anything else, his return to health and vigor was accelerated by his correspondence with Thomas Jefferson. The Jefferson-Callender correspondence was first collected from Jefferson's papers in the Library of Congress and published in the late nineteenth century by Worthington Chauncey Ford, a historian totally unsympathetic to Callender. Anxious to protect Jefferson from the stigma of associating with a scurrilous, libeling turncoat, Ford not only uncritically accepted his hero's later interpretation of the relationship, but he also silently glided over references in the correspondence inconsistent with this interpretation and failed even to consider the relationship from Callender's perspective.

While in Philadelphia, Jefferson had closer relations with Callender than Ford, and most historians since, was willing to admit. Their correspondence from September 1798 to April 1801 clearly shows that the bond forged between them in Philadelphia was strengthened in the years leading up to Jefferson's election victory and that Callender—in his activities as a Republican propagandist in Virginia—with good reason believed he had the support and encouragement of Jefferson.

Between May 1801 and July 1804 Jefferson offered a consistent explanation of his long-term liaison with Callender in letters to Madison, Monroe, and Abigail Adams. To each he excused himself by claiming his financial support for Callender during Adams's administration reflected his habitual charity to the needy—of any or no political persuasion—and pity for "a man of genius suffering under persecution." He flatly denied paying Callender for his political work and sought to convince Mrs. Adams that "nobody sooner disapproved of his writing than I did." He conceded meeting Callender on a few occasions in Philadelphia, but thereafter, although Callender in Virginia pestered him with unwelcome letters, political comments, newspapers, and galley proofs of his writings, Jefferson replied only thrice. In a final comment to his old adversary's wife, Jefferson suggested that ultimately his motives "must be decided by a regard to the general tenor of my life. On this I am not afraid to appeal to the nation at large, to posterity, and still less to that Being who sees himself our motives, who will judge us from his own knowledge of them."[4]

A number of characteristics of the Jefferson-Callender correspondence, however, strongly suggest the possibility—from Callender's perspective at least—of a very different interpretation. Quite the most expressive and salient aspect of the letters is the easy familiarity in which they are couched. An intimacy between the correspondents is apparent, surprising if their association had been fleeting and totally inappropriate if Callender were merely the recipient of charity, or even believed himself to be so. At all times respectful, Callender never descended to flattery, fawning, or self-pity but embarked on a correspondence, not of equals, but of mentor and acolyte.

In one sense the intimacy was that of the confessional, for Callender unburdened his hopes and fears to Jefferson. He was not afraid to express his disappointment with the Philadelphia Republicans for their neglect of his interests: with Giles, who had united with William L. Smith to ruin Callender's career as a congressional reporter yet "offered afterwards to speak to me in the street," and with Bache, who refused to print Callender's account of the Leesburg incident and allowed him to be blamed for some of the more scurrilous paragraphs in the *Aurora* written by other people.[5]

Callender also confided his future plans to Jefferson. Quoting Ossian's statement that "I am alone in the land of strangers," he expressed his determination to abandon political writing, which he had taken up not from choice but from necessity. His ultimate objective, once "matters clear up on the other side of the Atlantick," was to return home to Scotland. In the meantime, and here he sought Jefferson's aid and advice, schoolteaching or assisting in a store "in any part of the country, where I could be permitted to live in peace," appeared attractive possibilities.[6]

Jefferson's response was to have fateful consequences, for he expressed sympathy, support, and consolation for Callender, encouraging him to have confidence in "his power to render services to the public liberty." He condemned "the insult committed on you" following the Leesburg incident and offered an explanation for events in Philadelphia sufficient temporarily to diminish, if not eliminate, Callender's intense antipathy toward the moderate Republicans. He also sent Callender $50, to be drawn on the Richmond merchant George Jefferson. Jefferson concluded by expressing his "great satisfaction" at the possibility of their meeting again in the next few months.[7]

Whatever Jefferson may have hoped to achieve—and it is hard to reconcile this letter with the motives he expressed at a later date—he inspired Callender, whisking him out of his slough of introspection and depression and giving the unqualified impression of the Republican leader's need of him to continue the battle against Federalism. At no time before Callender's break with him in 1801 did Jefferson ever hint of his disapproval of the tactic of personal attacks on leading Federalists; the impression he gave Callender was of benign support for his activities. Nor, at this time, should Callender have anticipated otherwise. The Republican party was being buffetted by the storms created by the High Federalists; it was in danger of being utterly destroyed. Jefferson himself was undergoing one of his periodic flirtations with radicalism, invoking "the Spirit of '76" and helping to prepare the Virginia and Kentucky Resolutions, which asserted states' rights and threatened to undermine the sanctity of the Federal Constitution. In this crisis, Jefferson's encouragement of one of his most effective writers to resume duties is explicable, as is Callender's renewed enthusiasm for political activity, generated by the exquisite feeling of once again being needed. It is sufficient merely to view Callender's past life to understand why he cherished so strongly this evidence of his social acceptability.

Callender began to ransack Mason's library, seeking materials for "an Address to the Citizens of Virginia on the present state of public affairs," which later was published as the first volume of *The Prospect before Us.* A few months' work, he told Jefferson, and he would be "ready to give our readers such a Tornado as no Govt ever got before, for there is in American history a species of ignorance, absurdity, and imbecility unknown to the annals of any other nation." He had no intention of returning to Pennsylvania; he remembered Leiper's parting words: "There is no more safety in Philadelphia than in Constantinople." Although he continued to fear the prospect of living in any town, at least "till the tide turns," Richmond offered opportunities for reprinting his old books and an audience previously unexposed to his political writings. His books were "poor enough," he admitted to Jefferson, "yet they at least are better than the common rubbish of newspapers."[8]

Senator Mason, who had to return to Philadelphia for the reopening of Congress, had anticipated that Callender would leave Raspberry

Plain with him in the late fall, doubtless in the belief that the Federalist hue and cry would by then have dissipated. Callender, however, still nervous of the outside world and engrossed in note-taking in Mason's library, wished to stay longer. It appears he continued to live on the plantation—paying $15 a quarter for board—until early spring, when he moved to Petersburg.[9]

In February he had been confronted with the choice of two jobs, one in New York, the other in Virginia. The New York position became available as a result of the high mortality among printers and editors who had bravely remained at their posts during the yellow fever epidemic of 1798. In Philadelphia, both Bache and his opponent Fenno had succumbed. The latter's son took over the *Gazette of the United States*, while Bache's widow—with the assistance of Duane, who later married her—continued the *Aurora*. In New York, the most ardent Republican editor, with the possible exception of the United Irishman John Daly Burk, had been Thomas Greenleaf, who published the twice-weekly *Greenleaf's New York Journal* and the daily *Argus*. Following his death, his widow valiantly took up the reins, with the help of her journeymen. She clearly needed experienced editorial assistance, however, and it was this position that was offered to Callender.[10]

Although confident that Ann Greenleaf would accept his terms of employment, Callender nevertheless finally determined to remain in Virginia. Most probably he was unwilling at this stage to face the martyrdom almost inevitable for an editor prepared to defend Republican principles in Alexander Hamilton's own backyard. If so, it was a judicious decision. By the end of 1799 Ann Greenleaf was under indictment and her journeyman David Frothingham was in prison charged with sedition.[11]

The position offered in Virginia appeared to be politically safer; Callender believed the state's Federalists to be too weak to test the Sedition Act locally. But financially there was more risk, for the job entailed working in a new and speculative enterprise with James Lyon, who only migrated to Virginia from Vermont once he managed to employ Callender. James was a committed Republican, a son of the notorious Colonel Matthew ("Spitting") Lyon, who had been involved in two fracases in Congress with arch-Federalist Roger Griswold and was currently imprisoned under the Sedition Act. James Lyon had ambitious plans for publications in Richmond, including a monthly magazine to gather together the best Republican writings from around the country.[12]

Another offer from Meriwether Jones of Richmond made Callender's decision easier. Jones (1766–1806) was a friend of Jefferson, a former member of the Virginia House of Delegates who had recently resigned from the Executive Council after his appointment as printer to the Commonwealth. In December 1798, in partnership with John Dixon, he had established in Richmond the semiweekly and ardently Republican newspaper the *Examiner*. He first corresponded with Callender in the spring of 1799 and, knowing of his partner's imminent retirement and with little personal experience of conducting a newspaper, mentioned the possibility of work. The offer interested Callender; the prospect of earning between $12 and $14 a week from Lyon and Jones together raised the hope of bringing his children to Virginia. Unfortunately, Jones felt unable to pay a regular salary until his newspaper achieved profitability, although he arranged with other printers for a joint payment for reporting the debates of the next state assembly. At the conclusion of the session he would, he hoped, be able to offer Callender $10 a week for his services. In the meantime he would try to help Callender if he came to Richmond.[13]

Under these very uncertain conditions, with apparently little understanding of how he was to live before the House of Delegates met in December, Callender arrived in Richmond on 25 May 1799, ready once more to wage war under Jefferson's banner.[14]

II

Late eighteenth-century Richmond struggled to live up to the honor and dignity of being the capital of the Commonwealth of Virginia. It was, said one visiting Englishman, "one of the dirtiest holes of a place I ever was in." Although a new penitentiary and a new arsenal—both in a curious sense reflecting some social progress—were opened while Callender was in residence, the capital had few impressive public buildings. The Capitol, symbolically situated high on Shockoe Hill, whence society's leaders could look down on their masters, was appropriately both difficult to reach and partly unfinished. Equally symbolic of the contradictions in a society where the new concept of popular sovereignty coexisted uneasily with the old reality of a planter oligarchy, the governor's house was an uninspiring frame building. Only "Brick Row"—actually Main Street but popularly known thus in deference to the unusual solidity of its building materials—gave any sense of *gravitas* and permanence.[15]

In this rude, overlarge village—despite its menial size, it was one of the larger settlements in Virginia—with its creeks and gulleys and unpaved roads, between 5,000 and 6,000 people lived, one-third of them slaves and about one-sixth white males over the age of sixteen. Strategically placed at the falls of the James River and the hub that joined Tidewater, Piedmont, and Southside, Richmond served as an entrepôt for the products of the surrounding countryside. Merchants, many of whom were Scottish or Scotch-Irish, traded in corn, wheat, and tobacco and carried on the commission trade, acting as agents for British mercantile houses. They were, however, only part of the elite of Richmond society; they rubbed shoulders with the local planters who visited Richmond for its social gatherings and entertainment and with the legal profession, who made up one of the most brilliant and socially prestigious bars in the country. Between 1789 and 1826 it produced two Supreme Court justices, two United States attorneys general, and two secretaries of state. In his years in Richmond, Callender was to generate considerable work for this legal fraternity.[16]

Culturally, Richmond was only superficially sedate. As among Virginians in general, the inhabitants of Richmond wore their religion lightly. Until 1800, when a Methodist chapel was opened, they were served only by a small Baptist meetinghouse and the Episcopalian church of St. John's. This, too, was tiny, but according to one visitor in the 1780s it was "spacious enough for all the pious souls of the place and the region."[17] Respectable tea gardens and a theater offered further innocent recreations, but they were outnumbered by the more raffish pleasure outlets patronized by the young lawyers and the planter aristocracy. All the main features of Virginia's planter culture were present in Richmond: horse racing, gambling, and the social interaction of market days and the assizes. As integral a part of this culture, but representing its darker side, were the black dances, usually attended by white males also; the rougher animal bloodsports; and the "code duello," which reached a peak at this time. This was a very different world from that of Philadelphia, more hedonistic, more stratified, and more dissembling; it was not one that was to appeal to Callender's innate puritanism. In the years following his arrival he was to come close to destroying Richmond society by concentrating his fire on the contradictions within this culture.

On Callender's arrival in Richmond, Meriwether Jones immediately invited him to live with his family, an offer the roving Scotsman was happy to accept. He remained there for the next six months, repaying the cost of his board by producing articles for the *Examiner*. Taking stock of his new surroundings, the impression first gained in Loudoun County, that Virginia—although Republican in political orientation—possessed a significant Federalist minority, was reinforced. Richmond, in fact, was nearly evenly divided between the two parties. La Rochefoucauld had noticed the lack of unity when he explored the capital a few years earlier. "The men who belong to opposite parties seldom visit each other," he noted. But, he continued, "when they happen to meet, they treat each other with all the politeness and civility of well-bred people"; by 1799 this courtesy was no longer observed.[18]

Supporting the Federalists in Richmond were two newspapers, the *Virginia Gazette*, edited by Augustine Davis, and the *Virginia Federalist*, edited by William Rind and Jack Stuart. The editors were to be prime targets for Callender's pen and the objects of a partisan Republican onslaught from 1799 on. Both Davis and Stuart fell victims to the strategy of Madison and Jefferson of turning Virginia into a Republican stronghold from which to launch an assault on the presidency. Davis lost to Jones his position as printer to the Commonwealth, and Stuart was dismissed as clerk to the House of Delegates (being replaced by the soon-to-be-famous orator-lawyer William Wirt). The Republicans for the time being were unable to touch Davis's federal position of Richmond postmaster. With the prospect of Jefferson winning the presidency, the Federalist editor moderated the views expressed in his newspaper before the election, but he lost the postmastership after 1801. Rind and Stuart were equally unfortunate. The former moved to Washington in 1800, and the latter within a few years had become a sea captain.[19]

The Republican press in Richmond consisted of Jones's *Examiner* and the Quaker Samuel Pleasants's moderate *Virginia Argus*. James Lyon's press did not produce a newspaper—*The Friend of the People*—until 1800, but the first edition of his *National Magazine* was published in July 1799. Writing for this magazine remained Callender's only source of cash until he began reporting the debates of the state assembly. Copies of the magazine are no longer extant, but presumably Callender contributed material similar to that later contained in the two-volume *Prospect before Us*.[20]

Callender's initial foray into Virginia's political disputes was typically devastating, swiftly crystallizing the anger and frustrations of the increasingly beleaguered Federalists. In the middle of June 1799 he began his campaign to put Jefferson into the presidency by publishing a major critique of President Adams's administration in the *Examiner*. Claiming that "there exists a conspiracy against the liberties of this country," Callender pointed to the presence of "a junto, the members of which feel the utmost solicitude to calumniate Mr. Jefferson. Nay we solemnly believe that, next to the merit of knocking down Republican printers, the shortest and surest road to the favour of certain great personages is by publishing falsehoods, and ribaldry, against the Vice-President." In reality, he continued, "it is impossible to arraign this amiable Virginian, whose character, with spirit gentle, and with wisdom gay, forms an acquisition to society, and an ornament to human nature."

The contrast between Jefferson and Adams was stark. The former, by questioning the legality of the Alien and Sedition Acts, had remained consistent in his republican principles; Adams, however, since 1789 had turned his coat. The former advocate of the right of resistance against a corrupt government, Adams now happily presided over an arbitrary tyranny. But perhaps there was no need to worry, concluded Callender with tongue in cheek; "in the vicissitudes of electioneering, we do not despair of seeing Mr. Adams once more A VIOLENT DEMO-CRAT. Always in the cellar, or the garret, seems to be the rule with some characters."[21]

Callender's determination "to return blow for blow" enraged some of the younger local Federalists. Meeting in the Swan Tavern soon after the *Examiner*'s publication, they formed themselves into the "Rich-mond Associators," drawing up a plan to drive Callender out of town on the evening of the twenty-second. Rumors of the plot swiftly spread, and Callender prudently absented himself from Jones's shop, leaving the owner to prepare the next day's newspaper himself. Acting, as he later said, on the principle "that no man on earth, shall injure [me], or [my] men, in the discharge of their duty . . . , unless [I] am first deprived of the power of resistance," Jones and his friend Alexander McRae, a lawyer and a member of Virginia's Executive Council, warned the mayor of the possibility of a mob attack and judiciously surrounded the *Examiner*'s printshop with armed Republicans. The preparations were unnecessary, for the Federalists aborted their plan.[22]

The affair was a potential propaganda coup for the Republicans. The Federalists had shown themselves in their true colors: superior to the law, nativist bullyboys, and intolerant of opposing opinions (Call-ender's writings had not been scurrilous but concerned with political interpretation). In an attempt at damage control, the Federalists estab-lished a committee which issued a statement that "their object was not to raise a nocturnal riot, nor indeed [to cause] the smallest violation of decency and good order, but [was] only designed, by peaceably convey-ing this political imposter out of the limits of our city, to manifest to the world, that the vengeance of an injured people does not always sleep." This effort to concentrate attention on Callender was only partly suc-cessful. "A Friend to the Sovereignty of the People" pointed out that the Associators, if they objected to comments in the *Examiner*, ought to direct their complaints to Meriwether Jones, as the owner, and not "to poor Callender, a perfect stranger here, a man totally defenceless and destitute of friends, except such as the duties of humanity, and an attachment to the rights of man shall call to his assistance."[23]

Nevertheless, the Richmond Republicans failed to make political capital from the incident: it was scarcely reported in the local news-papers (although news of it did reach Philadelphia). Possibly most moderate Republicans were wary of extending a crisis which centered around a writer about whom they had mixed feelings. Certainly Callender felt he had not been properly supported.[24]

Republican tentativeness became clear in early August when Alexander McRae was brought before three magistrates to comment on allegations—made in four depositions published in the *Virginia Gazette*—that on 24 June at Colonel Goodall's tavern he had said he would have brought 3,000 men into Richmond "to tear down every house in Brick Row" if Callender or Jones's printshop had been harmed. Several witnesses gave evidence on McRae's conversation that night, but they were unable to clarify whether he had been merely expressing a belief that men would have spontaneously marched on Richmond or had threatened to lead them personally. The "trial" fizzled out when Meriwether Jones admitted to having overreacted by placing armed men around his shop. He was, he claimed, expecting a mob, not the Associators, whom he now accepted were respectable gentlemen.[25]

In Richmond both the Republicans and the Federalists were finally grateful to allow the incident to fade away. In his cups McRae not only had ruined whatever opportunity the Republicans had for a propaganda coup, but he had also highlighted the potential dangers that might arise if political partisanship was taken too far. Ever present in the minds of Virginia's elites was the fear of social upheaval, which gentry disharmony might spark off and which was to be confirmed a year later with a slave insurrection. Callender was a stranger; moreover, he was a militant. In the final analysis social cohesion was more important than cheap political points.

Callender had been both badly frightened by the episode and disappointed by the temperate response of the Republicans, especially Jones. One consequence, as he told Jefferson in August, was his reluctance to continue as a newspaper propagandist. "While I am in danger of being murthered without doors," he commented, "I do not find within them any very particular encouragement to proceed." He decided, therefore, to halt his paragraphs for the *Examiner* and concentrate on preparing his book and his articles for Lyon's magazine.[26]

Once again Jefferson came forward to encourage Callender to continue his important propaganda work. In addition to sending the Scotsman another $50—as advance payment for copies of *The Prospect before Us*—he boosted Callender's sense of importance in a comment extraordinary in its exaggeration:

> The violence which was meditated against you lately has excited a very general indignation in this part of the country. Our state from it's

first plantation has been remarkable for it's order and submission to the laws. But three instances are recollected in it's history of an organized opposition to the laws. The first was Bacon's Rebellion; the 2d. our revolution; the 3d. the Richmond association who, by their committee, have in the public papers avowed their purpose of taking out of the hands of the law the function of declaring who may or may not have free residence among us. But these gentlemen miscalculate the temper and force of this country extremely if they supposed there would have been a want of either to support the authority of the laws: and equally mistake their own interests in setting the example of club-law.[27]

To compare the rodomontade in Richmond with the Revolution was manifestly to overestimate the former's importance, but Jefferson achieved his major objective of persuading Callender to maintain his newspaper writing, even if it was at the price of inflating the Scotsman's ego and strengthening the mentor-acolyte link. In September, Callender informed Jones of his decision to settle permanently in Richmond. He then sent proofs of a number of pages of *The Prospect before Us* to Jefferson, asking him for information on certain political points. In his reply Jefferson cemented his relationship with Callender. He gave him the information he sought, which he had found among his papers "after a very long search," and warmly approved of the proofs of Callender's book. "Such papers cannot fail to produce the best effect. They inform the thinking part of the nation." He concluded by warning Callender that because of "the curiosity of the post offices," he intended drastically to reduce the number of letters he sent to his colleagues in the future.[28]

Jefferson by his support and encouragement was cajoling Callender along the path that was to lead to his eventual martyrdom. Henry Pace, Callender's partner in 1802 and 1803, later claimed that the Scotsman "has not perseverance, he has not spirit. . . . Why need I say—HE HAS NOT STEADINESS."[29] There is much to be said for this assessment. When combined with a certain timidity in the face of physical danger and a growing tendency to seek escape through the bottle, this evidence of a lack of self-confidence helps to explain why Callender usually performed at his best when he had someone to lean on. Lord Gardenstone performed this function in Scotland, Thomas Leiper was his helpmeet in Philadelphia, and Jefferson acted as his mentor in Virginia. All can be said to have fulfilled the role of father figure to Callender. When the prospect of political martyrdom arose in the next few months, Callender was eagerly to embrace it, for it gave him the opportunity of demonstrating his filial affection and of shedding his reputation for fickleness and lack of courage.

III

In her analysis of Jeffersonian Republicanism in the 1790s, Joyce Appleby has argued that Jefferson's victory in the presidential election of 1800 was achieved by the creation of "a movement that was national in scope and universal in its ideological appeal." Success was won with words:

> those printed words that had for so long been owned and exchanged by the world's elites. With words in resolutions, toasts, orations, pamphlets, newspapers and broadsides, they took up positions on the French alliance, relations with Great Britain, the excise tax, and the president's conduct of foreign affairs. When this impertinence was construed as a crime, they engaged the nation in debate on the functional meaning of natural rights. With words they formed a democratic network, with words they created loyalties among strangers, with words—often anonymous words—they defied their social superiors, with words they repelled intimidation.[30]

Callender was only one of many agitators—both native and immigrant—who in the last years of the century used the medium of print to set up Jefferson's victory. But he was one of the most successful and certainly was one of the first to perceive the vital importance of creating a national network of Jeffersonian propaganda. At the state level, the *Examiner* became a major force in the second half of 1799. Callender, as "A Scots Correspondent," averaged five columns of political analysis a week. Each edition of the newspaper consumed forty-seven quires of paper (compared with twenty-seven before he began writing), which represented a gain of about 400 new subscribers. Callender modestly accepted that "all this cannot, with justice, be ascribed to any single pen." Meriwether Jones, however, was more generous. Celebrating the first anniversary of the newspaper's life, he wrote: "I fought for, and obtained the aid of a person well versed in the detail of American affairs, and therefore . . . well qualified to expose the improper designs of those in power, should such designs occur." In the local newspaper war for the hearts and minds of Virginians, Callender "has been completely victorious over the editor of the *Virginia Federalist* in every literary combat."[31]

Callender fully appreciated, especially once the Republicans had ensured that voting for Virginia's presidential electors would be on a statewide basis, that his efforts were being spent on a population almost certain to give a unanimous electoral college vote to Jefferson. To have the greatest impact, his writings had to be distributed in the more marginal states, especially Pennsylvania. The custom of editors reprinting articles from other newspapers was one way of spreading information, and Callender was gratified to see his work reprinted even in Connecticut. However, William Duane's failure to copy from the *Examiner* greatly disappointed him. To Jefferson he complained: "I expected that Duane would copy from us more than he has done. I think some of our columns would have been more to the purpose than his endless trash about Arthur McConnor [O'Connor] and Hindustan. He began to copy from us, and sickened I believe at hearing that the things were good. Thus the interest, or what I considered as the interest of the cause was betrayed from the meanest personal jealousy of me. I thank heaven that I feel none at him."[32]

In this statement Callender allowed his paranoia to overwhelm his political sense. Duane's audience in Philadelphia had a significant Irish element. News of the tragedy of the 1798 Irish rebellion and its aftermath appealed to the thousands of United Irishmen who were flocking into Pennsylvania. Even information from "Hindustan," in which Duane—having been thrown out of India in 1795—had a personal interest, could be used effectively in the propaganda war against the pro-British party in America. But Callender, probably as a side effect of his rigid anti-imperialist opinions, never fully appreciated the importance of foreign affairs as a political weapon. When writing for the *Aurora*, he had rarely commented at length on the French Revolution. He continued to believe, and on balance he was probably correct, that electoral success would be determined by victory in the contest over internal affairs.

Nevertheless, the problem of maximizing the effectiveness of propaganda continued to haunt Callender. Professional jealousy and the financial insecurities of the publishing world were realities that would continue to hinder the efficient and national distribution of political information. In 1800 Callender finally came up with a possible solution, although it required the collaboration of editors in every state. If a particularly important article was written in, say, New York, numerous copies of it should be sent to one or two sympathetic editors in every state before publication. They in turn would make further copies to distribute to the other Republican editors in the state, and on a specified day all the newspapers would publish the work simultaneously. "By their receiving, and publishing all these articles at the same time," wrote Callender,

> the jealousy of competition would have been destroyed; while the federal editors were to struggle after them, at the distance of several days, and very often of several weeks. The effect of such an arrangement must have been infinitely superior to the present disorderly crowd of republican newspapers. . . . What is the line of battle firing in platoons, or the ship that pops by single guns, compared with the

impression of a general attack, or a series of full broadsides? The result is very much the same in printing, as in fighting.[33]

Callender never attempted to implement this form of synchronized syndication, for by the time he was in a position to suggest it, he had begun to disassociate himself from the Republicans and to establish himself as a writer independent of both parties. Nevertheless, that he worked out such a plan demonstrates his awareness of the importance of nationwide propaganda for the development and success of a popular political party. Immigrant newspapermen brought a number of new ideas and techniques to America in the 1790s, some that lowered the tone of the press and some that made it more effective. This plan of Callender's, in an age before the electric telegraph, offered one possible way of maximizing a scarce resource, effective and rousing propaganda.

In the absence of such a system, the widespread influence of newspaper articles depended on chance: the swift arrival of newspapers from other states, the cooperation of local postmasters (those leaning toward the Federalists occasionally "mislaid" Republican sheets), and the concurrence of editors in what was a cutthroat business. Pamphlets, however, properly marketed across state boundaries, had the potential to be productive. When the first volume of *The Prospect before Us* was published by James Lyon in Richmond in February 1800, Callender sent copies to all the booksellers in Philadelphia (as well as a complimentary copy to John Adams!). This ploy's effectiveness was diminished by the local Federalist authorities, who in a "pitiful and illegal proceeding" forbade Philadelphia booksellers to sell it on pain of prosecution.[34]

One has a twinge of sympathy for the Federalists who were desperately trying to foil Callender in the lead-up to the presidential election, for contrary to the opinions of historians, who have dwelt on its occasional scurrility and lack of coherence, *The Prospect before Us* was a useful piece of propaganda. Its purpose, claimed Callender, was "to exhibit the multiplied corruptions of the Federal Government, and more especially the misconduct of the President, Mr. Adams." Its organization was deliberately fragmentary, for Callender assumed his audience's short attention span. "By [a] desultory mode of writing, by passing so frequently from one end to another of federal history, something may be lost in point of regularity, but much more is gained in the superior probability of fixing the reader's attention. When you cannot guess what is to come in the next page, your mind is kept more upon the watch."[35]

The Prospect may be seen as the final version of Callender's political history of the 1790s, whose earlier drafts were the pamphlets pub-

lished in Philadelphia between 1796 and 1798. Many of the same topics—the funding system, Jay's treaty, and the Algerine tribute—were
reexamined, but from a perspective more likely to appeal to south-
erners than his earlier works. The story of Federalist wickedness was
brought up-to-date, to include an examination of the XYZ affair and the
Alien and Sedition Acts.

In Callender's opinion the Alien Acts, whose penalties he had
avoided in June 1798 only by naturalization and flight, were aimed at
specific individuals, none of whom threatened the security of the political system. The Sedition Act was both unconstitutional and partial;
John Ward Fenno and Cobbett had violently attacked Adams in 1799,
yet neither was prosecuted under the legislation. Callender accepted
the value of personal reputation to a political figure but denied it to be
more important than a private individual's. No special legislation was,
therefore, necessary to augment the laws of slander and libel. "A PRESI-
DENT has, in strict justice, no more title to make a statute for the
peculiar protection of *his own* character, than for the peculiar punishment of stealing *his own* horses."[36]

The nucleus of *The Prospect*, as in all his work, was Callender's
constant preoccupation with the ubiquity of corruption in American
political life. His fixation with government maladministration and
malfeasance—only his support for Jefferson's presidential candidacy
prevented him from slipping into anarchism—was both a weakness and
a strength. Because he could find nothing positive to say of Adams's
administration, his work never rose above the level of propaganda,
however often he claimed to have given Republican congressmen "hard
rubs, or rather knocks." Nor is his claim to have converted Federalists
likely to be accurate; his writings were too blatantly partisan.[37]

On the other hand, by his deliberate appeal to the baser instincts of
his readers, to their love of sensationalism, and to their inherent suspicion of power and the powerful, he made a strong case against the
Federalist administrations under Washington and Adams. Callender
was particularly dangerous because of the plausibility and the slipperi-
ness of his criticisms. He had the unerring ability to focus on particular
issues and to twist them into shapes that conformed to his predeter-
mined conclusions. Even seemingly minor issues, such as the number of
outfits taxpayers funded when John Quincy Adams rapidly moved from
one European ambassadorial post to another or Abigail Adams's refur-
bishment of the president's residence, were used to pile up evidence of
Adams's purported misappropriation of funds. This tactic was very
effective, because the Federalists had no simple counter to use. They
were caught between denying every claim Callender made, which involved further publicizing the charges, with no certainty of being be-

lieved, or ignoring them altogether, thereby leaving the field to him. Either way, the Federalists were permanently on the defensive, as Callender gleefully harassed them from all sides. As a purely destructive force, but with a unerring instinct for knowing what his democratic constituency wanted to read, there was no one to compete with Callender in America in 1800.

Callender gave the Federalists little option but to invoke the Sedition Act against him. In August 1799 Secretary of State Timothy Pickering—in Adams's cabinet the most zealous pursuer of the seditious—ordered Thomas Nelson, federal district attorney of Virginia, to check each edition of the *Examiner*. Because it was "a virulent *Jacobin*, or if you please, *French-devoted* paper," he demanded its prosecution if any libels against the government or any of its officers were discovered. Nelson, living in Yorktown and thus unable to obtain regular copies of the newspaper, handed the task over to Daniel Call, a prominent Federalist lawyer and member of the Richmond Association. With the determination of a man deprived of his prey once before, "that sorry understrapper of Federal usurpation," as Callender called him, systematically began to stalk his quarry.[38]

He was not difficult to locate. Although Callender left Jones's household in December 1799, he took up lodgings in Richmond with no intention of disappearing. Jones later claimed that Callender's departure from his home resulted from embarrassment at having drunkenly entered the Virginian's bedchamber late one night to demand the whipping of a recalcitrant servant. In an age of heroic drinkers Callender compared favorably with William Pitt, Henry Dundas, Thomas Paine, and Chief Justice John Marshall; but it is equally likely that he left partly out of a disgust with Jones's household arrangements and partly because of a temporary political disagreement. Jones seems to have suffered a loss of nerve in January 1800, publishing an editorial in which he expressed reservations about the overzealous nature of current political debate in the newspapers. In a rare editorial statement he wrote: "It is time that the American press should assume a new character, and rescue itself by an effort no less easy than honorable, from that odium and persecution which its occasional irregularities may have contributed to produce. The enemies of freedom will thus be deprived of their only pretext for an invasion of the rights of the press, and the sedition bill itself, so far as it relates to libels, will be rendered as inactive as it is unconstitutional."[39]

The specter of Call perusing his newspaper for signs of disaffection did not, however, prevent Jones from keeping his promise to employ Callender at $10 a week in the ensuing months. Nor did Callender agree to temper his opinions. Indeed, the reverse happened; following the publication of *The Prospect before Us* he deliberately set himself up for prosecution under the Sedition Act. "It is time," he wrote in the *Examiner*, "for Americans to cast aside that trimming tone of sycophancy, which is too well calculated to oil the wheels of despotism."[40]

Federalist newspapers began a smear campaign, dredging up the false stories of his career in Edinburgh first published by Cobbett. Callender reveled in "A Federal Republican's" belief that he was one of "three foreign emissaries, . . . under the *Chief Juggler*" (Jefferson), who between them had divided the country into "three Grand Departments" for the purpose of spreading Jacobin principles. Callender ran the southern department, Duane the eastern, and Thomas Cooper, the English radical friend of Joseph Priestley, the western.[41]

Republicans associating with Callender also suffered harassment. In Staunton, one of the editors of the *Scourge of the Aristocracy*, for whom Callender wrote paragraphs, was assaulted by a local printer, illegally ordered to appear before local magistrates under the Sedition Act, and threatened with the destruction of his shop. No intimidation, however, could deter Callender. To Jefferson he wrote: "Every engine has been set to work to do me all kinds of mischief since I came here; the satisfaction of knowing that they are exceedingly provoked is to me a partial compensation for the inconvenience of being belied and stared at, as if I were a Rhinoceros. They are chop fallen, and many turn round that were very bitter against me at first."[42]

Publicly, Callender continued to project the image of an independent commentator ready to suffer for his political opinions. He had been "calumniated and persecuted by men of all parties, for he [had] told much that no party could deny, and which no party wished to hear." He would "proceed in line of his duty, without regard to all the shots that malice or stupidity may discharge against him." Privately, he deliberately sought prosecution in order to promote Jefferson's election. He wrote to Duane in April: "Let us, by one grand effort, snatch our country from that bottomless vortex of corruption and perdition which yawn[s] before us. The more violence, the more prosecutions from the treasury, so much the better. Those of yourself and Cooper will be of service. You know the old ecclesiastical observation, that *the blood of the martyrs was the seed of the church*."[43]

The net by now was closing around Callender. John B. Walton, a federal place seeker, had kept Pickering informed of the progress of *The Prospect before Us* since before Christmas, sending him a copy on publication. The Federalists, not wishing to risk confusion over authorship, decided to use this pamphlet, rather than articles in the *Examiner*, as the basis for their prosecution of Callender. On 24 May the Richmond grand jury approved an indictment in which Callender was accused, on the basis of twenty passages from *The Prospect before Us*, of inciting the American people to hatred of their president and of printing and publishing these false, scandalous, and malicious statements. Three days later Callender was arrested in Petersburg, where he had been visiting James Lyon to organize the publication of the second part of *The Prospect*. Brought before Supreme Court Justice Samuel Chase, Callender was released overnight on $400 bail.[44]

Meriwether Jones, relieved that his newspaper had been saved from prosecution but concerned that Callender's arrest might lead to violence, immediately called for calm and restraint. With the sangfroid possible only from a man not in the firing line, he wrote: "Let us then be temperate—he who cannot submit to a few years of incarceration for the good of his country, degrades the Dignity of Man." For Callender this was the moment of truth. On two previous occasions when faced with arrest, he had fled to safety; on this occasion, he stood his ground, ready to sacrifice himself for his mentor, Thomas Jefferson.[45]

IV

An overwhelming consenus of opinion among historians concedes the unfair treatment Callender received at his trial in June 1800. Charles Jellison, for example, whose most favorable feeling for Callender is pity, has commented: "Few more unsavory and generally obnoxious figures than James Thomson Callender have ever set foot on American soil, but even he deserved something better than he received from American justice. His trial . . . was from beginning to end little more than a mockery." In a major sense, however, rather than the trial proceedings, it was the nature of the Sedition Act and the exigencies of both political parties that determined Callender's fate. The Sedition Act, as an integral part of High Federalist strategy since 1798, was a blatantly partisan attempt to crush opposition to Adams's administration. There was little, if any, legal justification for its enactment. The common law offense of seditious libel was available for use both in state and federal courts in the 1790s. Indeed, several Republicans, including Bache and Frothingham, were indicted under the common law rather than the Sedition Act. But as Leonard W. Levy has stated, "It was politically advisable in the 1790s to declare public policy in the most unmistakable terms by the enactment of sedition statutes. Legislation helped ensure effective enforcement of the law, stirred public opinion against its intended victims, and in every way served party objectives."[46]

The Sedition Act's justification was thus purely partisan; it enabled the Federalists, who controlled the federal courts, to prosecute dangerous opponents in regions where they did not control the state courts. This fact alone made its implementation in the Republican stronghold of Virginia imperative if the Federalists were to fulfill their aim of completely crushing their political opponents. The act also consolidated in law the Old Whig perception that persistent and organized opposition to a properly constituted government was factious and therefore seditious, that is, disloyal to the state.[47] As Callender and many other Republicans pointed out (at least before they assumed power in 1801), such an opinion failed to distinguish between the system of government under the Constitution and an administration which happened to be in power at any particular time.

Most Republicans, including Jefferson, were far from wanting to overthrow the Constitution; rather, they wished to win power and operate within its framework. It is understandable, however, why Callender became a major Federalist target. Since his first attacks on Washington in 1795, he had constantly exposed the Federalists' strategy of using the symbolism of the Constitution to protect their leaders. Moreover, although some Republicans such as John Taylor and Edmund Pendleton in Virginia wished the Constitution to be amended, few followed Callender in openly criticizing it and calling for its radical reconstruction. *The Prospect before Us*, with its open attack on the Constitution, was thus, if not seditious by advanced libertarian standards, clearly subversive of the accepted political order.[48]

Callender's prosecution served two functions for the Federalists: it enabled them to raise their banner in the Republicans' stronghold, and it offered an opportunity to settle scores with a particularly dangerous adversary. Their angel of vengeance was Supreme Court Justice Samuel Chase (1741–1811), a belligerent, passionate, and boisterous Marylander. A signer of the Declaration of Independence, an unsuccessful speculator, and an Antifederalist in 1788, Chase had switched to the Federalists in the 1790s and, like many converts, swifty became more zealous than the orthodox faithful. Strangely, he reminded Joseph Story of Callender's first literary adversary: "He loves to croak and grumble, and in the very same breath he amuses you extremely by his anecdotes and pleasantry. His first approach is formidable, but all difficulty vanishes when you once understand him. In person, in manners, in unwieldy strength, in severity of reproof, in real tenderness of heart, and above all in intellect, he is the living, I had almost said the exact, image of Samuel Johnson. To use a provincial expression, I like him hugely."[49]

Chase's main purpose as a politicized judge was to protect society from the licentiousness and Jacobinism of the Republicans by encouraging the use of the Sedition Act. In Newcastle, Delaware, he refused to dismiss the grand jury until a local Republican newspaper had been examined for possible seditious sentiments. Of the fourteen cases tried under the Sedition Act between 1798 and 1800, Chase was involved in some of the most important. In June 1799 he presided over the trials of two Republicans involved in the erection of a liberty pole in Dedham, Massachusetts. One defendant, a wealthy local farmer, was treated leniently after he expressed remorse for his conduct. The other, however, a semiliterate, itinerant radical called David Brown, who in addition had sermonized the locals into frenzied political excitement, was fined $480 and imprisoned for eighteen months. In April 1800 Chase had his first opportunity to deflate Jefferson's Jacobin triumvirate of "foreign emissaries" when he presided over Thomas Cooper's sedition trial in Philadelphia, fining him $400 and imprisoning him for six months following his inevitable conviction.[50]

From Philadelphia, Chase moved on circuit to Annapolis, where his old friend and state attorney general, Luther Martin, gave him a copy of *The Prospect before Us* to read on the coach to Richmond. The book enraged the justice; it was "a libel so profligate and atrocious, that it excited disgust and indignation in every breast not wholly depraved." Publicly he asserted his determination to apply the Sedition Act in Virginia if the state was "not too depraved to furnish a jury of good and respectable men." Discussing *The Prospect* with another traveler in the coach, Chase was informed of Callender's arrest in Leesburg in 1798. "It is a pity you have not hanged the rascal," he is said to have replied.[51]

Chase's arrival in Richmond on 21 May 1800 to assert the full majesty of the Sedition Act thus signaled the culmination of a concerted Federalist campaign of intimidation against the Republican opposition. The ritual theater of federal authority was augmented by the presence nearby of a regiment of regular federal troops, whose officers, "who appear to have been all Virginians, were Federalists to a man."[52] Understandably, historians have viewed Callender as the unfortunate victim of a legal process perverted by political intrigue and necessity, with Chase as the wicked manipulator. There is no doubt that at one level this is a sustainable interpretation of the trial. But at another level a different plot can be discerned, in which one victim was Justice Chase, and another the authority of the Sedition Act (and thus Federalism). In this scenario, the drama that unfolded in the Richmond courthouse was choreographed, openly by the defense counsel and more circumspectly by Jefferson and Governor James Monroe. From Callender's defeat, they created a victory for Republicanism. At both levels Callender was a victim, but in the latter version he was a not unwilling one, prepared for martyrdom in a cause at whose head stood his mentor, Vice-President Jefferson.

The first scenes of this alternative scenario were played out in the spring of 1800, while Callender was extolling the virtues of martyrdom, Thomas Cooper was being tried by Chase, and Jefferson was surreptitiously sending eight dozen copies of Cooper's tract, *Political Arithmetic*, to Philip Nicholas in Virginia for distribution among the county committees. The vice-president was mulling over ways to build up popular enthusiasm for Republicanism in the lead-up to the presidential election. To Monroe he mused: "I know that sometimes it is useful to furnish occasions for the flame of public opinion to break out from time to time; and that that opinion strengthens and rallies numbers in that way." Although he hated personal publicity and disliked "being the mannequin of a ceremony," he hinted to Monroe that his journey from Philadelphia to Monticello at the end of the Senate's session might be a suitable occasion to boost Republican morale.[53]

Monroe was shocked that Jefferson could even consider such an unrepublican venture as a triumphal journey through the countryside. Jefferson swiftly backtracked, claiming Monroe had misunderstood him. "My query," he wrote, "was meant for the single spot of Richmond, where I had understood was a great deal of federalism and Marshalism, and this latter spirit I thought nothing should be spared to eradicate. I did not know whether any question of republican demonstrations might not be of service towards drawing over some of his [John Marshall's] less inveterate supporters." On second thought, he concluded, he did not wish to be included in any electoral venture.[54]

Monroe, nevertheless, began to plan a grand "Union dinner" for when Jefferson passed through Richmond; he was expected to arrive on 21 or 22 May, coincidentally at about the same time as Chase entered the town. By that time, such was the ugly mood in Richmond that— confronted with a Federalist threat of a rival dinner in honor of John Marshall, the new secretary of state, and nervous about the impact of Chase's charge to the grand jury, in which a thinly disguised Jefferson was accused of atheism—Monroe canceled the dinner. Jefferson remained in the vicinity, visiting his daughter and son-in-law.[55]

Callender's trial, however, raised the possibility of fanning "the flame of public opinion" without openly involving Jefferson. The possibility of popular agitation in favor of Callender had to be resisted strongly, lest an opportunity be given to discredit the Republicans or to warrant federal military intervention. The crisis called for a more subtle approach, one that gave symbolic meaning to the trial. Perhaps the most appropriate means, wrote Jefferson in answer to Monroe's request for advice, was for the state authorities to demonstrate their commitment to Callender by assisting in his defense. The three defense counsel who came forward offering their services for free—Philip N.

Nicholas, Virginia's attorney general, William Wirt, clerk to the House of Delegates, and George Hay, Monroe's son-in-law—represented just such an affirmation of the Republicans' championing of Callender as "the cause of the Constitution."[56]

The defense counsel were aware of the almost impossible task confronting them. The Sedition Act made it a crime to conspire to oppose the laws or the government; to incite any unlawful combination or riot; "to write, print, utter, or publish . . . any false, scandalous, and malicious writing" against the government, the president, or either house of Congress with intent to defame or to bring them into disrepute; to excite against them the hatred of the people; or to stir up sedition. Callender was charged under two counts: one of attempting to defame President Adams by writing and publishing the twenty passages mentioned in the indictment, which had been taken from *The Prospect before Us*, and one of causing these same extracts to be printed and published. Although Levy, with tongue in cheek, has pointed to the libertarian aspects of the Sedition Act—the acceptance of truth as a defense, the need to show criminal intent, "the power of the jury to decide whether the accused's statement was libelous as a matter of law as well as of fact"—the odds nevertheless were heavily stacked against Callender.[57]

The defense lawyers' opening gambit on 28 May, before the jury had been sworn, was to move that the trial be postponed until the next session in November. Success would have ensured that the trial coincided with, and thus possibly influenced, the presidential elections. Their argument stood on firm ground. Postponement was common practice in Virginia's state courts when, as in Callender's case, documentation had to be collected and witnesses rounded up. The custom in federal courts was much less clear, but the procedure in the 1790s had been to follow the practices of the state in which the court was sitting. Chase, however, was known to disapprove of this, and had been the first Supreme Court justice to codify, for Georgia in 1797, federal procedural rules. Moreover, in Cooper's trial, with which the defense was fully familiar, Chase had ruled against a similar argument, although he had given the defense a few days' grace to assemble witnesses.[58]

Nicholas and Hay were aware, therefore, that their plan had little chance of success, but it did give them the opportunity of informing "the very numerous assembly of citizens who were present" of the reasons why particular witnesses would be called and what evidence they would give. This was important, because they knew some of the witnesses were most unlikely to attend. Thus, in a long opening speech, Attorney General Nicholas presented the evidence of William Gardner and Tench

Coxe—both of whom would testify that public officials were dismissed
if their politics did not conform with Adams's—and of General Samuel
Blackburn, who would testify to Adams's perpetual irritation with
opposing opinions. In addition, Nicholas claimed that the evidence of
Timothy Pickering—recently dismissed as secretary of state—was
necessary to prove Callender's contention that Adams actively sought
war with France in 1798. Of these four potential witnesses, only one,
Blackburn, lived in Virginia. Pickering was in Massachusetts, Gardner
in New Hampshire, and Coxe in Philadelphia. None was likely to attend
as a witness, especially Gardner and Pickering, who were Federalists.[59]

The jury, of course, was not impaneled at this point, so the "evidence" presented by Nicholas could not influence them. But to regard
this as important is to miss the point of the Republicans' strategy
throughout the trial. Their aim was not to save Callender—his position
was considered hopeless—but to discredit Chase and the Sedition Act
and hopefully to create propaganda useful in the election campaign. The
stronger they could make the case for postponement, the worse Chase
would appear when he refused their request, as he did, although he
adjourned the hearing until Monday, 2 June. In the meantime, sub-
poenas were issued for William B. Giles, John Taylor of Caroline, and
Stevens Thomson Mason.

Only Taylor and Mason were present when the court reconvened
on 2 June. Claiming that Giles may have been but temporarily delayed
by inclement weather—although in reality he had no intention of attending to defend Callender—the defense sought a further adjournment, which Chase allowed, until the following day. On 3 June, Hay
supported Nicholas's request for a postponement in a speech which was
significantly more in the order of a defense summation than a simple
argument for delay. His main thrust concerned the need to distinguish
between facts and opinions. The assertion of the former "was the
assertion of that which, from its nature, was susceptible of direct and
positive evidence; everything else was opinion." Most of Callender's
statements in the indictment were opinions, not demonstrable facts,
and therefore incapable of proof and not subject to the Sedition Act.[60]

Such an argument, of course, had little to do with the need for a
postponement. If Callender's statements were opinions, not facts, neither documentation nor witnesses were needed to prove the defense's
case. Also irrelevant to the case for postponement but of great moment
for the defense's overall strategy were Hay's deliberate use of extracts
from Adams's speeches to demonstrate that he had used "the language
of passion and malignity," of which Callender had accused him, and his
assertion that the Sedition Act was unconstitutional. Slightly more

relevant but particularly disingenuous was Hay's claim "that he was but little acquainted with the doctrine of libels," primarily, he pointedly noted, because libel laws had never been invoked in Virginia. To claim inexperience may have been good tactics, aimed at gaining the sympathy of his audience, but it was palpably untrue. In 1799, as "Hortensius," Hay had published a series of addresses, first in the *Aurora* and then as a pamphlet entitled *An Essay on the Liberty of the Press*, in which he had condemned the Sedition Act as unconstitutional and demonstrated a deep knowledge of the law of libel.[61]

If the object of the defense counsel's speeches was to rile the judge, they can be accounted a success. In rejecting the plea for postponement, Chase, whose biographers claim that "he had all the qualities of an outstanding judge except a judicial temperament," allowed his contempt for the Virginia bar and his determination to chastise the Republicans to overwhelm his good sense. He patronizingly corrected the defense on points of law and made abundantly clear his opinion that the statements attributed to Callender were defamatory, false, scandalous, and malicious.[62]

Defense counsel, belittled but unbowed, continued to draw Chase onto dangerous ground when the jury was called. A subsequent claim by a local lawyer to have heard Chase order the federal marshal to omit from the panel "any of those creatures or people called democrats" cannot be verified, but certainly the final twelve were all Federalists. Chase clashed with defense counsel again over how prospective jurors should be examined and what questions could be asked of them. He denied them the right to discover if any juror had preconceived notions of *The Prospect before Us*, confining their questions to charges in the indictment, which the jurors had never seen and which did not include the name of Callender's book. When one of the panel said he had formed the opinion that *The Prospect* came within the scope of the Sedition Act, Chase refused to disqualify him, thus creating the first of five charges stemming from this trial for which he was to be impeached in 1804.[63]

The prosecution case was straightforward: instead of proving Callender's statements libelous, Thomas Nelson, the government prosecutor, shifted the onus of proof onto the defense. It was, writes James Morton Smith, "the clearest statement of presumptive guilt made by any district attorney prosecuting a case under the Sedition Law. The indictment which accused Callender of making seditious statements with bad intentions was presumed true until proved untrue by the defendant. . . . This concept . . . can only be described as 'guilt by association.'"[64]

The prosecution needed, therefore, only to prove Callender to be the author and publisher of the seditious libels. Evidence given by local printers, including Meriwether Jones and James Lyon (who admitted publishing *The Prospect* jointly with Callender), quickly settled the issue of publication. The authorship of the book was confirmed by William Rind, who —gaining revenge for the mauling he had received from Callender in the newspaper war—offered as evidence part of the manuscript in Callender's handwriting.[65]

To seal the case against Callender, Nelson needed to confirm the presence of the indictment extracts in *The Prospect*. When he produced the book, however, Hay rose to protest its admissibility, claiming that the fact that it was not mentioned in the indictment demonstrated its irrelevance. Using precedents from English libel trials, Hay argued that the absence of the title from the indictment violated the requirement of literal exactness in the libel being judged and raised the possibility of double jeopardy. Chase, interrupting Hay, correctly rejected the defense's argument; but in so doing he gave erroneous justifications for his decision. Nelson proceeded to complete the prosecution case by discussing each of the twenty libelous statements as found in Callender's work.[66]

The case so far had been punctuated by wordy disagreements between the defense and Chase on the interpretation of the law, but it degenerated even further once Nicholas, Hay, and Wirt began their defense. In reality, they had little to offer. They could not throw doubt on Callender's authorship of *The Prospect*, and they had to prove the truth of all twenty statements in the indictment. This they manifestly could not do. Their first witness, John Taylor, was expected to give evidence supporting only one part of one of the libels, regarding Adams's supposed aristocratic leanings. Most probably he would have recounted his conversation in 1794 with Adams, who apparently had expressed pessimism for the future of republican government in America. But Chase, having demanded to see the defense's questions in writing, adjudged Taylor's testimony inadmissible, on the faulty grounds that he could not refute the whole charge. In the arguments that followed, the justice openly suggested, probably correctly, that defense counsel were deliberately misinterpreting the law and "press-[ing] your mistakes on the court."[67]

The final card played by the defense, which brought the trial to a melodramatic climax, was to argue that the jury—on the basis of their right as judges of the law as well as of the facts—should declare the Sedition Act unconstitutional and refuse to enforce it. As a legal argument, the defense's case was untenable, raising the specter, as Chase rightly pointed out, of anarchy as juries around the country unilaterally selected which laws they personally wished to enforce. The defense, naturally, appreciated this, but they had their eyes fixed on the political consequences of their arguments. Chase was trapped; as he, of necessity, continually interrupted their repetitive arguments, the disdain and irritation he felt broke through in his comments. True, he had the satisfaction of slapping down the cream of the Virginia bar, calling their actions "disrespectful, irritating, and highly incorrect," but this is precisely what they sought. At the most dramatic moment, when Chase had once again interrupted, Hay "folded up and put away his papers, seeming to decline any further argument." As in the Cooper trial, defense counsel walked out of Chase's court, leaving the field to him but taking the political rewards with them. It is difficult to deny the careful stage management of their actions.[68]

Callender, meanwhile, was left sitting in the dock. He played no role at all in the trial. He neither gave evidence nor spoke when the verdict was given. Temperamentally, he was ill suited to the role of an injured and mistreated martyr. He disliked the limelight and felt uncomfortable without a pen, or a glass, in his hand. He was no poseur, nor had he the oratorical talents or the physical presence to influence an audience in his favor. His sole contribution to the entertainment in Chase's court was to have been the violator of the Sedition Act; the political warfare was conducted around him.

After Chase's summation of the evidence, the jury took two hours to return a verdict of guilty. In sentencing Callender, Chase emphasized the enormity of his offenses. He was "a well-informed observer," an "intelligent stranger," who must have been aware of President Adams's great services to his country, yet he had deliberately and maliciously maligned him for political purposes, ignoring the distinction between the liberty and the licentiousness of the press. The penalty Chase imposed, however—a $200 fine, a bond for good behavior for two years of $1,200, and a prison sentence of nine months—in comparison with other sentences he had given earlier does not appear to correspond with the supposed malignity of Callender's offenses. Admittedly, Chase was bound to take the defendant's personal condition into account when fixing a penalty, and the defense had claimed Callender to be poor and friendless, but the Scotsman was treated less harshly than the manifestly poor David Brown in Massachusetts, who was fined $480 and imprisoned for eighteen months. The maximum penalties under the Sedition Act were a fine of $2,000 and imprisonment for two years. The conclusion must be that Chase, having made his point of enforcing the act in Virginia and aware that the Republicans had outmaneuvered him, felt obliged to avoid making Callender too obviously a martyr. It was, of course, far too late to prevent that from happening.

V

As Callender was led from the dock to prison, he was reminded of his services to the cause of Republicanism by Senator Stevens Thomson Mason, who strode up to shake his hand. In Caroline County, John Taylor organized a subscription that raised $113 toward the fine (or, alternatively, in the event of Callender's death, toward the upkeep of his children). Republican members of the House of Delegates contributed another $200, of which Meriwether Jones became custodian. In addition, Jones was one of eleven sympathizers who agreed to cover the cost of Callender's board in prison.[69] The Virginia Republicans thus signified support for his political martyrdom in the most practical manner. Unfortunately, however, general Republican approval was to be conditional; when Callender reverted to his customary tirades of propaganda, he was to become once again comparatively isolated. In addition, arguments over the way the subscriptions were later used and the failure of some Republicans to honor their engagements were to be the source of friction between Callender and his erstwhile friends after he was released from prison.

Throughout his prison term Callender remained strapped for money. He was still obliged to pay Leiper for the care of his children, as well as the wages of two journeymen assisting him in the preparation of *The Prospect before Us*, volume two. In July, Jones publicly asked his patrons to pay their debts to Callender, then amounting to $400, but by October only $20 had been received. James Lyon had left for Washington owing Callender $70, and an advance of $14 to one of his journeymen had been lost when the man was "struck with the dead palsy." Finally, Callender was compelled to pay freight costs to and from Philadelphia when Duane, having asked for 100 copies of *The Prospect*, volume one, failed to advertise them, leaving most of them on his hands.[70]

Sentenced under a federal statute, Callender served his prison term not in the new state penitentiary, which was being constructed in accordance with some of Jefferson's "enlightened penological concepts," but in the old Richmond jail. It was an insalubrious place, where he was "surrounded by thieves of every description and unfortunate negroes." Callender had his own apartment, but in hot weather the atmosphere was oppressive and heavy, and "owing to the stink of this place," he soon succumbed to a fever, only slowly recovering. In colder weather the absence of a chimney made it impracticable to light a stove for warmth. "Unless a man has the constitution of a horse," wrote Callender, "he must in such lodgings either catch his death of cold, or think himself happy in escaping with a rooted rheumatism."[71]

Although conditions were uncomfortable in jail, Callender was never totally isolated or neglected. A small stream of visitors, including

Governor Monroe, Chancellor George Wythe, and Meriwether Jones, signified his good standing with the Republicans. Their visits raised his spirits, as did the appearance of three of his sons (the fourth had died the previous year). Callender had been planning to fetch the boys from Philadelphia at the time he was arrested; the disappointment had put him for some weeks "into an extasy of rage that no words can express." Their visit now, however, cleared away the gloom. "Still I hope," he informed Jefferson, "to be what I once was, one of the happiest of human beings; and which I alwise would have been, if fortune had been half as kind as nature."[72]

Callender was treated with kindness and care by his jailer, William Rose, Jefferson's "old acquaintance and protégé." During the hot weather he permitted his prisoner to visit his garden for fresh air. When news of this indulgence filtered out to the local Federalists, they complained to the marshal, who stopped the practice. "I do not believe that the world ever saw such a contemptible set of scoundrels," wrote Callender to Jefferson. In the *Examiner*, he vowed to revenge himself on these "Church and State Christians." At the completion of his sentence they "will suffer more from Callender's freedom, than even Callender has suffered from confinement."[73]

In September the jail was filled with prisoners from the abortive Gabriel slave insurrection. Callender's attitude toward slavery had changed since his arrival in the United States. As with other British-born radicals, such as Thomas Cooper and Matthew Lyon, Callender's initial opposition to the institution of slavery did not survive his first-hand experience of its role in southern society and culture. In Philadelphia he had called for the ending of slavery, believing it to be "a dark stain on our character," and for the suppression of slave importation, "a practice deserving the severest reprobation." Yet after eighteen months in Virginia he was openly expressing fears that the Alien Acts of 1798 might be used to prevent the landing of imported slaves and had imbibed most of the justifications for slavery expressed in the South, as well as the customary cries of regret at the original establishment of a slave society. The slave, he claimed, was generally well treated: "In Richmond, and Petersburg, at least, a much greater number of slaves has been spoiled by foolish and useless indulgence, than has ever been ruined by fetters and scorpions." His condition "is very often much more comfortable than that of his master" and was certainly superior to his counterpart's in Africa. Blacks were inherently inferior to whites; the black was "too stupid for acute reflection," had no sense of shame, and was concerned only with cramming food into his belly. Wrote Callender: "We do not know that a prostitute is likely to improve her morals by being left entirely to her own freedom, or that a fellow, who was too lazy to work for his master, will sharpen his industry by the absence of compulsion."[74]

Callender's attitude was determined by a number of factors: the normal process of acculturation that a newcomer undergoes in a new society; his role as a propagandist for the planter class; and a racism, expressed as a puritanical, almost pathological distaste for the libidinous ways of blacks, which Callender blamed for the promiscuity of the members of white society who fraternized with them. His solution to the problem of slavery and the black presence was heavily influenced by Jefferson's *Notes on the State of Virginia*. General emancipation ("this wild scheme") would be a fatal action, the consequence inevitably being "civil war, and there never could nor would be an end of the business, till the last of the black and yellow race was exterminated." Transportation back to Africa was impractical, but Callender supported two variants of this scheme: transplantation to "a sequestered part of the continent," where they might live "without intermingling with the whites," and the offer of graduated bounties to slaveowners to move their slaves farther westward, in order to diminish the proportion of blacks in Virginia's population.[75]

Fear lay at the root of Callender's desire to spread a diluted slavery over a wider area, a fear shared with most other whites after the exposure of Gabriel's plot. Callender showed not the slightest compassion for those sharing his prison. He approved of the hanging of these "African speculators in fire and blood" and regarded an appeal for clemency by some Richmond ladies as "very ill-timed." When the slaves, many of whom were Baptists, consoled themselves by hymn singing at night, Callender, "whose slender stock of patience was exhausted, went down stairs, and assured them that not one of them was to be hanged; . . . and [said] he hoped they would make less noise and permit him to enjoy a little quiet. The music immediately ceased."[76]

There was an irony, therefore, in the attempts by Federalist editors to blame the racist Callender for the slave revolt.[77] He found blacks physically repulsive, and he possessed none of the paternalism and anguished doubt that characterized the ambivalent position on slavery of Jefferson and others raised from birth in a slave society. As an outsider and in some respects a "poor white," Callender had little understanding of the complexities of master-slave relations. In the center of his vision lay the Gabriel insurrection; it defined both his fear and his loathing of black slaves. They were a threat to society, requiring firm, even harsh treatment in normal conditions and condign punishment if they stepped out of line.

Callender's report to Jefferson on the insurrection reflected these views and was spiced with relish for vengeance. He seems to have been unaware that his mentor, who advised Monroe to deport rather than execute the malefactors, was appalled by the number of hangings. Nor was Callender ever to be disabused, for throughout 1800 Jefferson continued his policy of not committing his thoughts and plans to the dangers and vagaries of the postal service. Nevertheless, unlike in 1796, he participated fully in the election campaign, sending confidential messages to his supporters by special messenger or trusted friends. Despite a request, however, Callender received no written or oral communication from Jefferson, although the Richmond merchant George Jefferson, who had previously acted as an intermediary between the two, did visit him in October. He also failed to receive any comment on the voluminous drafts, newspaper articles, and proofs he continued to send. He had to guess the burden of Jefferson's opinions in the months leading up to the presidential election. Although accepting that "neither the stile nor the matter [in *The Prospect*, volume two] could be exactly conformable to your ideas, or taste," he informed Jefferson of his hope "that upon the whole, they would not be disagreeable."[78]

In these circumstances, inevitably a gulf emerged between Jefferson's tactics and plans and Callender's conception of them. The Scotsman's view of Jefferson and Republicanism continued to be locked into the events of 1798; his mentor remained the radical of the Virginia and Kentucky Resolutions and of the revived "Spirit of '76." In March and April 1800, before Callender's arrest, Jefferson had indeed retained his radical mantle. He contemplated abandoning caution and considered the issuing in Congress of a declaration of constitutional principles aimed at resurrecting the "Spirit of '76" and forcing the Federalists to adopt an "antirepublican" position. Madison, however, wisely counseled caution, for with the Federalists in internal disarray, a low profile was seen to be the key to Republican victory. Thus, even when Jefferson was the victim of a vicious newspaper campaign during 1800, his policy was to ignore it; the "returning good sense of our country" following the delusions of 1798 rendered unnecessary a vigorous Republican campaign in response. When Gideon Granger informed him of a concerted attempt by New England clergymen to blacken him with accusations of atheism, Jefferson, although privately condemning them as liars, refused to allow public defense of his religious opinions.[79]

Callender, however—the recipient of only secondhand versions of political events and personally still committed to a radical politics— failed to move with the times. No one seems to have told him of the changed strategy, although Meriwether Jones sought in vain to persuade him of the counterproductive nature of his comments on certain local issues and personalities. Quite probably, Callender would have ignored any advice not coming from Jefferson himself. Intent only on revenge—"It is not only proper to knock an adversary down, but to keep him down"—Callender was blind to the political wind shifts. He had no faith in the moderate Republicans. In *The Prospect before Us*, volume two, published in November 1800, he wrote: "It is not in the power of these moderate republicans to think more despicably of me than I thought of them. I halt upon a kind of isthmus, between the two parties. From the aristocrats I can expect nothing but mischief; and I have studied farther to serve the republicans than they will ever study to serve me. But as I had never placed confidence in their gratitude, their friendship, or their justice, I am altogether exempted from the pangs of disappointment." In such a frame of mind, Callender was unlikely to heed those counseling caution and moderation.[80]

He had, moreover, a personal investment in continuing to beat the radical drum. His martyrdom had been the means of boosting his self-confidence and pride: "I would not, for the price of an estate," he told Jefferson shortly before his release from prison, "be divested of the self-congratulation that I feel, in being able to go straightly through this great national crisis, without having to look back upon one moment of trimming, or flinching." For a man with the reputation of cracking and fleeing in a crisis, his stance in 1800, although passive during the trial, represented a significant personal victory.[81]

If the moderate Republicans had hoped imprisonment might silence his extremist pen, they were to be disappointed, for his time in prison seemed to rekindle Callender's enthusiasm and drive, bringing to mind his statement that "writing and printing form not only the business, but the pleasure of my life. To me, all the comedians, painters, and architects in the world are not worth a careful compositor, and a clean proof sheet." In March 1800 he had been "firing through five port holes, at once," writing for the Richmond publications the *Examiner*, the *Friend of the People*, and the *National Magazine*, as well as Lyon's Petersburg *Republican* and Staunton *Scourge of the Aristocracy*. His imprisonment failed to check his output. Extracts and drafts of volume two of *The Prospect* were first published in these outlets. In addition, he furnished regular political commentary and argument for Jones's *Examiner*. While in jail he supplied, without receiving a cent in return, nearly ninety columns for Jones, raising the number of subscribers to 1,200.[82]

All his productions were fueled by his customary objectives: "to shake the pool of corruption to its bottom, to extinguish the torch of the incendiary . . . and go, right as a rifle-ball, through the heart of Presidential duplicity." *The Prospect before Us*, volume two, published in late 1800, followed the pattern of his previous pamphlets, being a contemporary history of the Federalist period. It added little to his earlier interpretations of his political enemies' activities and motives. But a large proportion of his contributions to the *Examiner* was concerned with a systematic defense of the character and politics of Jefferson, constituting Callender's response to a series of attacks by Rind and Stewart in their newly established *Washington Federalist*. That moderate Republicans felt this to be an unnecessary and potentially dangerous indulgence is suggested by Jones's disclaimer when the series first began: the author, he said, had expressly asked for no changes and thus would be "permitted to tell the story IN HIS OWN WAY."[83]

The fears of the Republicans had some grounding: hatred of Rind for his role in the sedition trial had blinded Callender. By systematically repudiating the *Washington Federalist*'s libels of Jefferson he fell into the trap of publicizing his opponents' propaganda. Thus he brought to his public's attention, at the very moment of the election, Jefferson's attitudes toward the Constitution, religion, Thomas Paine, party divisions, and slavery.

It is possible, of course, that this was a deliberate policy by Callender, for it enabled him to sustain an image of Jefferson the radical, a man in his own political image. He saw no need to dissemble; unhesitatingly he pursued every libel his Federalist quarry served up. Whether it was the letter to Mazzei written by Jefferson in 1796 in which he expressed fears of a monarchical party suborning the Republic; Jefferson's friendship with, and support for, Thomas Paine; his so-called atheism; or his dissatisfaction with the Constitution, Callender refused to fudge the issue. Jefferson's infidelism was defended as toleration of all religious opinions; he was a gradual, not an immediate emancipationist; the Mazzei letter contained "a correct sketch" of republican principles; and Paine, although not faultless, "had exposed the trades both of Priest and King with a depth of ingenuity, a dignity and sublimity of eloquence, which never will be refuted."[84]

On the issue of the sanctity of the Constitution, Callender most clearly espoused his belief in the radicalism of Jefferson. Repeating his claims that the role of the Senate and the presidential election process were only two of "an hundred . . . chasms, that call most loudly for amendment," Callender asserted that Jefferson had always been and still remained equivocal on many aspects of the Constitution. The people and been "juggled" into accepting it in 1788 by Federalists determined to raise the specter of anarchy. If Jefferson had been present at the Richmond ratifying convention, "we should have seen a less faulty constitution than what we now see." Fortunately, Callender continued, the Constitution offers a mechanism for amendments. He left his readers in little doubt of Jefferson's intention, as president, to revamp the Constitution along radically democratic lines.[85]

Callender's Jefferson was no caricature, nor did he excessively exaggerate the radicalism of his mentor. But for many in the Republican party, those aspects of his character that so impressed Callender were sources of uneasiness and concern, sometimes to be explained by Jefferson's "philosophic" nature, sometimes to be glossed over. Callender had little respect for the opinions of the moderates; in some ways they were as much in his sights as the Federalists. They had toadied to Washington and Adams; they had expressed the most "wretched timidity . . . and sycophancy" in the past ten years. They were, he trumpeted in a last-minute blast before the election, "trimmers, trucklers, apostates, turncoats, demi-democrats, water-gruel republicans, and half-way hobblers." Now was the moment for them "to make your peace with mankind, and with your own consciences, if you have any."[86]

When news finally arrived of Jefferson's victory over Adams, Callender was both exultant and convinced of his own vital role in the campaign. "And so the day's our own," he wrote in the *Examiner*. "Hurraw! How shall I triumph over the miscreants! How, as Othello says, shall they be damned beyond all depth! What a burst of rapture one feels in the embraces of Victory! She is certainly the most charming of all Goddesses, Venus and the graces not excepted."[87]

The dispute over the tied electoral votes for Jefferson and Aaron Burr brought him temporarily back into the lists, much to the alarm of Meriwether Jones, who felt the issue ought to be resolved without undue publicity. A euphoric Callender, determined not to lose the prize at the last moment, refused to hold back. Rather loftily, he forced Jones to retreat by asserting that "no fear of consequences should divert me from the prosecution of my purpose; that it was part of my intellectual constitution that the stronger opposition proved to be, I was only the more perfectly determined to strike it in the face; and that I would rather stay in prison for thirty years, than recede from one syllable, which had been wrote."[88]

Fortunately, however, Callender's prison term came to an end; he was released on 2 March 1801, having served his full term. As he blinked in the strong spring sunlight he felt immensely self-satisfied with the role he had played in the election of Jefferson. If he had doubts, they would have been erased by the toasts given at dinners celebrating Jefferson's victory. At Captain Stannard's, a general toast was given to the Republican printers; at Richard Price's tavern in Albemarle County, Captain Edward Moore's volunteer toast was to "James Thomson Callender, who looks down on his persecutors with their merited contempt." The future looked bright for one of the Republican party's most stalwart campaigners.[89]

7

"His Hand Should Be against Every Man, and Every Man's Hand against Him"

I

Any residual feelings of euphoria Callender may have felt did not long survive his first days of freedom. Not unexpectedly, he assumed his services to Republicanism would be officially recognized in a more substantial form than toasts to his health and success. While still in prison in the last months of 1800, Callender had begun dropping hints of the reward he anticipated. Privately to Jefferson he mentioned the cost of establishing a printing office and a newspaper in Richmond, as well as the propriety of dismissing the Federalist Augustine Davis from his position as Richmond's postmaster in the event of a Republican presidential victory. In his newspaper columns he called for the dismissal of all Federalists in public offices. He applauded Pennsylvania governor Thomas McKean's policy of a clean sweep through the state bureaucracy (although he appeared unaware of McKean's nepotism). His justification was revenge, to punish those who had victimized Republicans on partisan grounds. "Nothing," he wrote, "can be an act of more exquisite justice than that, as the poet Thomson phrases it, these tyrants *should feel the pangs they gave.*" He assumed that, for similar reasons, Jefferson, "unless he should be willing to degrade his own character to a level with [the Federalists]," would follow the same policy. Callender was encouraged when, within a month of Jefferson's inauguration, most of the federal marshals were dismissed. Gleefully he wrote of his old enemy: "D[avid] Meade Randolph in Virginia has gone, ha, ha!"[1]

Callender was, however, to be disappointed in his expectation of appointment as Richmond postmaster. Indeed, he received no reward at all, leaving him with a justifiable sense of grievance. The most recent research on Jefferson's patronage policy has shown that, contrary to earlier views which emphasized its moderation, it was distinctly partisan, involving the dismissal of hundreds of public servants, many solely for political reasons. As Carl Prince has noted: "Removals in one form or another for purely political reasons constituted the backbone of [Jefferson's] effort to break the Federalists' power." It was, therefore, within Jefferson's gift to reward Callender with a public position. Although he had devolved the power of choosing federal postmasters onto his postmaster general, Gideon Granger, the new president had ordered Federalist activists to be removed. Augustine Davis was to be one victim; if Jefferson had so suggested, undoubtedly Callender would have been his replacement.[2]

Ironically, however, Jefferson's patronage policy greatly favored the moderate rather than the radical Republicans, even though the latter were the most vehement in promoting a total removals policy. This may have made political sense while Jefferson still hoped to detach the more moderate Federalists from their leaders, but it was of little consolation to the radicals themselves. In particular, a number of British radical emigrants found themselves neglected. In New York, the former United Englishman James Cheetham, who coedited the *American Citizen*, promoted a full-scale removals policy, as did the defrocked priest and deist Denis Driscol in his Baltimore *American Patriot*. "It appears to us," wrote Driscol, "that Mr. Jefferson is a better philosopher than he is a General," for he had failed to disarm his opponents when the opportunity presented itself.[3]

Possibly neither Cheetham nor Driscol had strong expectations of receiving patronage in Jefferson's first term, for they had been in America only a short while. But for William Duane and Callender it was another matter; both had been in the van of Republican battles for a long time and had borne the brunt of Federalist hostility in 1798. Duane had opened a printshop and planned a newspaper in Washington under the impression that Republican patronage would make them profitable. In the event, almost all the printing patronage in the capital went to the American-born editor of the *National Intelligencer*, the moderate Samuel Harrison Smith. Duane was left with the paltry contract for supplying stationery to the Treasury.[4]

Others therefore may have shared Callender's disappointment at failing to obtain patronage in 1801, but he alone refused to swallow his pride and subsequently broke with the Republican party. His actions are understandable. He had never supported the moderate Republicans, whom Jefferson, perhaps reluctantly, now favored. In addition, his future prospects were more dependent on patronage than Duane's, Driscol's, or Cheetham's, for they either owned or partly owned printing establishments they could fall back on. Moreover, Callender had suffered more for the cause than most; of the four, only he had been imprisoned. As he told Jefferson in April 1801, "By the cause, I have lost five years of labor; gained five thousand personal enemies; got my name inserted in five hundred libels, and have ultimately got something very like a quarrel with the only friend [Leiper] I had in Pennsylvania."[5]

Above all, however, it was the apparent desertion by Jefferson, his father figure, that embittered Callender. He had opened his soul to the president and had suffered personally for him, not for the party. Even during the long silence from Monticello while he was in prison, Callender had not doubted his mentor's continuing support. That Jefferson might find it politically expedient to abandon him was unthinkable, yet this was the conclusion to which Callender was inexorably drawn.

Some historians have defended Jefferson by claiming that the president did his utmost to aid Callender in the weeks after the inaugural. According to both Charles Jellison and Virginius Dabney, Jefferson ordered that Callender be "set free"; they also point out that he personally paid part of the $200 fine. In reality, of course, Callender served his full sentence; Jefferson's pardon, issued on 16 March, was retrospective and merely erased Callender's conviction, not his sentence. Nor did Jefferson pay part of the fine, although he asked his secretary, Meriwether Lewis, to give Callender $50 in May 1801. Meriwether Jones paid the fine, from the subscription raised in July 1800, before Callender was released. Jefferson canceled a further draft for $50 that he had asked James Monroe to pay when he learned that Callender regarded it as hush money. But even this money was mere charity; by this stage Callender was convinced that his services deserved more than that.[6]

The rift between Callender and Jefferson, at least from the former's perspective, began within days of his release from prison when George Jefferson, reading from a slip of paper which he then threw into the fire, informed Callender of Jefferson's immediate intention to remit the fine. Callender took him at his exact word, expecting the fine to be returned within days. He was in urgent need of the money, because half of the Republicans who had subscribed to pay his prison debts reneged, leaving him to pay the balance out of his own pocket and thereby unable to settle his debt with Leiper in Philadelphia. After nine months' imprisonment, he was in no mood for further delays. Unfortunately, however, the fine had been paid to federal marshal Randolph, who had just been dismissed and was facing difficulties settling his accounts. He was only too happy to frustrate his hated kinsman Jefferson and the gloating Callender, which he did by seeking Attorney General Levi Lincoln's opinion on the legality of returning a fine that had been paid before the issuing of a pardon. Lincoln took nearly a month to resolve this conundrum, eventually favoring the remission of the fine as long as it had not been paid into the Treasury.[7]

Callender was aware of Randolph's mischief. But on the basis of the information George Jefferson had given him, he perhaps unreasonably expected Jefferson to repay the fine himself while the legal issue was being considered. In the middle of April, as he slowly began to appreciate that patronage might not flow his way, he wrote to Jefferson explaining his plight, pointedly exclaiming that "You may not suppose that I, at least, have gained anything by the victories of Republicanism."[8]

He received neither a reply nor any intimation of a swift remission of the fine. A fortnight later, his patience exhausted, he sent a stinging letter to Madison in which he accused Jefferson of ingratitude and indifference. As he wrote, the rage, despair, and venom he felt at his "betrayal" spilled out. He emphasized the "desperate lengths" to which he had gone for the party's benefit and pointed to Jefferson's previous acknowledgments of his services. Now, however, the president intended in return "to discountenance me and sacrifice me, as a kind of scapegoat to political *decorum* [and] as a kind of compromise to federal feelings." This, he hinted, would be a foolish policy, for not only was he "not the man, who is either to be oppressed or plundered with impunity," but also the Republicans would continue to require political writers in the future.[9]

In this same letter Callender openly sought the position of Richmond postmaster. He recognized his unsuitability for more prestigious posts requiring highly tuned social skills: "I am not, to be sure," he claimed with some truth, "very expert in making a bow, or at supporting the sycophancy of conversation. I speak as well as write what I think; for God, when he made me, made that a part of my constitution." He was, however, seeking only a minor position, from an administration that claimed to represent the ordinary people, not an elite. Jefferson, he continued, "should recollect that it is not by beaux, and dancing masters, [or] by editors, who would look extremely well in a muslin gown and petticoats, that the battles of freedom are to be fought and won."[10]

Nothing demonstrates more clearly Callender's naive view of his own position in the Republican party than his perception that it was his lack of social graces that alone prevented him from receiving patronage. Undoubtedly this was part of the explanation for his rejection; the moderate Republicans in particular refused to accept the full implications of the democratic message that had been circulated in their name during the past few years. They accepted in theory the doctrine of popular sovereignty but retained in practice the ideal of an educated social elite continuing to control the levers of power. But in Callender's case, perhaps of equal importance for his rejection was his reputation for militancy and scurrility, which were regarded as having been counterproductive. The Republicans believed they had succeeded not because of but in spite of Callender's contributions. To have appointed him to a federal post, however menial, would have conferred public approbation on his political ideas and conduct. As Meriwether Jones was later to explain, with a condescension that neatly encapsulated the moderates' inherent sense of superiority: "Callender was already too well known, and too much despised to be thought worthy of public trust: and Mr. Jefferson disdained employing any person who was unworthy."[11]

A week after writing his letter to Madison, Callender received a note from Randolph intimating that he would reimburse the $200 at the customs house in Petersburg on 6 May. Callender, then lodging in that town, refused to attend; he prudently kept away because statements in a Federalist newspaper of that day "recommended me to a drubbing." With the money still in Randolph's hands, Callender set off for Washington, determined to argue his case with the Republican leaders in person.[12]

In a later justification of his visit to the capital, Callender disingenuously claimed he went to discuss his plans for editorial unity among Republican newspapermen and to obtain state papers from John Adams's presidency in order to write another anti-Federalist broadside. Actually he had but one objective: to plead for the Richmond postmastership. He did not receive an interview with Jefferson but met with his secretary, who reported that Callender had threatened blackmail if his demands were not met. On three successive evenings Callender was closeted with Madison in the State Department, where he was finally convinced that the fine would only be repaid through Randolph and that the Richmond postmastership would never be his. "He is sent back in despair," wrote Madison to Monroe.[13]

Callender later wrote of the high-handed manner in which Madison treated him. The secretary of state "seemed to think that he had become a sort of semi-divinity, and that poor Callender was not worthy to be his foot-stool." It is unlikely that Madison was so condescending; nevertheless, Callender was devastated by his rejection. Whichever way he considered his prospects, they appeared worse than during his earlier low point in mid–1798. Then, at least, he could rely on the support of Stevens Thomson Mason. Now he was alone, again virtually penniless, with a very uncertain future. In desperation and rage he found solace in his old standby, the bottle. According to William Duane, after leaving Madison for the final time Callender made a disgusting spectacle of himself at Rhodes's Hotel in Washington: "You wallowed in your own excrement, while you lavished execrations on those who would not dishonor themselves by employing you."[14]

Revenge had always been a strong motivating force in Callender's life, but for nearly a year after his return to Virginia he held his tongue and suffered in silence. Randolph finally remitted his fine in June 1801, and although Callender was able to repay part of his debt to Leiper, he remained unable to visit his sons in Philadelphia. Oscillating between Petersburg and Richmond, Callender kept body and soul together by working for Samuel Pleasants, the only Richmond printer/editor with whom he had not quarreled. His low profile, as much the consequence of his depressed spirits as of a period of political quiescence, did not prevent the local Federalists from taunting him unmercifully for his misfortunes. Finally, in September 1801, he felt compelled publicly to seek a truce. In an unsigned letter to the *Examiner* he wrote:

> Sacred writ says that "the righteous shall rest from their labours, and their works follow them." Whether the writer of the Prospect is one of the righteous the public may judge; but it seems to be the determination of the federal party that his works shall follow him. The battle being now, in a great measure at an end, he was willing to let the opposite party alone. He has not, for many months, wrote one line with a design to offend them. He wished old scores to be, as far as possible, forgotten. But his silence seems to give as much occasion for calumny as his publications had formerly done. In prose and verse, his name continues to be bandied about through a shoal of newspapers. In the spirit of charity, he wishes these good folks to let him alone. . . . QUIESCAT.[15]

Callender's letter prompted Meriwether Jones to seek his old assistant's aid once again. In the months following the disappearance of Callender's byline, sales of the *Examiner* had plummeted, leaving Jones financially embarrassed. In September he reversed his decision not to publicize private quarrels, justifying himself by referring to "the barrenness of important news, and the want of money." The most persistent disparager of Callender had been William Rind, whose comments in the *Washington Federalist* were circulated by Virginia newspapermen. Among his strictures were claims that Callender had been heard to say that he wished for "fifty drops of Mr. Jefferson's heart's blood." In the hope of increasing subscriptions, Jones encouraged Callender to come out of retirement. For a few weeks Callender once more wrote for the *Examiner*. But he confined his comments to answering the personal attacks of his enemies. He no longer had the heart or the conviction to defend the Republican party. His paragraphs soon petered out, leaving Jones, who never had Callender's skill as a political journalist, to cast around for other ways of boosting sales.[16]

Ironically, the publication of exciting political disputes and spicy personal details, so vital for the healthiness of newspaper circulations at this time, was reintroduced in Virginia by Callender, but not in the columns of the *Examiner*. In the early summer of 1801 Henry Pace, who had settled in Richmond about a year earlier, decided to establish a newspaper. Pace was an English printer who had emigrated to America in about 1798 as a consequence of printing and uttering sedition in London. In July 1801 he issued the first number of the Richmond *Recorder: or Lady's and Gentleman's Miscellany*. Within a few months Callender was contributing the occasional paragraph.[17]

As the name of the new offering suggests, Pace initially had no intention of publishing a partisan political newspaper. Inevitably, he was soon in financial difficulties; Richmond did not possess the population base to support four newspapers. In February 1802, however, Pace formally went into partnership with Callender; Pace supplied the financing from his printshop, Callender supplied the editorial expertise.[18] Within a few weeks began one of the most vicious, unprincipled newspaper wars in American history, which in scurrility outstripped the editorial battles of the 1790s. By the time it ended, the dark side of Virginia society had been dragged into prominence, breaches of the peace had become commonplace, and the appetites of even the most avid consumers of personal gossip and scandal had been sated.

Callender began his career as joint editor of the *Recorder* by propounding the newspaper's policy of political impartiality. "We shall neither calumniate nor flatter men in office. We shall neither defame nor worship men that are out of it. The public shall see that, from whatever quarter imposture and falsehood may come, yet, if they force themselves in their way, it shall be our ambition to blast them with the lightning of truth." Impartiality was a consequence of independence: "[We] have no personal obligations to any party, although [we] are willing, if necessary, to contend occasionally for political principles." The *Recorder*, he claimed, would never "prostrate itself to the fanaticks of either party."[19]

Assertions of independence and impartiality from partisan newspapermen were notorious in this era, and most were taken with a grain of salt. In Callender's case, however, although less so with Pace, who was a moderate Federalist, there was an element of truth in his claim. Contrary to the views of some historians, who have accused him of deserting to the Federalists, after March 1802 Callender remained free of party entanglements. He had never been comfortable as a party writer, nor had he ever totally subordinated his own political beliefs to the needs of party. In truth, like Paine, Duane, and many other radicals of his generation, Callender was an oppositionist *tout court*; this alone probably would have guaranteed his ultimate break with the Jeffersonians, even if personal matters had not hastened the process. He switched to attacking the Republicans in 1802, but he did so without joining the Federalists and without compromising his militant, if cynical and idiosyncratic, republican ideals. His principles, he wrote, "were known to be not merely republican, but to be of that sort which invites and challenges tyranny to inflict its utmost, without flinching for a moment from the ground that had been taken."[20]

Callender's "impartiality" incorporated that deep suspicion of human motivation which he had expressed repeatedly since his first writings in Scotland. In 1802 he quoted Paine's dictum that "government, at best, is a choice of evils." It is "a sort of complex constable, a *something* hired to keep the peace, and nothing more." Paine's distinction that society arises from our wants and government from our vices "is perfect. Government is to society, what a bridle is to a horse, or a dose of salts to the human body." Unlike Paine, however, Callender denied that republicanism could ultimately avert the evils inherent in other political systems. Even in a republic, government was "a system of robbery, and of swindling." Corruption was inevitable, because human nature was fatally flawed: he had, he claimed with some personal justification, "but a very humble opinion of *patriotic* virtue." Both parties, he thought, "require a great deal of watching; . . . there is not a prodigious difference between the moral characters of the one and the other." The "factious and worthless ringleaders" of the parties had nothing but contempt for the people. "Every sensible *federalist* will tell you, and every candid *republican* tells you, that whenever a patriot talks about loving his country, he is understood to mean, that he has a very unaffected love for *himself*. He is understood to mean, that it requires an uncommon command of muscles, to keep him from laughing in the faces of his simpleton admirers." One could rely only on individuals. Individual effort alone would lead to improvement and prosperity.[21]

To emphasize the continuity of Callender's political thought is not to deny that a superficial glance at the *Recorder*'s offerings might not indicate a Federalist persuasion. In his very occasional paragraphs, for instance, Pace openly defended Federalist politicians, forcing Callender to deny his authorship. Many of the new subscribers picked up as the assaults on the Republicans intensified came from the Federalist ranks, but as Callender pointed out, they read the newspaper only because of the hostility of Jones's *Examiner*. Moreover, in such a cutthroat business as journalism, one did not ask a potential buyer for his political opinions before making a sale. In any case, wrote Callender with feigned innocence, did not Jefferson say we were all Federalists and all

Republicans? A truly impartial newspaper would naturally gain subscribers from both sides of the political fence.[22]

The *Recorder* appeared to be a Federalist organ primarily, of course, because the bulk of its political comment was hostile to the Republican administration. But as Callender observed, by holding all the levers of power, both at state and federal levels, the Republicans were the natural focus of criticism. In October 1802 he wrote: "If we seem to bear hardest upon the men, at present, in office, it is only because they are, at this time, more formidable and dangerous than their defeated adversaries. A few months of additional reading, a little candour and patience, an acquaintance with a hundred important facts . . . will convince the majority of our subscribers that neither the *ins* nor the *outs*, ever have deserved, or ever will deserve implicit confidence."[23]

Thus, as editor of the *Recorder*, Callender found himself for the first time in the United States unencumbered by political debts, free to develop those suspicions of power and the powerful that had always been implicit, and frequently explicit, in his writings since the 1780s. It was no coincidence that in 1802–3 his essentially destructive talents reached fulfillment, for now his personal resentments, unchecked by the moderating influence of a mentor, fueled his habitual rhetoric. In the last months of his life Callender did not turn his coat; he merely gave free rein to the spirit of Old Testament vengeance and the eighteenth-century oppositionist, Antifederalist features latent in his thought. His treatment by the Jeffersonians had confirmed his longheld conviction that political power always was used despotically. Filled with hatred, Callender systematically set out to pull down the pillars of society.

His strategy was two-pronged, aimed at undermining both the political and the social fabric of Republicanism. First in his sights was, unsurprisingly, Gideon Granger, whom he criticized for not dismissing Federalist postmasters, for his policy of not employing newspaper editors of either political persuasion, and for not rewarding those who "have been of ten times more service and some of them ten thousand times more service [to the Republicans] than Mr. Granger himself." He then turned his attention to state politics, and for several months Callender dwelt on his favorite issue, the ubiquity of corruption in political life. The cost of the new armory, the proposed merchant's tax, and government waste in general were examined. He also involved himself in the state election, supporting for the seat of Richmond not the official Federalist candidate, Dr. John Adams, nor the Republicans' George Hay, but the independent James Rind, whom the Republican press called a trimmer. Adams won quite comfortably, but Rind, whom

Meriwether Jones had wounded in a duel in 1800, got four more votes than Hay, much to Callender's glee.[24]

By early May 1802, as a consequence of his electioneering in the *Recorder*, Callender had stirred up a hornet's nest. One Republican had threatened to break "every bone in [Callender's] skin"; another, Skelton Jones, Meriwether's older brother, had threatened to horsewhip the Scot. Yet another, Lewis Harvie, soon to become Jefferson's private secretary and whose grandfather had been Jefferson's guardian, was bound over at Callender's request to keep the peace, after his threat during the election campaign to kill anyone who continued to attack in print his father, a prominent builder and former mayor of Richmond. Callender's use of the law to protect himself led Meriwether Jones to write: "The malignity of this wretch can only be equalled by his cowardice. If he sees a gentleman walking with more than ordinary speed, he immediately binds him over [to keep] the peace." His "morbid timidity" shielded him from "corporeal chastisement" and "his blasted fame from the importance of a newspaper investigation."[25]

Callender stimulated this outcry less by his political paragraphs than by his assaults on the very essence of Virginian society, the honor and virtue of the gentry. By 1800 the gentry's hegemony was under threat, partly from the growing importance of an ethnic, evangelical Baptist culture and partly from politically engendered fissures within the gentry order itself. In response, the normal means of promoting social deference and oligarchical authority—the theatrical tableaux of horse races, assizes, dances, and barbeques—took on greater symbolic meaning and significance.[26] Callender's strategy was aimed at exploiting the weaknesses of that public culture and demonstrating that in Virginia public virtue masked private vice. Indeed, his eventual indictment of Jefferson's personal life ought to be seen as a high point of his mission to destroy the cultural hegemony of the Virginia gentry as a whole.

Callender, with his Calvinism spurring him on, easily found ways to break through the crust and to expose the less salubrious regions of gentry culture. His determination to crucify his enemies, coupled with the gentry's divisions and willingness to accept and to spread gossip and innuendo, made exposure inevitable. There was much to be examined in the light of Truth and Justice. The Virginia elite, for instance, had a mania for gambling, not only on quarter-horse racing but also on "every imaginable game of hazard"; La Rochefoucauld-Liancourt noted that "gaming-tables are publicly kept in almost every town, and particularly at Richmond." This leisure activity ran counter to restrictive state gambling laws, which generally remained unenforced because most legislators and justices of the peace shared the gambling habit.[27]

Gambling inevitably led to quarrels and their resolution by dueling. The gentry held a very precious conception of honor and a highly developed sense of pride. In Callender's time duels appear to have occurred with increasing frequency, and the law was seemingly myopic. Both Skelton and Meriwether Jones eventually died on the field of "honor," as did John Daly Burk, the Irish radical immigrant and historian of Virginia. Newspapers reported duels with apparent equanimity; a letter from "Pacificus" to the *Virginia Federalist* opposing the practice, for instance, was rejected by William Rind because he was in the midst of a duel himself.[28] When to gambling and dueling are added the keenness of some of the gentry to attend slave dances and the widespread practice of miscegenation, the ease of Callender's task, to expose gentry culture as vice-ridden, corrupt, and lacking in the virtue necessary to sustain republican institutions, becomes clear. The key was to uncover vice and to convince the public of its ubiquity.

Ironically, however, the public exploration of this murky world, which undoubtedly existed, if not to the extent argued by Callender, began with a misunderstanding of something trivial that Callender wrote of Skelton Jones, who by April 1802, as coeditor of the *Examiner* with his brother, had taken the initiative in attacking Callender. In reply to a paragraph in which Skelton had accused Callender of apostasy, the Scotsman innocuously commented in passing that his opponent "wishes partly to retrace his steps." Jones's response seemed out of all proportion to the statement. "The fiend-like malignity of this allusion is well understood," he wrote. "Should I have the misfortune, to be engaged in a scene of the kind you mean, it would be [with] a far different subject from the editor of the Recorder, his correspondents, or coadjutors. A horse-whip would honor him; the knout is the adequate punishment for such abject pusillanimity, coupled with such base illiberality."[29]

Skelton Jones believed Callender was alluding to a duel in May 1801 in which he had killed Armistead Selden. Although Callender hotly denied this, his interest was raised by the vehemence of the response. Inquiries seemed to confirm that the circumstances of the duel offered an ideal way of exposing the profligate side of the gentry's cultural life. In the next issue of the *Recorder*, Callender laid bare his version of the events. Skelton Jones, that "Bloodyrun Marksman" and "Mulatto Dance Marksman," had quarreled with his friend Selden in an "African brothel" for "the possession of an African strumpet." After the duel, Jones and his second, Wiltshire Lewis, had fled, and the coroner had ordered their arrest. How then, asked Callender, was it possible for Jones to be moving freely around Richmond? "People talk of aristocracy! Was there ever a viler instance of its worst spirit than this, that a man who is understood to have killed another, under the most questionable circumstances, shall be endured to spit in the face of public justice, merely because he is the brother of a popular democratical printer? This is liberty and equality with a vengeance." When Meriwether Jones defended his brother's honor by denying that there had been a coroner's inquest, Callender reprinted the original warrant, which had been published three times in the *Virginia Gazette* in 1801.[30]

Having begun the war, the Jones brothers found themselves under siege. As soon as Meriwether publicly condoned Skelton's strictures, Callender pitilessly exposed his old employer's private life. Meriwether Jones's financial embarrassments, he wrote, resulted from lavishing money and presents on his slave mistress, commonly known as "Mistress Examiner," whom he had set up in an apartment. Jones was frequently seen at brothels, black dances, and horse races attended by his whore. He was, claimed Callender, incorrigible: "I have heard him, at his own table, and before his own lady, boasting that he never had any pleasure, but in a certain kind of woman; and that it was the custom of his family to be fond of the other colour." Callender had left Jones's household in December 1799 not because he had been drunk and had blundered into his employer's bedroom, but because Mistress Examiner had moved in when Mrs. Jones was out of town.[31]

Meriwether Jones was helpless before this savage onslaught, primarily because of its veracity. He denied only one of Callender's charges, that he had given a miniature self-portrait to his whore to wear round her neck. All he could do was lament Callender's desire for vengeance: "Men disposed to sacrifice private confidence, the offspring of regard and benevolence, to their revenge and chagrin, and to array trifles in the harsh language of crimination, may always make unpleasant assaults." The scion of one of the more prominent families in Virginia had thus been shown, with his brother, to be singularly lacking in virtue.[32]

There is no doubt that miscegenation and the mixing of races at low dances and bordellos deeply troubled contemporary Virginian society and that by highlighting them Callender had discovered an effective way of causing distress and anxiety. The blame, he argued, should be placed on the married gentry, who "not only behave wrong themselves, but . . . act as apostles and precedents in the cause of debauchery. They meet with abundance of disciples." Personally, claimed Callender, he did not object to the activities of the unmarried: "Boys and batchelors will take liberties." But the whorehouses and black dances had not been suppressed, as he had demanded since 1800, for there the magistrates and their social circle took their pleasures. In a number of issues of his newspaper Callender named those prominent members of Richmond society who had a "white wife and black concubine," who "dabble to some extent in African merchandize," and who sat in the blacks-only area at the playhouse with their whores.[33]

Callender's strategy of exposure fulfilled several functions: it satisfied personal revenge, it confirmed the virtue-vice dichotomy of oppositionist ideology, and it threw Richmond's Republican society into turmoil. To use a cant phrase, Callender knew where the bodies were buried. The prospects were frightening. As "A Federal Republican" wrote in September 1802: "Your productions, by infusing a vicious taste into society, have a tendency to destroy it. They constitute a species of debauchery, which will throw the body politic into a sickly habit, as excessive drinking does the human body." As far as Callender was concerned, this was precisely what he hoped to achieve.[34]

Callender's assaults on the Republicans soon received a national audience, as newspapers in other states avidly reprinted his copy. The Federalist press, however, remained suspicious of his motives and continued to attack him. For several months he felt like Ishmael, of whom it was foretold that "his hand should be against every man, and every man's hand against him." Nevertheless, the press in other states generally agreed that in his fight with Jones he was far ahead on points. The New York *Herald* wrote: "It must be allowed that [Callender] certainly has a faculty at 'hitting that particular knack, which is the soul of a newspaper.' Poor Jones has been so cut and bruised and mauled and gouged, in the battle, that he must be toughness itself, if he can carry it all off, without lasting and *irreparable* injury." Callender explained his success in terms of Jones's lack of capacity.

> He wants those habits of industry which are essential for the labour of collecting information; that unrelenting vigilence, which is ever on the wing; that sullen merciless sagacity, that suffers nothing to escape; that equally scorns to take, or to give quarter. Mr. Jones wants those abilities, without which knowledge is almost useless, and which in some measure, create it. He wants the talent of selecting, of combining, of charging home his information, that talent without which the fiercest assailant rebounds from his mark. . . . Mr. Jones wants that firmness which fights for the last inch of its ground.[35]

Undoubtedly Callender could claim all these qualities himself in 1802, although he underestimated the perseverance of Meriwether and Skelton Jones. Even while Callender was condemning Meriwether for leading a campaign aimed at discrediting his own father-in-law, Norfolk magistrate Dr. Read, Jones doggedly continued to fight. He had few weapons at his disposal; personal abuse, references to excessive drinking, and accusations of apostasy failed to hinder Callender's relentless progress. When, however, Callender accused the Federalist press of naively failing to attack Jefferson at his weakest point, Jones fell into the trap of unreservedly defending the president. "The fact is," he wrote, "that there is not *one* recorded or unrecorded truth which can in the smallest degree militate against the integrity or talents, the patriotism or wisdom of Mr. Jefferson."[36]

Callender's response cunningly drew the Republican press into a maze of accusations, counteraccusations, statements, and retractions, from which it emerged with its reputation in tatters. Initially he merely hinted at future revelations but coyly suggested the public was unready for them. More proof was needed "to get over honest prejudices"; a wider readership was required. A fortnight later, however, Callender published his assertion that Jefferson had financially supported Callender's political writings in the years before the election of 1800. The $100 Jefferson paid toward the two volumes of *The Prospect before Us* "attest, beyond a thousand letters of compliment, how seriously the president was satisfied with the contents of the book, and how anxiously he felt himself interested in its success." When Jones claimed the money had been given as charity, Callender quoted from Jefferson's letters. When Jones denied their existence, Callender published them in full. When Jones denigrated him for libeling Adams, Callender replied that "if there was guilt in the contents of the Prospect, then every [R]epublican in Virginia is a criminal; and Mr. Jefferson is by far the worst of them." The president was clearly exposed as the financial backer of Callender's libels. "It may be emphatically said," wrote William Coleman in the Federalists' major newspaper, "that Federalism has been lied out of power."[37]

Jones was out of his depth, but help began to arrive via Duane's *Aurora*, which included comments on Callender's past. Garbled versions of the Gardenstone affair were printed, and Callender was falsely accused of jumping bail before escaping to America (he was confused with one Alexander Callender). In August 1802 Duane turned his attention to Callender's career in Philadelphia, belittling his services to Republicanism and accusing him of threatening to switch to the Federalists in 1798 and of stealing mahogany from his lodgings on 12th Street.[38]

Jones regained his confidence with these exposés and began again to taunt Callender for more revelations on Jefferson's past. But Callender was in no hurry to publish his information. His intention, he later said, was to keep silent for eighteen months, until the next presidential election came due. But on 25 August, Duane published an article on Callender's dead wife. At the time Callender stole the mahogany, Duane asserted, his wife was being "overwhelmed by a created disease

[VD], on a loathsome bed, with a number of children, all in a state next to famishing . . . , while Callender [was] having his usual pint of brandy at breakfast." Three days later a copy of the *Aurora* arrived in Richmond, and Callender exploded in fury. On 1 September he published the first details of the Jefferson–Sally Hemings affair.[39]

III

The story of Jefferson's supposed long-term relationship with his slave Sally Hemings has echoed down the years since Callender first publicized it. An ideal subject for partisan exposition, it was used by British visitors to denigrate American democratic society in the 1830s, by abolitionists in the period around the Civil War, and by blacks in the late 1950s as part of the early civil rights campaign. As the story was repeated, it became burdened with more and more implausible embellishments, so that Callender's original and rather prosaic comments have been submerged in a welter of imaginative hypotheses. One of the most inventive explanations of the Black Sally story occurs in Fawn Brodie's psychological history of Jefferson's inner life, in which Callender's account of miscegenation, buttressed by evidence unavailable to him, is used to support the theory that Jefferson and Sally shared a thirty-eight-year-long love affair. Published in 1974, Brodie's book created considerable public interest, thereby confirming—nearly two hundred years later—Callender's conviction of the popular taste for private scandal.[40]

Except in the unlikely event of new evidence coming to light, the truth of Callender's accusations will never be known. Nevertheless, historians, skilled at reaching conclusions from limited evidence, have put forward various explanations for the undeniable fact that Jefferson's slave Sally Hemings had a number of mulatto children. Those most sympathetic to Jefferson have denied Callender's (and Brodie's) assertions; following the defense put forward by the president's descendants, they have placed the burden of paternity on one or both of his nephews Samuel and Peter Carr.[41]

It is sufficient to say that their evidence is no less circumstantial than Brodie's. Quite simply, the available data will not bear out Jefferson's innocence or guilt. The more general explanations in defense of Jefferson, however, are relevant, for their authority depends partly on a particular interpretation of Callender's character. As put forward by Jefferson's biographer Dumas Malone, a defense of Jefferson's honor may be premised on three general observations: "(1) the charges are suspect in the first place because they issued from the vengeful pen of an unscrupulous man and were promulgated in a spirit of bitter partisanship. (2) They cannot be proved and certain of the alleged facts were obviously erroneous. (3) They are distinctly out of character, being virtually unthinkable in a man of Jefferson's moral standards and habitual conduct."[42]

The third defense mentioned by Malone can be disposed of most swiftly. It is a clear tautology; Jefferson's high moral standards and habitual conduct depend on the presumption of his innocence of mis-cegenation. It also requires the glossing over of Jefferson's admission, after publicity by Callender, of an attempt to seduce a neighbor's wife when he was young and his wooing of Maria Cosway, a married woman, while in France.[43] Jefferson was not the paragon of virtue his defenders are so determined to create. Perhaps this is just as well; Jefferson's humanity stems from his weaknesses as well as from his virtues.

The other general defenses of Jefferson can best be answered after Callender's exact comments on the Jefferson–Sally affair have been examined. In the *Recorder* of 1 September he wrote:

> It is well known that the man, *whom it delighteth the people to honor*, keeps, and for many years past has kept, as his concubine, one of his own slaves. Her name is SALLY. The name of her eldest son is TOM. His features are said to bear a striking although sable resemblance to those of the president himself. The boy is ten or twelve years of age. His mother went to France in the same vessel with Mr. Jefferson and his two daughters. The delicacy of this arrangement must strike every person of common sensibilities. What a sublime pattern for an American ambassador to place before the eyes of two young ladies! . . . By this wench Sally, our president has had several children. . . . THE AFRICAN VENUS is said to officiate, as housekeeper at Monticello.[44]

In the ensuing months Callender did not add greatly to these "facts." In mid–September he stated that Sally had five mulatto children; and a month later, on the evidence of a gentleman who, at the district court, "bet a suit of clothes, or any sum of money" on the truth of the story, he corrected his statement that Sally had traveled to France in Jefferson's entourage rather than at a later date. A fortnight later Callender queried new information suggesting that young Tom was older than had been originally stated. "He is not big enough, at least our correspondent thinks so, to have been in existence fifteen or sixteen years ago. Our information goes to twelve or thirteen years." This brought the birth to 1789 or 1790, which coincides—according to her son Madison's account first published in the 1870s—with the date Sally gave her children for the birth of her first child by Jefferson.[45]

In the next issue of the *Recorder*, Callender informed his readers that "Sally's brother was set free by the president. He has an infirmity in one of his arms. During the sitting of the last assembly, he sold fruit in the capital. It is said, but we do not give it as gospel, that one of her daughters is a house servant to a person in this city. This wench must have been by some other father than the president." Finally, in December, Callender reprinted confirmatory evidence obtained by the editor of the Maryland *Frederick-town Herald.*

> Other information assures us, that Mr. Jefferson's Sally and their children are real persons, that the woman has a room to herself at Monticello in the character of sempstress to the family, if not as housekeeper; that she is an industrious and orderly creature in her behaviour, but that her intimacy with her master is well known, and that on this account, she is treated by the rest of the house as one much above the level of his other servants. Her son, whom Callender calls president Tom, we are also assured, bears a strong likeness to Mr. Jefferson.[46]

The "facts" presented here, the only ones vouchsafed by Callender personally, are—claim Malone and others—suspect because they came from a "vengeful pen" in a "spirit of partisanship." That Callender was suffused with the desire for revenge and that he was partisan are undeniable. Callender openly and honestly said so himself at various times. "The original and just cause for introducing the background scenery of Monticello" was Jefferson's connivance with the personal attacks by Republican printers, he wrote on one occasion. He "had it in his power, with a single word, to have extinguished the volcanoes of reproach," but "with that frigid indifference which forms the pride of his character, the president stood neuter." As a consequence, "chastisement was promised, and the promise has been kept with the most rigid punctuality. If [Jefferson] had not violated the sanctuary of the grave, SALLY and her son TOM would still, perhaps, have slumbered in the tomb of oblivion. To charge a man as a *thief,* and an *adulterer,* is, of itself, bad enough. But when you charge him with an action that is much more execrable than *an ordinary murder* . . . is the party injured not to repeal such baseness, with ten thousand fold vengeance upon the miscreant that invented it?"[47]

Unattractive as personal vengeance may be, the means used to assuage it are not necessarily suspect, especially if revenge is openly conceded to be a motivating force. Of all the facts published by Callender on the Sally affair, only one, suggesting that her daughter was in service, can be proved to be incorrect. In this instance, Callender specifically warned that it might not be true. Malone, Douglass Adair, Virginius Dabney, and John C. Miller support their assertion of Callender's unreliability (and deliberate falsehoods) primarily with a denial of the existence of such a person as young Tom: he was a figment of

Callender's imagination, they say. But the evidence that they all use is itself suspect, for they rely on Jefferson's own *Farm Book*, which fails to include a notation of Tom's birth. Adair writes of "the neutral statistics" and "independent records" in the *Farm Book*. How Jefferson's own records can be neutral and independent is difficult to imagine; if anyone had a motive for hiding Tom's birth, it was Jefferson. Against this evidence is Sally's statement to her son Madison that her first child, fathered by Jefferson, was born soon after her return from France and the undeniable fact that "white" slave children lived at Monticello, as the French émigré Volney noted when he visited in 1796.[48]

Undoubtedly the evidence supporting Tom's existence is inconclusive, but it ought not to be invalidated because Jefferson's own records are silent and because its first public airing can be attributed to Callender. Contrary to the opinion of Jefferson's admirers, Callender was not an incorrigible liar. His interpretations of facts frequently were strained and exaggerated, but there is little, if any, evidence of his purposeful invention of stories or falsification of facts. When his published facts, rather than opinions, were found to be false, he usually publicly corrected them. In the Hamilton-Reynolds affair his facts were correct, if his interpretation was possibly misplaced. Of the four major accusations he threw at Jefferson, only the Sally Hemings affair is in any doubt. What is surprising is not Callender's penchant for falsification, but his ability to uncover facts that have later been found to be true.

This is not to deny Callender's reputation as a scandalmonger, for he evidently obtained most of his information secondhand and published what most others would have ignored. But he did sift his material before publishing it, even if the mesh he used was wide. Perhaps more attention ought to be given to the sources of Callender's information. Undoubtedly these were members of the Virginia gentry, some living close to Monticello. Their motives can only be guessed at, but presumably envy, political discord, and moral righteousness should be considered. The rumor of Jefferson's affair with Sally was known to local Federalists in 1799. William Rind of the *Virginia Federalist* was acquainted with, but failed to publicize, it during the 1800 election campaign. Callender knew of it when he met Madison in Washington. "There is not an individual in the neighbourhood of Charlottesville who does not believe the story; and not a few who know it," he wrote in September 1802. By November, when he was publishing further exposés, Callender claimed to be receiving packets of information from numerous gentlemen.[49]

Adding to the tantalizing vagueness and ambiguity surrounding the Black Sally affair, on 1 September, the very day of Callender's bombshell, Meriwether Jones claimed that "General Barbecue" (Chief Justice John Marshall) had been seen at the office of the *Recorder*. "There is some person *behind* the curtain, who directs the operation of the Recorder. And the influence of this personage is connected with the influence of another personage [Hamilton] at New-York," he wrote. When, after a fortnight's hesitation, Jones finally commented on the affair, he accused Marshall of furnishing Callender "with matter for detraction, and joining their mighty wits together" to concoct the Sally story. Marshall's involvement in giving scurrilous information to Callender is possible but unlikely. Both Pace and Callender swore affidavits that the Chief Justice had never been at their office, did not subscribe to the *Recorder*, and had never written for it. This failed to prevent Jones from hinting that Marshall himself was "not invulnerable" to accusations of miscegenation.[50]

Jones's attempt to implicate Marshall in Virginia's culture of promiscuity was part of a feeble, if surprising, defense of Jefferson put up by the Republicans. The editor of the *Examiner* was compelled to acknowledge the existence of Sally's mulatto children—he did not, incidentally, deny the existence of Tom—but he refused to blame Jefferson.

> In gentlemen's houses everywhere, we know that the virtue of unfortunate slaves is assailed with impunity. White women in these situations, whose educations are better, frequently fall victims; but the other classes are attempted, without fear, having no defender, and yield most frequently. Is it strange therefore, that a servant of Mr. Jefferson's, at a home where so many strangers resort, who is daily engaged in the ordinary vocations of the family, like thousands of others, should have a mulatto child? Certainly not.

That a man from the Virginia gentry should so openly have accepted the ubiquity of master-slave sexual contact is startling, until the context of Callender's aspersions on Jones's own behavior is remembered.[51]

As Douglass Adair once amusingly stated, "Every man's knowledge of his paternity rests on hearsay." The difficulty for Jones and Duane lay in proving a negative, that the hearsay was wrong. Although it may not have been known at the time, Jefferson was present at Monticello nine months before the birth of each of Sally's children. His absence could not be used to prove his innocence. Understandably perhaps, therefore, Jones and Duane had to resort to maligning Callender and his supposed colleagues in an attempt to discredit the source and to hide the accusation amid a welter of others. Callender soon faced renewed accusations of infecting his wife, embellished by Jones's claim of hearing Callender screaming in his sleep as the clay-covered corpse of his wife attempted to embrace him. In prison Callender's "temporary companion" had been a runaway black slave, "an old deformed corn field labourer." Currently his "Penelope" was a lady called Darby, whose brothers were thieves. "This lady is faithful as the sun; she admits no negro—if he cannot raise twenty five cents."[52]

Never at a high level of sophistication or taste, the newspaper war in 1802 had degenerated into unadulterated muckraking. This, of course, effectively served Callender's ultimate purpose, to undermine society. As his readership increased and the rumors spread, more information on Jefferson's personal life was received and duly published in the *Recorder*. First came, via Bronson's *Gazette of the United States*, a report that Jefferson, at the age of twenty-five, had "offered love to a handsome lady," the wife of his neighbor John Walker. Thereafter, claimed Callender, Jefferson had passed Walker's house only at night, fearing retribution. The story was not unknown; Hamilton had apparently threatened to publicize it during the Reynolds furor in 1797. But its resurrection in 1802 caused Jefferson acute embarrassment and nearly resulted in a duel with Walker, who seemingly connived at the publicity for political purposes. To just what lengths Jefferson had taken his pursuit of Mrs. Walker can only be surmised, but privately in 1804 he was to acknowledge the impropriety of his actions.[53]

Callender justified the publication of the Walker story on his usual grounds—that the public had a right to know the character of candidates holding or standing for public office. In Jefferson's case such publicity was particularly appropriate. Similar means had been used by the Jeffersonians to discredit Hamilton in 1797: "What is sauce for the goose, is sauce for the gander." Having earlier outmaneuvered the Republican press by publishing letters (regarding Jefferson's payments to him in 1800) whose existence they had denied, Callender was able to blunt the opposition's replies to the Walker story by threatening to publish further letters that, quite possibly, he did not possess. Jones, Duane, and the lesser Republican printers were confused, bitter, and demoralized. If they had remained silent, perhaps—wrote Callender—the Walker story might not have emerged. "It never was our serious intention to have meddled with Mrs. Walker, but the president's *felo de se* defenders insulted the public with a denial of the fact. This compelled us to knock them down with the hammer of truth."[54]

Callender's trilogy of blows aimed at the president was completed by his publication of Jefferson's purported attempt during the Revolution to pay off a debt in depreciated currency. Most historians have asserted Jefferson's innocence of this charge, in that he finally repaid the debt to full value. Indeed, Callender himself admitted this, and he never claimed that Jefferson did more than attempt to use depreciated currency. In this he was correct.[55] As with the Walker affair, this episode rumbled on for many months, but it had less impact on a readership now expecting new sexual revelations with each newspaper edition. Unfortunately for the gossips and sensation seekers, Callender had no more tales of Jefferson to impart; he did not attempt to invent new stories.

In purely political terms Callender's accusations had little impact. The Republicans were successful in the congressional elections of 1802, and Jefferson easily won a second term in 1804. This is not to say that some people were unwilling to believe the stories. Federalists such as Gouverneur Morris, John Adams, and John Quincy Adams accepted the truth of the Sally Hemings story, and some historians today continue to believe that the balance of evidence supports Callender.[56]

For Callender, the failure of the Federalist party to capitalize on his revelations was of little concern. In one sense, of course, he was doing the opposition's job for them, but his aim was not to replace the corrupt Republicans with the equally corrupt Federalists. He was appealing over the politicians to the people, to convince them that behind the facade of public duty, politicians wallow in private vice. "For an 150th. time, we ask, we demand, what virtuous character has been destroyed by this paper? If seduction, and hypocrisy, if the grossest breach of personal friendship, and of domestic confidence, form a department in the new code of morality and virtue, it is indeed true, that the Recorder has overwhelmed them." Although Callender's own private humiliations were being requited by his revelations, one can still perceive the influence of his Calvinist background and the oppositionist concepts of virtue—taken to their outer limits—in his newspaper campaign in the final months of 1802.[57]

IV

By December 1802 Callender had reached the summit of his notoriety, reflected in the one thousand people subscribing to the *Recorder*, a very large number for such a new publication. Callender's articles were being republished throughout the Union, principally by Federalist editors keen to take advantage of his vendetta against the Republicans. His abilities as a political editor and the tactics he used to confound his Republican opponents were widely admired:

> At every step that Callender took, in this contest, he compelled his adversaries to change their ground. Sometime he suffered them to exult in the hope of victory; but in the midst of their triumph, he would come unexpectedly upon them, storm their entrenchments, and drive the whole army of democrats before him; until, by attacking them first

in one quarter, and then in another, carrying first in one point, and then in another, he has forced the whole troop, harassed and dispirited with repeated defeats, into bogs and quicksands, where they are completely hemmed in, and entirely at his mercy.

In Richmond the gentry watched his progress with fear and loathing, paralyzed by the prospect of swift public retribution if they crossed him. Dueling, their usual manner of dealing with such difficulties, was inappropriate, for Callender was no gentleman. He would, moreover, have scorned to accept a challenge. Retaliatory abuse had merely resulted in further unsavory revelations.[58]

But inevitably someone eventually took the law into his own hands. Ironically, it was George Hay, one of Callender's lawyers at his sedition trial and the author of the extreme libertarian *Essay on the Liberty of the Press* (1799), who sought to silence Callender by the simple expedient of assaulting him with a walking stick. Hay had not been a particular subject of Callender's wrath in 1802, but he was involved in the *Hermione* affair that was being used in the *Recorder* to embarrass Meriwether Jones. The dispute in which Callender chose to become involved was in one sense an intrafamily issue, for Meriwether Jones had publicly attacked his Federalist father-in-law, Dr. Read, for boasting of having given up to British justice and execution in the West Indies a mutineer from the frigate *Hermione*. According to Jones, Read had surrendered the wrong man, an innocent American national. Hay became involved when the Virginia Executive Council sent him to Norfolk to take affidavits on the case. According to Callender, he ignored evidence supporting Read and deliberately left the threat of prosecution hanging over the magistrate for the next fifteen months.[59]

Callender claimed Hay had been treated fairly in his newspaper, but the lawyer obviously disagreed. Hay's temper finally snapped when in late November Pace and Callender presented a memorial to the House of Delegates, offering to replace Meriwether Jones as public printer at a fee of $1,200 a year, less than half the fee established by law in 1798. They had little expectation of success; the memorial was a ploy to embarrass the Republicans and to highlight the existence of government financial waste and corruption. During the ensuing debate, Hay apparently insulted Pace. In consequence, Callender asked Augustine Davis to warn Hay that he would receive "a serve" in the *Recorder*.[60]

Hay shortly afterward had a furious argument with Callender in Pace's shop, his final statement as he stormed out being: "Pursue your course, and I will pursue mine." On 20 December, Callender was in Darmstadt's store seeking the translation of a document in Dutch. Suddenly, "I felt a violent stroke on my forehead. The blow was repeated three or four times. An immediate effusion of blood was so violent, that, for some moments, it was impossible for me to distinguish who my adversary was. . . . I had hitherto considered that high crowned hats were a mere species of foppery. But it was this kind of hat which saved my life." In a "cowardly attack from behind," Hay landed about six blows, including one on a finger Callender had already damaged on the printing press.[61]

Callender responded in his customary fashion by applying to Mayor John Foster for an order binding over Hay to keep the peace. Although he promised not to molest Callender "unless he gave the first attack," Hay was bound over in the sum of $500 with a similar surety until 2 January. Indignant that his word of honor and his high social position (he had just become a member of the Executive Council) had been disregarded, Hay countered by seeking a recognizance of Callender, preventing him from publishing anything detrimental to Hay's, or any other Virginian's, character. Foster, worried that such an undertaking might represent an illegal restriction on the freedom of the press, stalled until he could obtain further legal advice. Without waiting for the mayor's reply, however, Hay took his case to a more amenable arena, the Republican-dominated court in Henrico County.[62]

There Callender and Pace were represented by William Marshall—the Federalist clerk of the federal circuit court and the brother of John Marshall—and James Rind, a renegade Republican, whom Callender had supported for the seat of Richmond in the assembly elections held earlier in the year. Hay was represented by John Wickham and Alexander McRae, Callender's outspoken defender against the Richmond Associators in 1799. Hay and his colleagues supported their case by an interpretation of English common law, still applicable in Virginia state courts, which asserted "preventive justice," permitting persons of ill fame to be bound over on account of their bad reputations, even though they may never formally have been found guilty of libel. Callender and Pace, said the prosecution, were "evidently common libellers of all the best and greatest men in our country," a statement that Callender would have heard with equanimity. He also would have smiled at the description of Pace as equally as criminal as himself, "only more insignificant, being totally destitute of talents." The magistrates found in favor of Hay, binding over Pace and Callender to an amount similar to Hay's. Because the legality of the decision remained in doubt, it was decided to reconsider it at the next session of the full county court on 3 January. Pace made suitable arrangements to fulfill his recognizance; Callender refused and was committed to Richmond jail.[63]

The events of the past few days and the effects of Hay's attack had badly shaken Callender. Although the next *Recorder* was a black-bordered, half-size issue, in which he defiantly reported from "My Old Quarters in Richmond Jail," his comments reflected a temporary loss of nerve and commitment. He had, he admitted, preferred to go to jail rather than run the gauntlet of a mob that he believed was waiting for him outside the court and that represented a continuing threat to his safety in Richmond. The prospect of flight again appeared attractive.

> Whether the political condition of the citizens of Richmond can be sunk beneath its present point of depression, it is hardly worth while to investigate. The difference cannot be very important between nothing at all, and that which is next to nothing. We must not, we dare not speak, or even be suspected of speaking, one sentence, complaining of what we have been, or what we are likely to become. That such a paper as the Recorder should long be suffered to exist, in the centre of riot, of assassination, and of despotism, is what no rational being can be supposed to expect. If the torch of the press is not, as it almost has been, extinguished in the blood of its editors, we shall probably find it advisable to seek an asylum somewhere else. We shall find it advisable to attempt publication, and to look for protection in some happy corner of America, where the phantom of justice does not flutter upon the knots of a club, or the lock of a pistol.[64]

With Callender fearing the chastisement of a Republican mob, the respective counsel holding opposing political opinions, and the Federalists upholding the rights of a free press, it would be easy to conclude that the Hay affair was simply a partisan battle in which a Federalist Callender combated a Republican Hay. But Hay denied this, claiming he had decided to confront Callender for personal, not political, reasons. Much of the evidence supports his assertion or, at least, confirms Callender's innocence of acting for the Federalists by maligning Hay. For example, although William Marshall was a prominent Federalist, he did not defend the *Recorder*'s editors for political reasons. On the basis of a conventional interpretation of "prior restraint," he had argued at the first hearing in Henrico County only for the scheduling of a formal trial before the editors were bound over. He displayed no sympathy for his clients and fully expected them to be found guilty if sued for libel, a point that did not escape Republican editors, anxious to avoid claims of partisanship.[65]

More importantly, James Rind was no Federalist; rather, he was a democratic republican in Callender's mold. His defense speech was a classic democratic assault on English common law and its applicability to America, a position that defined the democrats as a minority faction on the fringes of the Republican party in the next decade. Rind had "vehemently, and with much declamation," opposed the common law, "which all good democrats had abused as a system of tyranny." Furthermore, in January 1803 he was probably the author of a series of anonymous articles in the *Virginia Gazette* which incorporated, suggests Steven Hochman, "the broadest construction of freedom of the press that appeared in the early national period." His theoretical position conformed exactly to Callender's practice in the *Recorder.* "I contend," he wrote, "that it is the right and duty of every man in society, to expose to *public* view all the vices and improper practices, even of private men, that threat[en] or tend in the smallest degree to injure that society."[66]

The libertarian defense of Callender explains why William Duane, also a democrat, held ambivalent views of the Hay affair. He wrote: "The press has indeed been prostituted to the basest purposes by Callender, but we doubt much whether the method taken to correct the evil will have any effect other than the contrary of what was intended, and whether the freedom of the press is not much endangered by it. It is to be lamented that at a moment when few continued to defend Callender, even among the federalists, that Mr. Hay should have contributed to drag him again before the public by whom his libels would not be believed." Duane himself was a staunch proponent of absolute freedom of the press and was never averse to maligning individuals in print. Between 1798 and 1806 he was the defendant in sixty libel suits. He too was a major opponent of the common law. His dilemma arose from his recognition that while Hay was a fellow Republican who required support, Callender's defense conformed with his own conception of the law on free speech and a free press. He thus implicitly acknowledged the fact that Callender remained the democratic libertarian of 1798–1801, except that his focus of attack had altered. If in the following years Duane, following Callender's example, was to break with moderate Republicanism by remaining consistent to the "Principles of '98," in the short term he resolved his dilemma by ignoring the events in Richmond in favor of publicizing the ideologically more straightforward financial scandal involving the New York Federalist editor William Coleman. He realized that the Hay affair was less a confrontation between Federalism and Republicanism than a fratricidal conflict between different versions of Republicanism, brought to a head by Callender's policy of using libertarian doctrine for personal revenge.[67]

Judicial interpretation of the law favored Callender and Pace, for a new bench of magistrates in Henrico County on 3 and 4 January rejected Hay's arguments and discharged Callender from custody. A week later Hay returned to the court in Richmond in an attempt to have his recognizance dismissed. Because his own position remained unaltered—he agreed only not to molest Callender unless attacked—and because Callender repeated his fear of molestation, Hay failed in his maneuver. He remained bound over for twelve months.[68]

It remains impossible to determine for certain why Hay assaulted Callender on 20 December. He claimed to have acted on the spur of the moment, but if so, his compulsion must have been fueled by the fear of what Callender might reveal of his personal life rather than anything that had already been published in the *Recorder*. Alternatively, he might have attacked Callender in revenge for the smears on Jefferson. Undoubtedly, many Republicans would have considered the beating justifiable in that light, although they failed to assist Hay when he pressed his case to curtail press freedom. Only two Republicans openly expressed their support for Hay by accompanying him to the court-house and acting as his securities. One was John Mercer, the other Peter Carr, Jefferson's nephew (and the purported father of Sally Heming's children). It would be mere speculation to suggest that Carr's presence represented anything other than his own personal desire to express solidarity with the one man courageous enough to stand up to his uncle's tormentor. He had a history of acting unilaterally—and rashly—in defense of Jefferson, as when, using the pseudonym of "John Langhorne," he had attempted to trick Washington into maligning his uncle in print. Whatever his role in the Sally Hemings affair, he could not resist the opportunity of publicly demonstrating his family's opposi-tion to Callender. In return, Callender, who believed Carr to be Jeffer-son's "confidential agent" in the House of Delegates, soon revived the issue of the Langhorne letter, further embarrassing the Republicans.[69]

V

Although bloodied by the encounter, Callender appeared to have had the better of the struggle with Hay. Public opinion predominantly supported him, Hay was humiliated, the Republicans were discomfited, and subscriptions to—and the crucially important advertisements in— the *Recorder* rose sufficiently for it to became a biweekly.[70] Neverthe-less, Callender's final collapse into ignomiy and degradation can be traced back to the first months of 1803. With hindsight his decline appears inevitable. However brilliantly he steered the *Recorder* in these months, his success depended on the steady flow of exposés to sate the appetites of his sensation-hungry readers. But Callender had already tapped every scandal that, as far as is known today, it was possible to uncover.

Compared with his revelations in 1802, those of 1803 were mere tittle-tattle. For many weeks he worked on Hay's reputation; he was "a notorious fibber," a "coward," and the "emperor of gamblers," who had set up a loo table in his house during the sitting of the General Assembly, at which he had cheated his opponents. Hay, having shot his bolt, was forced to suffer in silence. Callender then turned his attention back to Skelton Jones, claiming he had struck a mulatto woman with his sword cane during a public altercation. Not even Callender's greatest admirers could claim that these "scoops" had much public relevance.[71]

At the same time the atmosphere in Richmond remained heavy with menace. Both Pace and Callender kept firearms in their house. Toward the end of March, "two persons came to this office enquiring for one of the editors. They threatened to set the house on fire, and threw a large stone at two of the young men belonging to the office. Muskets were brought, and the fellows were followed into the street, where three of their companions were waiting for them. . . . A proper enquiry will be made about these ruffians. This is your *republican* liberty of the press." Callender soon discovered they were young law students, most of them attached to Hay's firm, who had attended a Republican festival on the evening of the attack. They must have been drunk, for they had also apparently accosted a woman in the street, forced her to strip, and burned her shift. Their names were like a roll call of the prominent Virginia gentry: a Pendleton, a Randolph, a Harvie, a Lindsay, and a Cary (the last being Peter Carr's nephew).[72]

Ironically, not only the threats from the young Republican hotheads but also his own success led to Callender's undoing. One prominent feature of his character was a disregard of money. Even Meriwether Jones acknowledged that Callender appeared unmindful of its importance, being content if he had enough to support his immediate needs. Only his family commitments appeared sufficiently compelling to force his attention toward the resolution of his habitual financial insecurity. Early in 1803, possibly as a consequence of his assaults on Jefferson, his boys left Leiper's home in Philadelphia and traveled to Richmond. The additional responsibilities made Callender consider anew his articles of agreement with Pace. The *Recorder* being now profitable, he not unexpectedly hoped to receive half of the profits. But Pace, who felt that his financial support of the newspaper when it was struggling gave him the right to keep the profits, rejected Callender's request for a statement of accounts.[73]

The arguments began in February. Who was in the right is now impossible to ascertain, although Meriwether Jones surprisingly sympathized with Callender. After the students' attack on the office of the *Recorder* at the end of March, Callender apparently withdrew his services, either from fright, disgust, or sickness. For six weeks he failed to offer any original paragraphs to the newspaper. He later explained that he had met with an accident by which he lost nearly "four pounds weight of blood" and nearly died. But according to Pace, Callender had embarked on a monumental binge.

> While writing at another's risk, Callender is bold, is sometimes capable of supporting the fatigues of business. But this is only when he is sober, which seldom lasts more than three or four weeks at a time. [It must be recollected, by those who have never seen Callender, that what is called soberness in him, would make any two men constantly drunk. For at his sober periods, he never gets drunk above once a day, which he will do contentedly, by taking a quart of rum, one hour, and get sober in the next.] To see him constantly drunk . . . is nothing new.

For whatever reason, the impact on the *Recorder* was immediate; without Callender's pen it subsided into repetition and vacuity.[74]

A reconciliation of sorts took place in May but lasted less than a month. By mid–June the dispute was on public display, with Callender publishing his version of events in the *Virginia Gazette* and Pace replying in the *Recorder*. Callender proudly asserted that "the success of [the *Recorder*], since I became connected with it, exceeds everything that had previously been heard of in this state. . . . The Recorder has been read with attention and avidity by persons of all classes, and of all parties. Its circulation has extended from Maine to Georgia, to the remotest corners of the state of New York, to Vincennes, and to Kentucky." It now had a circulation of 1,500. Unfortunately, however, Pace had refused to settle accounts. "I have a family to provide for," explained Callender, "and the subscribers cannot expect that I am to continue to labour without adequate compensation." In his attempts to bilk Callender of his rightful compensation and to thwart his other creditors, Pace had followed the common practice of debtors in Virginia of "selling" his movable property to another and leasing it back, in order to prevent its being distrained.[75]

In response, Pace emphasized Callender's drinking habits and ingratitude: "The truth is, Callender has been envious that I should receive any profits from this paper. He has long endeavoured to vilify and defame my character." His object was to take over the *Recorder*; he would not succeed, however, for by his absence he had broken his agreement, thus dissolving the partnership. His claim that Pace had "moved [his] visible property away from creditors" was untrue; "if I hear of any more such language, I shall clap him in jail."[76]

The Jones brothers watched this dispute with growing amazement and fascination. They eagerly reported every accusation and counteraccusation, especially when, after Callender's statement that Pace's former partner had acted as his pimp, Pace asserted that Callender had attempted to sodomize Pace's brother. The irony of these self-destructive exposures was not lost on the Republicans, particularly on the long-suffering Jones brothers. Such they wrote, " are the base foreigners whom ye have indirectly hired to calumniate the worthiest characters of our country."[77]

Surprisingly, Meriwether Jones sided with Callender against Pace. His admiration for his talents as a polemicist overrode his resentment at the treatment he had personally received. "However barefaced [Callender's] falsehoods, or atrocious the calumnies," he wrote, "they were undeniably dictated with an energy of thought, and expressed with a grace of style which was calculated to make an impression, in proportion to the penetration, impartiality or prejudices of the persons who perused them." In contrast, the avowed Federalist Pace had no saving graces. "For the little pimp to talk of Callender's ingratitude, and of supporting him from starving is ridiculous enough. Everybody knows that Pace was much nearer starving than Callender [in 1802]. Pace, indeed, if there is any difference between them, is the more infamous of the two, since he has no talents to redeem any of his grovelling and numberless atrocities." When he met Pace at the ten-pin ground at Bacon Branch in July, Jones drew his knife before beating him up.[78]

The end came with startling suddenness but in a not unexpected manner. Early in the morning of Sunday, 17 July, Callender was observed wandering the town in a drunken state. Soon after, his body was found floating in the James River. A doctor "tried every method to restore him to life—but all his efforts proved ineffectual." After a hurried coroner's inquest, which recorded accidental drowning while drunk, Callender was buried that same day in the local churchyard. It was as if the citizens of Richmond could not wait to destroy all evidence of his existence.[79]

Epilogue

Six weeks after his death, a letter from Callender was published by Skelton Jones, now sole editor of the *Examiner* following his brother's retirement. Initially intended for publication in the *Recorder* (it was rejected by Pace), the letter referred to Skelton Jones's duel with Armistead Selden, the original cause of the newspaper war in Richmond.

Daily experience proves to us, the [*illegible*] and variableness of everything which relates to human affairs. Nobody is more sensible of this than the writer of this article; nor is there anyone more willing to repair his errors when they are known. An occasion of this sort now occurs; justice and generosity points the way, and it is performed with that sort of satisfaction which can only be conceived by the heart of sensibility, by a heart which gives no room to passions of unyielding malignancy, and implacable revenge. It is well known that the columns of this paper [*Recorder*], as well as those of the *Examiner*, have been often filled with subjects of a personal nature, in which the community had no substantial interest. They related to the private and unimportant affairs of individuals. They were filled with disputes between the Editors of the Examiner and the writer. It is not now necessary to ascertain, which party was the aggressor, or which has been most to blame. It will be recollected that virulence, invective and recrimination, have appeared upon each side. To ascertain which party has been victorious, will add nothing to the splendor of talents, or to private worth. It will be best for criticks to determine as they please. It remains with me to close the scene as far as I can. One thing however deserves particular notice; it deserves recantation, and that is made because it will tend, in some degree, to restore to the good opinion of mankind, a young man of ardent mind and promising talents, whose name and whose feelings have both been severely affected. I mean Mr. Skelton Jones, in relation to his unfortunate quarrel with Mr. Armistead Selden. Harsh and acrimonious as the publications on the subject have been, until very lately, the writer always considered that the facts were correctly stated, that opinion, added to the inveteracy of which the papers had descended, is offered as the excuse for extraordinary severity. At this time the facts are known. They give very

different impressions. They extort the belief that Mr. Jones's character has been improperly injured, and a sense of Justice, which I have
no wish to suppress, urges me to make a suitable reparation. . . . These
declarations are the voluntary effusions of my own heart. They have
obtained my own approbation and I hope will be properly appreciated
by those whom they most concern. Having succeeded as to these
points, the rest will be left to fate. Here I mean to drop the controversy with Mr. Skelton Jones, at least as to this point, forever.[1]

Some historians, ignorant of this letter and the tragedy implicit in
it, have excoriated Callender for failing to make similar reparation to
the likes of Alexander Hamilton, John Adams, and Thomas Jefferson.
"Of all the foreigners who were connected with journalism in the
United States at the beginning of the century," writes one, "James
Thomson Callender was easily the first in the worst qualities of mind
and character." He was "a journalistic janizary . . . a hardened and
habitual liar, a traitorous and truculent scoundrel." "The most out-
rageous and wretched scandalmonger of a scurrilous age," Callender
was "drunken, vicious and depraved, albeit talented." Of all the public
figures in the era of the American Revolution, perhaps only Benedict
Arnold has suffered from such unrelenting obloquy.[2]

Such a consensus among historians is unusual. Even Aaron Burr,
whom both political parties despised for his alleged opportunism, treason, and murder of Hamilton, has found sympathetic advocates willing
to defend his controversial career. Burr could kill Hamilton yet receive,
in some quarters, compassionate understanding; Callender, in concert
with Jeffersonian partisans, publicized Hamilton's extramarital affair
and has been pilloried. Burr could silently acquiesce in the Federalists'
attempts to overthrow the popular choice of Jefferson as president in
1801 yet still receive sympathetic treatment. Callender, using information given to him by members of the Virginia gentry, accused Jefferson
of miscegenation and has ever since been castigated as an unmitigated
liar and scoundrel. The double standard at work here, of which Callender remains the victim, is based on an artificial distinction between
public and private virtue.

Callender has suffered from what has been called "the side-road
assassination technique," whereby "relatively minor characters with
whom the historian does not sympathise are taken into a short paragraph where they are made to look wicked or ridiculous or very very
small in a couple of sentences, almost in a couple of words; and done
away with. There is no argument, no balancing of good and bad, no fuss.
It is casual, almost off-stage. The victims have been shot down before
you notice. Falsehood is not required, for a partial truth will do." The
urge among historians to deal with Callender in this manner has been

strong, partly because the reputation of the founding generation relies heavily on the integrity and virtue of the men whom he openly suggested had feet of clay. To assert the incorrigible wickedness of Callender is by implication to reinforce the respectability of the Founding Fathers. Historians have easily found contemporary comments hostile to Callender, who at various times enraged the penmen of both parties; uncritically they have accepted them as fair and appropriate.[3]

But to examine Callender's career only from the perspective of his periodic tirades against prominent figures would be to emphasize his methods at the expense of his message. His importance lies primarily in his awareness of the potential contradictions within a political society which, founded on the doctrine of popular sovereignty, was only slowly coming to terms with that doctrine's implications. If the people were truly to influence the future development of their society, traditional deference to the rich and the wellborn had to be eliminated. Callender was one of a group of democrats who perceived that even among the Republicans many gave unquestioning endorsement to the view that a republican society still ought to be dominated by a natural aristocracy. To combat this heresy, Callender invoked the language and ideology of the eighteenth-century opposition, taking its essentially pessimistic outlook to a logical and democratic conclusion. To this he engrafted the ideas of Paine, rejecting only his optimistic belief in human nature. From this mixture, to which he added arguments from the Antifederalists of 1787–88, he concluded that the United States ought to be broken up into its component parts; only then could the people hope effectively to regulate their representatives and to regain control of their own destiny.

It is unnecessary to point out that Callender failed in his objective of convincing the people that "Republicans are found to be just as corruptible as the rest of mankind." Partly this was because his message was too monolithic and doctrinaire to be easily believable (were all politicians inevitably corrupt?), and partly because he too often allowed his own resentments to intrude. But, in addition, his failure can be attributed to his concentration on attracting a receptive audience for his democratic message. His effort to gain readers justified his emphasis on the publicizing of private scandal, but it ultimately became an end in itself, relegating his political message to limbo. In the process, however, Callender discovered an enduring truth, that scandal and private tittle-tattle are of compelling interest to many people. "If there were no buyers" of newspapers, he pointed out, "there could be no sellers." Meriwether Jones was forced to agree. Callender's tactics had greatly increased the *Recorder's* circulation. "And this stands upon record, to the eternal disgrace, shame and infamy of those that patronized, or in any way supported a paper so eminently noxious and pestilential to the harmony and morality of society." It is not difficult to understand why, within weeks of Callender's death, the *Recorder* had collapsed and Pace was in jail for debt.[4]

If Callender was a pioneer of muckraking journalism, he ought also to be remembered for forcing a reconsideration of what limits should be put on freedom of the press. In defense of his writings, and those of a similar extremism, a corpus of libertarian doctrine emerged which, although not immediately influential, offered an alternative to the conventional interpretation of free speech as put forward by Blackstone. Callender himself played little role in advancing this doctrine. Generally, he felt that expressions of controversial opinions in print should be responded to in the same medium, not in the courts. He acknowledged a distinction between liberty and licentiousness but felt that there was no clearly acceptable dividing line. In one of his last political salvos he wrote: "Licentiousness is nothing more than a ricketty, or dropsical species of liberty. It is liberty swelling beyond its proper limits; and upon enquiring at the first ten men you meet with, it will be hard to find four that will agree, where such limits are to be placed." He personally defined licentiousness very narrowly, leaving a wide field for the free exercise of liberty. All "true" facts, of a public or private nature, and all opinion were grist to an editor's mill.[5]

The problem of editorial independence was, argued Callender, of much more relevance to political progress than a legal definition of free speech. His dream of becoming independent can be traced back to his days in Edinburgh, and his fears of literary dependence to his understanding of Swift. In the United States his expectations were for many years unfulfilled; whenever he acted unilaterally, he was condemned as a trimmer or lambasted for naïveté. He took the role of newspapers in a democratic society very seriously; they were the one major channel whereby the political delusions of the people might be corrected. Unfortunately, virtually every newspaper was attached, by patronage in various forms, to one party or another. "Each editor," claimed Callender, "says all he can say to defend his friends, and to blacken his enemies. His accusations are often true; his encomiums almost never. . . . If a plain reader buys papers on both sides, they stand in such irreconcilable contradiction that he can be sure of almost nothing but this, that neither printer deserves his confidence." Only with the *Recorder* did Callender belatedly gain the opportunity to assert a truly independent line. But it was at a significant cost; with no patronage to fall back on, he had to raise subscriptions and advertising revenue by appealing to the baser interests of a mass audience. He had, of course, no compunction in so doing. He was for a while brilliantly successful.

The editors of the yellow press later in the century could have looked to Callender as an exemplar. If in his politics he looked to the past for a message foreshadowing the future, as an editor he was far in advance of his time.[6]

Callender was forty-five years old when he died. He had fled to the United States in the expectation of finding freedom and personal independence. He was destined to find neither. But as happened to so many immigrant families, the second and third generations of the Callender clan found the key to personal success in the New World. Callender's son Thomas moved to Nashville in 1817, where he became a tobacconist and merchant. Like his father a Presbyterian, he served as an alderman for several terms and as a member of the county court before dying a respectable member of the community in 1851.

His son, John Hill Callender, found the social success that always eluded grandfather James. He received his M.D. from the University of Pennsylvania in 1855. In the same year he followed his grandfather's footsteps, becoming joint proprietor and editor of the *Patriot*, a Nashville newspaper which he continued until 1858. After briefly serving as a surgeon in the Confederate army during the Civil War, between 1865 and 1869 he became connected in an editorial capacity with another Nashville newspaper. In the following decade he held various university medical chairs, in 1881 becoming the youngest president of the Association of Medical Superintendents of American Institutions for the Insane. In that capacity he was one of the witnesses to give testimony on the sanity of Charles J. Guiteau, President McKinley's assassin.

John Hill Callender achieved all that his grandfather could merely dream of. He even married a great-grandniece of Thomas Jefferson! With many of his grandfather's qualities—"a comorant, both as student and reader, of boundless memory and wonderful power of analysis; as a writer . . . graceful, fluent and exhaustive"; of an "ardent nature, intensely individual and positive in his opinions and character"—he had also the inestimable advantage of being "a finished gentleman." He nevertheless was felt to have "proved himself worthy to follow the footsteps of his distinguished grandfather."[7]

Appendix
Abbreviations
Notes
Bibliography
Index

Appendix

According to William Burroughs, "A satire must offend, it must be crude, it must be humorous, it must be philosophical. But above all, it must be written with consummate skill. . . . Satire is a form expressly developed to describe the complexity of civilisation in decline, by a man who has felt it in his own personality." Few writers have been consistently successful when using this genre; Callender was no exception. Often his satire collapsed into mere sarcasm and raillery. His lampooning was heavy-handed, reflecting the lack of subtlety characteristic of the humor of his times. He was unable to produce an extended piece of effective satire, but on occasions Callender found it possible to write biting, crude, and effective satirical squibs for the newspapers. Rather too ponderous for modern taste, they nevertheless would have been appreciated by his contemporaries. The following are a selection.

1. From the AURORA, 19 August 1794.

This was written when Washington's administration espoused a policy of neutrality toward the belligerents in Europe but was seemingly sympathetic to the British. At this time Ambassador Jay was in England seeking to resolve the many differences between Britain and the United States. British orders-in-council (the proclamations) and impressment of sailors from American ships were major causes of friction in the seaports, leading to several outbursts of anti-British sentiment, including, in this instance, the burning of the Union Jack.

> *The unparalleled insult offered to his majesty's flag* . . . by burning it publicly in Market Street, is certainly an offence of a very serious nature, and no doubt will be properly resented. Indeed it may be a question whether it is not a violation of our neutrality, and punishable by *proclamation*; for it is no excuse to say, that as it was done by boys, the offence is the less. If a boy commits murder or a robbery, he is punished, and why ought he not to be equally amenable to the law or the *proclamation* for such an unparalleled aggression. Our government will no doubt feel as sensibly on this as they have on other occasions, and as they have on one occasion endeavoured to convert a citizen into a *subject* [by handing him over to the British], they will now transform a boy into a man, and punish him accordingly.

2. From the AURORA, 8 June 1796.

This paragraph, headed "Congressional Prudence," highlights both Congress's unwillingness to antagonize Britain and the failure of Jay's treaty to resolve the problem of impressment.

How abominable it is in many of our *mad caps* to blame Congress for a non-completion of the frigates which they voted should be commenced and fitted out as speedily as possible. Would these hair-brained politicians give themselves the trouble to reflect they might inform themselves, that the suppression of frigate building was the most *wise* and the *most prudent congressional act* of this session. For who would build a house and have nobody to live in it? Why certainly no man in his senses. Upon this principle it was that Congress gave up the idea of building the frigates; for we trust, that by the time the frigates might be built the *tender receptions* of our seamen on board of British fleets would not leave us sailors enough to hoist a sail on board of them. Those frigates now on the stocks when finished can be hauled to anchor after launching by *farmers*, where they can remain as *empty* documents that the United States have a fleet of frigates.

3. From the AURORA, 27 February 1797.

Robert Goodloe Harper, a High Federalist representative from South Carolina, entered Congress only in 1796 but quickly became a frequent debater. He was in the forefront of the attacks on the "Jacobin" emigrants to America; in 1798 he strongly supported the Alien and Sedition Acts.

A very modern historian of this country has made an allusion to "the aspen tongue of ROBERT GOODLOE HARPER." During the last session, it is computed that this gentleman cost the country at least 6000 dollars worth of time, by making superfluous motions for the sake of making superfluous speeches about them. In the present session, he has repeated one speech . . . at four different times, in the course of little more than a month. He has a very pretty delivery, if any obliging friend would supply him with a suitable stock of ideas. If he could be contented with repeating the same thoughts, not oftener than five times in the course of fifteen minutes, he would not so barbarously drive the members from their benches, nor run himself into so many scrapes with the Speaker, as to wandering from the question. In an antediluvian Congress, when people lived to an age of a thousand years, one might have found leisure for hearing him to an end. Our span of threescore and ten years is too narrow for the torrent of his eloquence.

4. From the AURORA, 25 May 1797.

Republican hopes that the new president, John Adams, might be more sympathetic than his predecessor to the French were dashed within months, and a policy of opposition was renewed in Republican news-papers from May 1797. This passage reflects the Republicans' conviction that Adams, under the guise of neutrality, supported Britain.

What a patriot is not Mr. Adams! He is all *American*! With what indignation did he not dwell on the treatment which we have received from the belligerent powers! The robberies of *Great Britain* called all the patriot and revolutionary blood into his cheek! With what *feeling* and with what *firmness* did he not expatiate on the *impressment of American seamen* by *British* ships of war, and his determination to relieve them from their cruel bondage, and obtain security for them in future! With what energy did he not retrace the savage conduct of Great Britain when she aided the Indians *with her own troops* in murdering our frontier citizens in time of *peace*! With what manly indignation did he not picture them instigating the Algerine pirates to filch us of our property, and to load our citizens with chains! How he kindled with ire when he took a view of *British robberies* under the *British Treaty*! To arms! to arms! was his language—let us repel those tyrants who endeavoured to enslave us during the revolution; who massacred our citizens, burned our towns, murdered our warriors by inches in prison ships and jails and desolated our country! Reverse the picture and hear him speak of France who aided us in our revolutionary struggle! Hear him expatiate on Frenchmen who fought, bled and died for American liberty! His notes are like those of the dying swan, they charm the soul of sensibility and gratitude! Frenchmen, contending in the same cause for themselves in which they contended for us, awake all the sensibilities of the soul! He has demonstrated himself the friend of liberty, the enemy of tyranny and the steady adherent to those maxims and principles which he professed during the late revolution! What a friend to the *Rights of Man*, to the *Republic of France* and to the *peace* of the United States is not JOHN ADAMS!!!

Abbreviations

Am. Cit.	New York *American Citizen*
Am. Pat.	Baltimore *American Patriot*
DNB	*Dictionary of National Biography*
Exam.	Richmond *Examiner*
Gaz. U.S.	Philadelphia *Gazette of the United States*
HSP	Historical Society of Pennsylvania
JTC	James Thomson Callender
LC	Library of Congress
NLS	National Library of Scotland
PMHB	*Pennsylvania Magazine of History and Biography*
"Pol. Prog."	[JTC], "On the Political Progress of Britain," *Bee*, Feb.–June 1792
Pol. Prog.	[JTC], *The Political Progress of Britain*
Porc. Gaz.	Philadelphia *Porcupine's Gazette*
PP	*Parliamentary Papers*
PRO	Public Record Office, London
Rec.	Richmond *Recorder*
SRO	Scottish Record Office
Va. Fed.	Richmond *Virginia Federalist*
VMHB	*Virginia Magazine of History and Biography*
WMQ	*William and Mary Quarterly*

Notes

CHAPTER ONE

1. *Rec.*, 12 Jan. 1803; [JTC], "The Present State of Parnassus," in *Miscellanies in Prose and Verse; Including Remarks on English Plays, Operas, and Farces, and on a Variety of Other Modern Publications by the Honourable Lord Gardenstone*, ed. [JTC], 2d ed. (Edinburgh, 1792), 327.

2. In May 1796 JTC wrote that he was in his thirty-ninth year (JTC to Madison, 28 May 1796, in "Thomas Jefferson and James Thomson Callender," ed. Worthington C. Ford, *New England Historical and Geneological Register* 51 [1896]:325). For Stirling as his birthplace, see P. Ross, *The Scot in America* (New York, 1896), 354.

3. Robert Anderson, *Life of Samuel Johnson, LLD*, 3d ed. (Edinburgh, 1815), 231; *DNB*, s.v. "Thomson, James." According to Dr. Samuel Johnson, *Lives of the Poets*, 2 vols. (London, 1964), 2:348, Thomson was one of nine children.

4. Johnson, *Lives of the Poets* 2:348–49; [JTC], *Deformities of Dr. Samuel Johnson, Selected from His Works*, 2d ed. (London, 1782), 84; [JTC], *A Critical Review of the Works of Dr. Samuel Johnson* (Edinburgh, 1783), 22; *The Bee, or Literary Weekly Intelligencer*, 15 Feb. 1792, pp. 235–37. Both *Deformities* and *A Critical Review* have been reprinted by Garland Publishing, 1974, in their Johnsoniana Series, vol. 13.

5. In particular, the eccentric earl of Buchan was promoting Thomson; see chap. 2.

6. *Exam.*, 21 Nov. 1800; Gerald R. Cragg, *The Church and the Age of Reason, 1648–1789*, 2d ed. (London, 1983), 84–87; Bruce Lenman, *Integration, Enlightenment, and Industrialisation: Scotland, 1746–1832* (London, 1981), 12; *The Oxford Dictionary of the Christian Church*, ed. F. L. Cross and E. A. Livingstone, 2d ed. (London, 1974); J. H. S. Burleigh, *A History of the Church of Scotland* (Edinburgh, 1960), chap. 2.

7. See Christina Bewley, *Muir of Huntershill* (Oxford, 1981), 1; Richard B. Sher, "Moderates, Managers, and Popular Politics in Mid–Eighteenth Century Edinburgh: The Drysdale 'Bustle' of the 1760s," in *New Perspectives in the Politics and Culture of Early Modern Scotland*, eds. John Dwyer et al. (Edinburgh, 1982), 202–3.

8. W. R. and C. H. Brock, *Scotus Americanus* (Edinburgh 1982), 19.

9. JTC to Madison, 28 May 1796, in Ford, "Jefferson and Callender," 325–26. Toward the end of his life JTC wrote that he had been "bred to the law" (*Rec.*, 30 April 1803).

10. Lenman, *Integration*, 35–36; Bewley, *Muir*, 9. See also Michael Miles, "'A Haven for the Privileged': Recruitment into the Profession of Attorney in England, 1709–92," *Social History* 11 (1986): 197–210.

11. JTC, *Deformities*, vii.

12. Charles A. Jellison, "That Scoundrel Callender," *VMHB* 64 (1959): 295, was thus wrong when he wrote that JTC "apparently spent the years of his youth and early manhood in drifting aimlessly from place to place and from one thing to another."

13. JTC to Andrew Stuart, 5 Dec. 1789, NLS, MS 8621, fol. 59.

14. Davis D. McElroy, *Scotland's Age of Improvement: A Survey of Eighteenth-Century Literary Clubs and Societies* (Pullman, Wash., 1969), 71.

15. JTC, *Deformities*, 66, iv, 88.

16. Ibid., 58, 65, 68, 20, 34.

17. Lenman, *Integration*, 60–62, 67; Albert Goodwin, *The Friends of Liberty: The English Democratic Movement in the Age of the French Revolution* (London, 1979), 282; John Cannon, *Parliamentary Reform, 1640–1832* (Cambridge, 1973), 108–11; Henry W. Meikle, *Scotland and the French Revolution*, 2d ed. (London, 1969), 1–2.

18. JTC, *Deformities*, v. See also Helen L. McGuffie, "Dr. Johnson and the Little Dogs: The Reaction of the London Press to 'Taxation No Tyranny,'" in *Newsletters to Newspapers: Eighteenth-Century Journalism*, ed. Donovan H. Bond and W. Reynolds McLeod (Morgantown, W.Va., 1977), 192.

19. JTC, *Deformities*, 12, 27, v, 89. Smith was not a zealous partisan of the American patriot cause; on the other hand, he did not believe that American independence would cause major economic problems for Britain.

20. Ibid., 11–12.

21. Bernard Tucker, *Jonathan Swift* (Dublin, 1983); Richard I. Cook, *Jonathan Swift as a Tory Pamphleteer* (Seattle, 1967); Jonathan Swift, "Verses on the Union," in *Swift on His Age: Selected Prose and Verse*, ed. Colin J. Horne (London, 1953), 127; JTC, *Deformities*, 12.

22. Tucker, *Swift*, 87–88.

23. JTC, *Deformities*, viii, vii, 87, iii.

24. JTC, *Critical Review*, iii.

25. Ronald M. Sunter, *Patronage and Politics in Scotland, 1707–1832* (Edinburgh, 1986), 7; Alexander Murdoch, *"The People Above": Politics and Administration in Mid–Eighteenth Century Scotland* (Edinburgh, 1980), 140–45; William D. Rubinstein, "The End of 'Old Corruption' in Britain, 1780–1860," *Past and Present* 101 (1984): 55–86; Roy Porter, *English Society in the Eighteenth Century* (London, 1982), 133.

26. M. Livingstone, *A Guide to the Public Records of Scotland Deposited in H.M. General Register House, Edinburgh* (Glasgow, 1905), 166–72; J. Maitland Thompson, *The Public Records of Scotland* (Glasgow, 1922), 105–9; Lewis Ockrent, *Land Rights: An Enquiry into the History of Registration for Publication in Scotland* (London, 1942), 101–8; [Alexander Robertson], Memorial Relative to an Improvement in the System of the Records of Scotland, 16 Oct. 1788, SRO 1/109, pp. 7–9.

27. Meikle, *Scotland and the French Revolution*, 9–10; William Ferguson,

"The Electoral System in the Scottish Counties before 1832," *Stair Society* 35 (1984): 261–94.

28. Ockrent, *Land Rights*, 101–8; Return of the Salary and Emoluments of the Register of the Sasines in Scotland . . . , *PP* 14 (1821): 472.

29. Return of the Salary and Emoluments . . . , *PP* 14 (1821): 472; Return of the Total Number and the Names of all and each of the Officers, Clerks and other Persons composing the several Establishments and Offices in Scotland . . . , *PP* 39 (1837): 7; Account Books of Andrew Stuart and Cash Books of Andrew Stuart, NLS, MSS 5398, 5394–95.

30. *History of the Society of Writers to His Majesty's Signet* (Edinburgh, 1936), 336, 267; *DNB*, s.v. "Stuart, Andrew," and "Davidson, John"; Correspondence of Andrew Stuart, NLS, MS 8261, fols. 28, 60.

31. Bewley, *Muir*, 8; Henry Cockburn, *Memorials of His Time* (1856; rept. Edinburgh, 1971), 27; *Edinburgh and Leith Trade Directories*, 1786–88, 1790–92; *History of the Society of Writers*, 328.

32. Account Books of Andrew Stuart, Cash Books of Andrew Stuart, and Bank Book of Andrew Stuart, NLS, MSS 5398, 5394–95, 8282.

33. *First Annual Report of the Deputy Clerk Register of Scotland* (Edinburgh, 1807), 11; *Second Annual Report of the Deputy Clerk Register of Scotland* (Edinburgh, 1808), 33–34; JTC to Stuart, 5 Dec. 1789, NLS, MS 8261, fol. 65. The deputy clerk register admitted in 1807 that "the Operative Hands [in all the Record Offices] are hired at the ordinary, often the lowest Rate of the Market, without sufficient regard to their qualifications."

34. JTC to Stuart, 19 Dec. 1789, NLS, MS 8261, fol. 73.

35. *Second Annual Report of the Deputy Clerk Register*, 1808, 10.

36. Joel Hurstfield, *Freedom, Corruption, and Government in Elizabethan England* (London, 1973), 137–62.

37. JTC to Stuart, 5 Dec. 1789, NLS, MS 8261 fols. 59, 61.

38. Ibid.

39. Ibid., fols. 61–62.

40. Ibid., fol. 65.

41. Ibid., fol. 59; JTC to Stuart, 12 Dec. 1789, ibid., fols. 63, 64, 70; JTC to Stuart, 19 Dec. 1789, ibid., fols. 72–73.

42. JTC to Stuart, 12 Dec. 1789, ibid., fol. 71; JTC to Stuart, 19 Dec. 1789, ibid., fols. 72–73.

43. The Court of the Lord Lyon, Edinburgh, Records of Messengers' Admission, Jan. 1778 to Oct. 1815, p. 168; William Bell, *A Dictionary and Digest of the Laws of Scotland* (Edinburgh, 1861), 565; James J. Darling, *The Powers and Duties of Messengers at Arms, Sheriffs, and Burgh Officers* (Edinburgh, 1840), 12.

44. Darling, *Powers and Duties*, 10–11.

45. Fourteen messengers-at-arms are listed in *Williamson's Edinburgh Directory*, 1788–90. JTC's name is not among them.

CHAPTER TWO

1. JTC to Stuart, 10 Dec. 1789, NLS MS 8261; General Register of Sasines, Edinburgh 5916; *DNB*, s.v. "Webster, Alexander"; Sir James Fergusson, *Balloon Tytler* (London, 1972), 20.

2. Richard G. Gallin, "Scottish Radicalism, 1792–1794" (Ph.D. diss., Columbia University, 1979), 23; William Hazlitt, "On the Aristocracy of Letters," in *Table-Talk: Essays on Men and Manners* (London, 1905), 278.

3. Lenman, *Integration*, 44; Nicholas Phillipson, "The Scottish Enlightenment," in *The Enlightenment in National Context*, ed. Roy Porter and Mikulas Teich (Cambridge, 1981), 19; Rosalind Mitchison, "Nineteenth Century Scottish Nationalism: The Cultural Background," in *The Roots of Nationalism: Studies in Northern Europe*, ed. R. Mitchison (Edinburgh, 1980), 131.

4. [JTC], "The Political Progress of Britain," *Bee*, 18 April 1792, 234; JTC to Jefferson, 22 Sept. 1798, in Ford, "Jefferson and Callender," 328. For his puritanical outlook, see JTC, *Critical Review*, 35; *Pol. Prog.* 1:33–34; *Pol. Prog.* 2:29–30.

5. Phillipson, "Scottish Enlightenment," 26–27; John A. Fairley, "The Pantheon: An Old Edinburgh Debating Society," *The Book of the Old Edinburgh Club* 1 (1908): 47, 50, 70, 72; McElroy, *Scotland's Age of Improvement*, 92–93.

6. Fergusson, *Tytler*, 20; Bewley, *Muir*, 8; Cockburn, *Memorials of His Time*, 169–70; Robert Chambers, *A Biographical Dictionary of Eminent Scotsmen*, 4 vols. (Edinburgh, 1835), 3:282; Mathew Carey to JTC, 28 May 1794, Lea and Febiger Collection, HSP.

7. Nicholas Phillipson, "Adam Smith as Civic Moralist," in *Wealth and Virtue: The Shaping of Political Economy in the Scottish Enlightenment*, ed. Istvan Holt and Michael Ignatieff (Cambridge, 1983), 199; Lenman, *Integration*, 96; John D. Brims, "The Scottish Democratic Movement in the Age of the French Revolution" (Ph.D. diss., University of Edinburgh, 1983), 98; William Thomas, *The Philosophic Radicals: Nine Studies in Theory and Practice, 1817–1841* (Oxford, 1979), 17.

8. Chambers, *Biographical Dictionary* 3:280–82.

9. William Gillan to JTC, 14 May 1792, PRO HO 102/7.

10. McElroy, *Scotland's Age of Improvement*, 87; Nicholas Phillipson, "Towards a Definition of the Scottish Enlightenment," in *City and Society in the Eighteenth Century*, ed. Paul Fritz and David Williams (Toronto, 1973), 137–38.

11. Fairley, "Pantheon," 65; Anand C. Chitnis, *The Scottish Enlightenment: A Social History* (London, 1976), 61–62; *Edinburgh Evening Courant*, 6 Sept. 1794.

12. John Ramsay, *Scotland and Scotsmen in the Eighteenth Century*, 2 vols. (Edinburgh, 1888), 1:370–79; *Scots Magazine* 51 (1789): 411; William R. Fraser, *History of the Parish and Burgh of Laurencekirk* (Edinburgh, 1880), 290–91; William Forbes to George Chalmers, 21 May 1794, University of Edinburgh Special Collections Department, MS La.11.451/2; John Kay, *Original Portraits*, 2 vols., (Edinburgh, 1877), 1:24.

13. JTC to Stuart, 5 Dec. 1789, NLS, MS 8261, fol. 69; Gardenstone to JTC, 21 Aug. 1790, University of Edinburgh Library MS.

14. Gardenstone to JTC, 21 Aug. 1790, University of Edinburgh Library MS.

15. See, for example, "On Moses," a weak satire on Pitt and the wealthy in the *Bee*, 4 July 1792, p. 329.

16. Examples from *Miscellanies* include "The Progress of Virginity, a Tale," "To the Male Virgins," and "An Index to Female Virtue."

17. "Pol. Prog.," 22 Feb. 1792, p. 270.

18. JTC, "On Good Nature," *Miscellanies*, 11.

19. JTC, "On the Death of a Friend," ibid., 16.

20. Ibid., 17.

21. Ibid., 35–38, 307–19.

22. "Society of Ancient Scots," *Lives of the Scottish Poets*, 3 vols. (London, 1822), 3:96; JTC, "Horace, lib. 1, ode 3," *Miscellanies*, 80–83.

23. Gardenstone to JTC, 21 Aug. 1790, University of Edinburgh Library MS; "Society of Ancient Scots," *Lives of the Scottish Poets* 3:90; JTC, "Peculiar Disadvantages of a Modern Poet," *Miscellanies*, 8.

24. W. J. Murray, "Poetry and Politics: Burns and Revolution," *Studies in the Eighteenth Century* 4 (1979): 57–82; Ramsey, *Scotland and Scotsmen*, 379.

25. "On the Diversities of Life," *Miscellanies*, 36; see also "Primum Mobile," ibid., 35.

26. Timothy Thunderproof [JTC], "To the Printer," ibid., 62; see also "A Poetical Prospect," ibid., 18–19.

27. [JTC], *An Impartial Account of the Conduct of the Excise towards the Breweries of Scotland* (Edinburgh, 1791), 25–26, 34–35.

28. Ibid., 43. JTC's authorship is confirmed in [JTC], *A Short History of the Nature and Consequences of Excise Laws* . . . (Philadelphia, 1795), 43.

29. JTC, *Impartial Account*, viii, x–xiii, 37, 68.

30. Ibid., 1, 22.

31. Brims, "Scottish Democratic Movement," 314; JTC, *Short History of Excise Laws*, 43.

32. Robert Cantwell, *Alexander Wilson: Naturalist and Pioneer* (Philadelphia, 1961), 65; Chambers, *Biographical Dictionary* 1:41; Gillan to JTC, 20 March 1792, PRO HO 102/7; Kay, *Original Portraits*, vii.

33. Gillan to JTC, 20 March 1792, Robert Dundas to Henry Dundas, 13 Jan. 1793, PRO HO 102/7; John Pringle to Henry Dundas, 7 Jan. 1793, PRO HO 102/5.

CHAPTER THREE

1. "Pol. Prog.," Feb. to June 1792.

2. *Pol. Prog.* 1:3.

3. *Pol. Prog.* 2:2.

4. Robert Darnton, *The Literary Underground of the Old Regime* (Cambs., Mass., 1982), 1. Most of the French hacks died on the guillotine.

5. *Pol. Prog.* 2:3; John Kenyon, *The History Men* (London, 1983), 53–55; Fergusson, *Tytler,* 51; JTC to Mathew Carey, n.d (1797?), James Carey to Mathew Carey, n.d (1800?), Lea and Febiger Collection, HSP.

6. *Pol. Prog.* 1:19; *Pol. Prog.* 2:6.

7. *Pol. Prog.* 2:6–7; Kenyon, *History Men,* 65–66. Ironically, Macpherson forged Ossian's poems.

8. "Pol. Prog.," 4 April 1792, p. 169; Victor G. Wexler, *David Hume and the History of England* (Philadelphia, 1979), 8; *Pol. Prog.* 2:51.

9. "Pol. Prog.," 20 June 1792, p. 243, 14 March 1792, p. 46; *Pol. Prog.* 1:3. For the use of Smollett, see "Pol. Prog.," 14 March 1792, p. 46. J. C. D. Clark, *English Society, 1688–1832* (Cambridge, 1985), 322, notes that late eighteenth-century radicals "enlisted Walpole's Tory critics into their radical pantheon."

10. See Harry T. Dickinson, *Liberty and Property: Political Ideology in Eighteenth-Century Britain* (New York, 1977), chap. 8; Gayle T. Pendelton, "English Conservative Propaganda during the French Revolution, 1789–1802" (Ph.D. diss., Emory University, 1976); Clark, *English Society,* chap. 4.

11. "Pol. Prog.," 29 Feb. 1792, p. 307.

12. Ibid., 20 June 1792, p. 241; *Pol. Prog.* 1:77, 30.

13. *Pol. Prog.* 1:12–13; "Pol. Prog.," 29 Feb. 1792, pp. 310–11, 9 May 1792, pp. 21, 26.

14. *Pol. Prog.* 2:5; *Pol. Prog.* 1:5–7. For similar critique of mercantilism and the wastage of wars to JTC's, although without the radical nationalist conclusions, see John Knox, *A View of the British Empire, More Especially Scotland . . .* (London, 1784). JTC may have read Knox's work, but it is more likely that he obtained information from it through Dr. James Anderson's work on Scotland, which he did use extensively. Anderson used Knox's writings without attribution. See A. J. Youngson, *After the Forty-Five: The Economic Impact on the Scottish Highlands* (Edinburgh, 1973), 87–89.

15. *Pol. Prog.* 1:74, 16–17, 78.

16. "Pol. Prog.," 22 Feb. 1792, p. 271, 14 March 1792, p. 45, 9 May 1792, p. 21, 20 June 1792, p. 241; *Pol. Prog.* 1:11–12.

17. See, especially, Bernard Bailyn, *The Ideological Origins of the American Revolution* (Cambridge, Mass., 1967); J. G. A. Pocock, *The Machiavellian Moment: Florentine Republican Thought and the Atlantic Republican Tradition* (Princeton, N.J., 1975); Pocock, *Virtue, Commerce, and History* (Cambridge, 1985).

18. Janice Lee, "Political Antiquarianism Unmasked: The Conservative Attack on the Myth of the Ancient Constitution," *Bulletin of the Institute of Historical Research* 55 (1982): 166–79; Eric Foner, *Tom Paine and Revolutionary America* (New York, 1976). For JTC's views on aristocracy, see *Pol. Prog.* 1:17: "The British aristocracy consider the rest of the nation, as a commodity bought and sold."

19. *Pol. Prog.* 2:55–56.

20. *Pol. Prog.* 1:77, 18–19; "Pol. Prog.," 29 Feb. 1792, p. 311, 20 June 1792, p. 242.

21. "Pol. Prog.," 22 Feb. 1792, pp. 265–66; *Pol. Prog.* 1:58.

22. *Pol. Prog.* 1:62, 43–45; "Pol. Prog.," 22 Feb. 1792, p. 267; *Pol. Prog.* 2:85. JTC's plans for domestic improvement were taken from the writings of John Knox and Dr. James Anderson (see Youngson, *After the Forty-Five*, chaps. 4 and 5). Neither Knox nor Anderson, of course, favored an independent Scotland; rather, they expected action and finance from the government in London to promote internal improvements in Scotland.

23. *Pol. Prog.* 1:64; "Pol. Prog.," 14 March 1792, p. 45. Paine's views on America can be followed in *Rights of Man (The Life and Major Writings of Thomas Paine*, ed. Philip S. Foner, 2 vols. [Secaucus, N.J., 1974], 1:360, 371).

24. Brims, "Scottish Democratic Movement," 45–47; Gallin, "Scottish Radicalism, 1792–1794," 82–89; Cockburn, *Memorials of His Time*, 81; Sher, "Moderates, Managers and Popular Politics in Mid–Eighteenth Century Edinburgh," 180. See also Sunter, *Patronage and Politics in Scotland*, chaps. 10–12.

25. *Scots Magazine* 51 (1789): 412; Gallin, "Scottish Radicalism," 90–94; Brims, "Scottish Democratic Movement," 52; John Dwyer and Alexander Murdoch, "Paradigms and Politics: Manners, Morals, and the Rise of Henry Dundas, 1770–1784," in Dwyer et al., *New Perspectives on the Politics and Culture of Early Modern Scotland*, 235–37.

26. *European Magazine and London Review* 6 (1784): 216; Grace Webster, *Memoir of Dr. Charles Webster* (Edinburgh, 1853).

27. *Gentleman's Magazine* 87 (1817): 647–48; Chambers, *a Biographical Dictionary* 7:378–79; *The Annual Biography and Obituary for the Year 1818*, 2 vols. (London, n.d.), 2:83–89; George Dempster to William Pultney, Dec. 1792, PRO HO 102/6. Other links between the London Scots, including Thomson and Christie, and reformers in Scotland are noted in David V. Erdman, *Commerce des Lumières: John Oswald and the British in Paris, 1790–1793* (Columbia, Mo., 1986), chap. 3. I am grateful to Dr. John Dinwiddy for this last reference.

28. Brims, "Scottish Democratic Movement," 117–22; Lucyle Werkmeister, *A Newspaper History of England*, 1792–1793 (Lincoln, Neb., 1969), 76.

29. William Gillan to JTC, 14 May 1792, PRO HO 102/7; Daniel L. McCue, "Daniel Isaac Eaton and *Politics for the People*," 2 vols. (Ph.D. diss., Columbia University, 1974), 1:38.

30. Gallin, "Scottish Radicalism," 48; Brims, "Scottish Democratic Movement," 49.

31. Brims, "Scottish Democratic Movement," 148: J. C. D. Clark, *Revolution and Rebellion: State and Society in England in the Seventeenth and Eighteenth Centuries* (Cambridge, 1986), 53.

32. Brims, "Scottish Democratic Movement," 147; Gallin, "Scottish Radicalism," 103.

33. JTC, *Impartial Account*, 51; Brims, "Scottish Democratic Movement," 159.

34. Brims, "Scottish Democratic Movement," 173.

35. Ibid., 181; Gallin, "Scottish Radicalism," 47.

36. Gallin, "Scottish Radicalism," 4–5.

37. Brims, "Scottish Democratic Movement," 226–27.

38. Report of the Friends of the People Convention of Delegates, 28 Nov. 1792, PRO HO 102/6; Thomas Muir to John Millar, Jr., July 1796, NLS, MS 3825, letter 1, p. 3; JTC to Thomas Jefferson, 26 Oct. 1798, in Ford, "Jefferson and Callender," 330.

39. Brims, "Scottish Democratic Movement," 295; Gallin, "Scottish Radicalism," 129.

40. *The Parliamentary History of England, from the Earliest Period to 1803*, 34 vols. (London, 1816–18), 24:315–17; Brims, "Scottish Democratic Movement," 315.

41. Brims, "Scottish Democratic Movement," 315–16; Meikle, *Scotland and the French Revolution*, 108; P. Beresford Ellis and Seumas Mac-A'Ghobhainn, *The Scottish Insurrection of 1820* (London, 1970), 36; Edward Hughes, "The Scottish Reform Movement and Charles Grey, 1792–94," *Scottish Historical Review* 35 (1956): 34.

42. The prosecution of JTC and Tytler had their effect. John Pringle, the deputy sheriff of Edinburgh, informed Henry Dundas, after the flight of JTC and Tytler, that at the latest meeting of the Friends of the People "their tone is much lowered. . . . Many who were formerly most violent and seemingly most determined will have been intimidated by the vigorous measures lately adopted and have withdrawn themselves altogether from the association" (John Pringle to Henry Dundas, 7 Jan. 1793, PRO HO 102/5). Pringle was wrong to think the most violent had gone; it was the Foxite Whigs who gave up. Tytler's broadside is reprinted in Fergusson, *Tytler*, 149–53.

43. *Pol. Prog.* 1:3; T. B. and T. J. Howell, *A Complete Collection of State Trials*, 34 vols. (London, 1817), 23:82.

44. See below, chaps. 6 and 7.

45. Anderson was interviewed several times between 29 Dec. 1792 and 1 Jan. 1793 (PRO HO 102/7).

46. Chambers, *Biographical Dictionary* 1:41; Meikle, *Scotland and the French Revolution*, 114: Andrew Hook, *Scotland and America: A Study of Cultural Relations 1750–1835* (Glasgow, 1975), 239.

47. JTC's comments added to Samuel H. Smith to JTC, 15 April 1801, in Ford, "Jefferson and Callender," 25; Hook, *Scotland and America*, 251.

48. In his first article in the *Bee* in 1790, Anderson called Cullen "the most eminent preceptor and disinterested friend he ever had in the world."

49. *Porc. Gaz.*, 19 July 1797.

50. Philadelphia *Aurora*, 4 Aug. 1802; see also ibid., 26 Oct. 1802; *Am. Cit.*, 6 Aug. 1802.

51. Examinations of James Robertson and Walter Berry, 29 Dec. 1792, PRO HO 102/6; Howell, *State Trials* 23:79–115.

52. James Anderson to Lord Gardenstone, 31 Dec. 1792, Gardenstone to Anderson 31 Dec. 1792, Anderson to JTC, n.d. [31 Dec. 1792], PRO HO 102/7.

53. Examinations of Alexander McCaslan and James Anderson, 1 Jan. 1793, ibid.; examination of JTC, 1 Jan. 1793, PRO HO 102/6.

54. Examination of Lord Gardenstone, 2 Jan. 1793, Robert Dundas to Evan Nepean, 3 Jan. 1793, William Scot (an informer) to Robert Dundas, 3 Jan. 1793, PRO HO 102/7.

55. *Rec.*, 4 Aug. 1802; Robert Dundas to Evan Nepean, 3 Jan. 1793, Dundas to Home Office, 4 Jan. 1793, PRO HO 102/7; Howell, *State Trials* 22:83; Court Book of the Court of the Lord Lyon, vol. 5, 1770–1818, Edinburgh, 12 March 1793, p. 135.

56. David F. Hawke, *Paine* (New York, 1974), 20–21.

57. Michael Durey, "Thomas Paine's Apostles: Radical Emigrés and the Triumph of Jeffersonian Republicanism," *WMQ*, 3d ser., 44 (1987): 661–88.

CHAPTER FOUR
1. Durey, "Thomas Paine's Apostles," 661–88; Richard J. Twomey, "Jacobins and Jeffersonians: Anglo–American Radicalism in the United States, 1790–1820" (Ph.D. diss., Northern Illinois University, 1974).

2. Michael Durey, "Transatlantic Patriotism: Political Exiles and America in the Age of Revolutions," in *Artisans, Peasants, and Proletarians, 1760–1860: Essays Presented to Gwyn A. Williams*, ed. Clive Emsley and James Walvin (London, 1985), 7; *Rec.*, 1 Dec. 1802; Fergusson, *Tytler*, 131–32; Gallin "Scottish Radicalism," 151; James Kennedy, *Treason!!! or Not Treason!!! Alias The Weavers Budget* (London [1795?]).

3. *Edinburgh Evening Courant*, 21 Feb. 1793. News of JTC's escape to the United States first became public in Scotland in September 1793; a spy confirmed this report for the government more than a year after JTC's outlawry (*Glasgow Courier*, 28 Sept. 1793; J. B. to William Scot, 24 Jan. 1794, NLS, HO (Scottish) Correspondence, RH 2/4/74. I am grateful to Dr. John Brims for these references).

4. *Rec.*, 9 Feb. 1803; *Aurora*, 18 April 1794; Brims, "Scottish Democratic Movement," 296–97.

5. Records of the Navigation Commission for the Delaware River and Its Navigable Tributaries: Health Officer's Register of Passengers' Names, 1792–94, Pennsylvania Historical and Museum Commission, Harrisburg RG-41, 1723; *Rec.*, 28 July 1802.

6. Brock and Brock, *Scotus Americanus*, 13; Richard G. Miller, *Philadelphia: The Federalist City* (Port Washington, N.Y., 1976), 4.

7. Ethel Rasmusson, "Capital on the Delaware: A Study of Philadelphia's Upper Class, 1789–1800" (Ph.D. diss., Brown University, 1962), 42–46.

8. Miller, *Philadelphia*, 4; William B. Wheeler, "Urban Politics in Nature's Republic: The Development of Political Parties in the Seaport Cities in the Federalist Era" (Ph.D. diss., University of Virginia, 1967), 27–28, 47.

9. Miller, *Philadelphia*, 4; Boston *Polar Star*, 6 Oct. 1796; Alexander Wilson to parents, 25 July 1794, Wilson to Alexander Wilson, Sr., 22 Aug. 1798,

in *The Life and Letters of Alexander Wilson,* ed. Clark Hunter (Philadelphia, 1983), 150, 156; Durey, "Thomas Paine's Apostles," 673–74; Charles W. Janson, *The Stranger in America, 1793–1806* (1806; rept. New York, 1971), 21.

10. Alexander Wilson to Orr, 12, 23 July, 7 Aug. 1801, 14 Feb. 1802, in Hunter, *Wilson,* 182–84, 187, 191; Brock and Brock, *Scotus Americanus,* 17.

11. *Rec.,* 28 July 1802; Mathew Carey to JTC, 5 Oct. 1793, Lea and Febiger Collection, Letter Book 4, 1st ser., HSP. See also Edward C. Carter II, "The Political Activities of Mathew Carey, Nationalist, 1760–1814" (Ph.D. diss., Bryn Mawr College, 1962).

12. *Rec.,* 28 July 1802; Philadelphia *American Daily Advertiser,* 26, 12 June 1793.

13. See Miller, *Philadelphia,* 52–56; Martin S. Pernick, "Politics, Parties, and Pestilence: Epidemic Yellow Fever and the Rise of the First Party System," *WMQ,* 3d ser., 29 (1972): 561; Paul M. Spurlin, *The French Enlightenment in America* (Athens, Ga., 1984), 24–25; Joyce Appleby, "The New Republican Synthesis and the Changing Political Thought of John Adams," *American Quarterly* 25 (1973): 591–92.

14. Jefferson to Madison, 3 April 1794, Thomas Jefferson Papers, LC; Oliver Wolcott, Jr., to Oliver Wolcott, Sr., April and May 1794, quoted in J. Wendell Knox, *Conspiracy in American Politics, 1787–1815* (New York, 1972), 43; Fisher Ames to Thomas Dwight, 12 Dec. 1794, in *Works of Fisher Ames as Published by Seth Ames,* ed. W. B. Allen, 2 vols. (Indianapolis, 1983), 2:1084; Nathan O. Hatch, *The Sacred Cause of Liberty: Republican Thought and the Millennium in Revolutionary New England* (New Haven, 1977), 137–38; Linda K. Kerber, *Federalists in Dissent: Image and Ideology in Jeffersonian America* (Ithaca, N.Y., 1980), 1–23; Gordon S. Wood, "Conspiracy and the Paranoid Style," *WMQ,* 3d ser., 39 (1982): 407.

15. David Hackett Fischer, *The Revolution of American Conservatism: The Federalist Party in the Era of Jeffersonian Democracy* (New York, 1965), 13, 17; John Zvesper, *Politics, Philosophy, and Rhetoric: A Study of the Origins of American Party Politics* (Cambridge, 1977), 93. JTC's perception of equality has similarities with Allan Bloom's interpretation of modern-day Americans' perception of the democratic principle "that denies greatness and wants everyone to feel comfortable in his skin without having to suffer unpleasant comparisons" (*The Closing of the American Mind* [New York, 1987], 66).

16. Monroe to Jefferson, 3 March 1794, Jefferson Papers, LC; Jacob E. Cooke, *Tench Coxe and the Early Republic* (Chapel Hill, N.C., 1978), 280.

17. See, for example, the speech of Dexter in [JTC], *The Political Register; or, Proceedings in the Session of Congress, Commencing on November 3d, 1794, and Ending March 3d, 1795* (Philadelphia, 1795), 383; Stephen Higginson to Timothy Pickering, 29 Aug. 1795, quoted in John R. Howe, "Republican Thought and the Political Violence of the 1790s," *American Quarterly* 19 (1967): 150.

18. John H. Powell, *Bring Out Your Dead: The Great Plague of Yellow Fever in Philadelphia in 1793* (Philadelphia, 1949); Pernick, "Politics, Parties, and Pestilence," 559–87.

19. Pernick, "Politics, Parties and Pestilence," 580; Jacob Axelrad, *Philip Freneau: Champion of Democracy* (Austin, Tex. 1967), 261.

20. Marion Tinling, "Thomas Lloyd's Reports of the First Federal Congress," *WMQ*, 3d ser., 18 (1961): 520.

21. Nelson S. Dearmont, "Secrecy in Government: The Public Debate in Congress during the Formative Years of the American Republic" (Ph.D. diss., City University of New York, 1975), 44–49.

22. Thomas Scharf and Thompson Westcott, *History of Philadelphia, 1609–1884*, 3 vols. (Philadelphia, 1884), 1:489; JTC, *Political Register*, 31–32.

23. [JTC], *The History of the United States for 1796; Including a Variety of Interesting Particulars Relative to the Federal Government, Previous to That Period* (Philadelphia, 1797), 279–80.

24. *The Debates and Proceedings in the Congress of the United States* (hereafter *Annals of Congress*), 42 vols., (Washington, D.C., 1834–56), 4:425; George C. Rogers, Jr., *Evolution of a Federalist: William Loughton Smith of Charleston (1758–1812)* (Columbia, S.C., 1962), 267. Smith was burned in effigy in Charleston in 1794, together with the images of Benedict Arnold and the Devil (*New Letters of Abigail Adams, 1788–1801*, ed. Stewart Mitchell, 2d ed. [New York, 1973], 195).

25. Jefferson to Madison, 3 April 1794, Jefferson Papers, LC; John C. Miller, *The Federalist Era, 1789–1801* (New York, 1963), 143.

26. Monroe to Jefferson, 3 March 1794, Coxe to Jefferson, 22 Feb. 1794, Jefferson Papers, LC.

27. JTC, *History of 1796*, 279; JTC, *Political Register*, vi; [William Cobbett], *Summary of the Proceedings of Congress, during the Session Which Commenced on the 4th of November, 1794*, in *Porcupine's Works*, 12 vols. (London, 1801), 2:157. The *Gaz. U.S.* gave only the barest details of the debates in December 1794 and January 1795, while the *Aurora* did not report them at all.

28. JTC, *Political Register*, 190–91, 252–53, 442–44; Fisher Ames to Thomas Dwight, 7 Jan. 1795, *Works of Fisher Ames* 2:1095.

29. JTC, *Political Register*, 178, 371, 403, 123–25, 434, 412. For Giles's "rambling speech" on Washington's Address, see Leonard W. Levy, *Emergence of a Free Press* (New York, 1985), 293.

30. JTC, *Political Register*, 172, 383, 403, 432. For the defense of Dexter, see *Gaz. U.S.*, 5 March 1795; Fisher Ames to George R. Minot, *Works of Fisher Ames* 2:1101. Dexter had been accused of holding antirepublican principles in December 1793 ("Gracchus" in *Aurora*, 1 Jan. 1794).

31. JTC, *Political Register*, 127, 133, 369–70, 471.

32. *Gaz. U.S.*, 5 March 1795; *Annals of Congress* 4:1268–69, 1242, 1280–81; Dearmont, "Secrecy in Government," 49; *Aurora*, 7 March 1795; JTC, *History of 1796*, 280.

33. *Gaz. U.S.*, 29, 30 Jan., 1 Feb. 1796.

34. Ibid. A similar account of Lyman's speech can be found in *Annals of Congress* 5:279–80. For Harper, see JTC, *History of 1796*, 281; *Annals of Congress* 5:277.

35. *Gaz. U.S.*, 4, 1 Feb. 1796.

36. *Aurora*, 11, 18 March 1795; *Exam.*, 28 Nov. 1800.

37. JTC, *History of 1796*, 281; JTC to Jefferson, 26 Oct. 1798, Jefferson Papers, LC; see also *Rec.*, 26 May, 27 Oct. 1802.

38. [William Cobbett], *Political Censor*, no. 2, in *Porcupine's Works* 3:267.

39. Cobbett, *Summary View*, ibid., 2:217; Dice R. Anderson, *William Branch Giles: A Study in the Politics of Virginia and the Nation from 1790 to 1830* (1914; rept. Gloucester, Mass., 1965), 16; *Rec.*, 27 Oct. 1802.

40. Giles to Jefferson, 4 Jan. 1794, Jefferson Papers, LC.

41. JTC to Madison, 28 May 1796, in Ford, "Jefferson and Callender," 326; *Sketches of Prominent Tennesseans*, ed. William S. Speer (Nashville, 1888), 59; Cantwell, *Alexander Wilson*, 89.

42. Mathew Carey to JTC, 25 April, 28 May 1794, Lea and Febiger Collection, HSP.

43. Bache's newspaper underwent several name changes between 1793 and 1798; I refer to it throughout as the *Aurora*.

44. In July 1802 William Duane, Bache's successor, said that these paragraphs were placed anonymously in Bache's letter box; he denied they were in JTC's handwriting (*Aurora*, 16 July 1802).

45. Miller, *Federalist Era*, 141–46.

46. *Aurora*, 17, 18 March 1794.

47. Ibid., 18, 24 March 1794.

48. Ibid., 17, 22, 25 March, 3 April 1794.

49. Miller, *Federalist Era*, 151; *Annals of Congress* 3:535; *Aurora*, 31 March 1794.

50. *Aurora*, 20 Feb., 28 April 1794, 19 Oct. 1796.

51. Ibid., 24 March 1794; see also ibid., 26 Aug. 1794.

52. Ibid., 21, 18 April 1794; see also ibid., 26 Aug. 1794.

53. See, for example, *Works of Fisher Ames*, ed. Allen; Charles Warren, *Jacobin and Junto: or Early American Politics Viewed in the Diary of Dr. Nathaniel Ames, 1758–1822* (New York, 1970); *New Letters of Abigail Adams*, ed. Mitchell, 117, 124, 126–27, 147, 216; Fischer, *The Revolution of American Conservatism*, 36–37, 112; Howe, "Republican Thought and the Political Violence of the 1790s," 147–65. For the French revolutionaries' enslavement by fears of plots, see D. M. G. Sutherland, *France, 1789–1815: Revolution and Counterrevolution* (London, 1985).

54. Richard Hofstadter, *The Paranoid Style in American Politics and Other Essays* (New York, 1965); Lance Banning, "Republican Ideology and the Triumph of the Constitution, 1789 to 1793," *WMQ*, 3d ser., 31 (1974): 171; David Sisson, *The American Revolution of 1800* (New York, 1974), 130–32; Vernon Stauffer, *New England and the Bavarian Illuminati* (1918; rept. New York, 1967); Knox, *Conspiracy in American Politics*, 69, 91, 114, 124; Lynn Hunt, *Politics, Culture, and Class in the French Revolution* (Berkeley, 1984), 42–47; Wood, "Conspiracy and the Paranoid Style," 427, 429.

55. Fisher Ames to Thomas Dwight, 11 Sept. 1794, *Works of Fisher Ames* 2:1049.

56. *The Democratic Republican Societies, 1790–1800,* ed. Philip Foner (Westport, Conn., 1976), 439–41.

57. *Aurora,* 28 Jan. 1794, 2 March 1795. Cobbett later satirized the Republican penchant for celebration. "I believe from my soul," he wrote in 1795, "there have been more cannons fired here in celebration of [the conquest of Amsterdam] than the French fired in achieving it. . . . I have counted 22 grand civic festivals, 51 of an inferior sort, and 193 public dinners" (Peter Porcupine [William Cobbett], *A Bone to Gnaw for the Democrats,* vol. 2 [Philadelphia, 1795], 51).

58. [William Cobbett], *A Bone to Gnaw for the Democrats: or, Observations on a Pamphlet, Entitled The Political Progress of Britain,* [vol. 1] (Philadelphia, 1795), 11; *Aurora,* 20, 26 Aug., 3 Oct., 8 Nov. 1794.

59. *Aurora* 27 Oct. 1794.

60. Ibid., 4 March, 16, 18, 20 June 1795.

61. James D. Tagg, "Benjamin Franklin Bache and the Philadelphia *Aurora*" (Ph.D. diss., Wayne State University, 1973), 451–55; *Aurora,* 27, 29 June 1795.

62. Walter F. Brown, Jr., "John Adams and the American Press, 1797–1801: The First Full-Scale Confrontation between the Executive and the Media" (Ph.D. diss., University of Notre Dame, 1974), 28; Miller, *Federalist Era,* 168.

63. *Aurora,* 5 Aug. 1795.

64. Ibid., 22 Aug. 1795.

65. Ibid., 29 Aug. 16 Sept. 1795.

66. Tagg, "Benjamin Franklin Bache," 527–28.

67. For examples of Callender's satire, see the Appendix.

CHAPTER FIVE

1. David Loth, *Chief Justice: John Marshall and the Growth of the Republic* (New York, 1949), 252; JTC to James Madison, 28 May 1796, in Ford, "Jefferson and Callender," 325.

2. JTC to James Madison, 28 May 1796, in Ford, "Jefferson and Callender," 325.

3. "An American," *Gaz. U.S.,* 24 April 1798; JTC, *Sketches of the History of America* (Philadelphia, 1798), 28, 207; *Rec.,* 23 March 1803; [JTC], *The Prospect before Us,* 2 vols., (Richmond, 1800), 2:34; Tagg, "Benjamin Franklin Bache," 134–36; Peter J. Parker, "Asbury Dickins, Bookseller, 1798–1801, or the Brief Career of a Careless Youth," *PMHB* 94 (1970): 464–83.

4. John Ashworth, "The Jeffersonians: Classical Republicans or Liberal Capitalists?" *Journal of American Studies* 18 (1984): 425–35; Joyce Appleby, *Capitalism and a New Social Order: The Republican Vision of the 1790s* (New York, 1984), 48; Wheeler, "Urban Politics in Nature's Republic," 55–57. For the Antifederalists, see Gordon S. Wood, "Interests and Disinterestedness in the Making of the Constitution," in *Beyond Confederation: Origins of the Constitution and American National Identity* ed. Richard Beeman, Stephen Botein, and Edward C. Carter II (Chapel Hill, N.C., 1987), 69–109.

5. Roland M. Baumann, "John Swanwick: Spokesman for 'Merchant-Republicanism' in Philadelphia, 1790–1798," *PMHB* 97 (1973): 139; Roland M. Baumann, "The Democratic-Republicans of Philadelphia: The Origins, 1776–97" (Ph.D. diss., Pennsylvania State University, 1970) chap. 10.

6. Edmund Berkeley and Dorothy Smith Berkeley, *John Beckley: Zealous Partisan in a Nation Divided* (Philadelphia, 1973), 67.

7. Ibid., 284 and passim; Cooke, *Coxe*, 283.

8. Cooke, *Coxe*, 283. There are two letters from JTC to Coxe dated 1794 in the Tench Coxe Papers, HSP. JTC also gave Coxe advice on Edinburgh booksellers (JTC to Coxe, 2 Dec. 1796, ibid.).

9. Cooke, *Coxe*, 237; Thomas Carey to Mathew Carey, 17 July 1792, Lea and Febiger Collection, HSP; James Carey to Mathew Carey, 9 Aug. 1795, Edward Carey Gardiner Collection: Carey Section, box 34A, HSP; Charleston *Daily Evening Gazette*, 10 Jan. 1795; JTC to Jefferson, 26 Oct. 1798, Jefferson Papers, LC. There is a brief, not totally accurate, account of James Carey in Carter, "Matthew Carey," 103.

10. Kim T. Phillips, "William Duane, Revolutionary Editor" (Ph.D. diss., University of California, Berkeley, 1968), chaps. 1–2; Jasper Dwight [William Duane], *A Letter to President Washington* (Philadelphia, 1796); Richard J. Twomey, "Jacobins and Jeffersonians: Anglo–American Radical Ideology, 1790–1810," in *The Origins of Anglo-American Radicalism*, ed. Margaret Jacob and James Jacob (London, 1984), 293–97.

11. JTC to James Carey, 22 Feb. 1799, Edward Carey Gardiner Collection, HSP; Baumann, "Swanwick"; Baumann, "Philadelphia's Manufacturers and the Excise Taxes of 1794: The Forging of the Jeffersonian Coalition," *PMHB* 106 (1982): 3–39; Cobbett, *Bone to Gnaw*, 1:56; [William Cobbett], *The Political Censor, or Monthly Review of the Most Interesting Political Occurrences Relative to the United States of America* (Philadelphia, 1796), 189. Robert Liston, British minister to the United States, informed Foreign Secretary Lord Granville in 1796 that Swanwick was "a man of doubtful morality, and little respectability of character" (Liston to Granville, 13 Oct. 1796, PRO FO 5/14).

12. [JTC], *British Honour and Humanity; or, The Wonders of American Patience* (Philadelphia, 1796); Peter Porcupine [William Cobbett], *The Life and Adventures of Peter Porcupine* (Philadelphia, 1796); JTC, *History of 1796*, 165–67; JTC, *Prospect*, 1:57–58. James Carey wrote on Swanwick's death that "he died a victim of political persecution; a model of unshaken patriotism, and a martyr in the cause of civil liberty" (Philadelphia *Carey's United States Recorder*, 2 Aug. 1798).

13. *DAB*, s.v. "Leiper, Thomas"; Baumann, "Philadelphia's Manufacturers," 18–19; Scharf and Westcott, *Philadelphia* 1:451, 2:1465; *Rec.*, 20 Oct. 1802; Callender, *Prospect*, 1:33.

14. Foner, *Democratic Republican Societies*, 439–41; Carter, "Mathew Carey," 131, 137, 142–43, 211; Cooke, *Coxe*, 201–26; Baumann, "Swanwick," 144–45; *DAB*, s.v. "Leiper, Thomas"; Scharf and Westcott, *Philadelphia* 1:465.

15. Baumann, "Philadelphia's Manufacturers," 15.

16. See, for example, *Aurora*, 7 May, 5 Aug. 1794.

17. JTC, *Short History of Excise Laws*, 11, 116.

18. Ibid., 3–4; Forrest McDonald, *Novus Ordo Seclorum: The Intellectual Origins of the Constitution* (Lawrence, Kans., 1985), 65; D. D. Raphael, *Adam Smith* (Oxford, 1985), 2, 82–83; Donald Winch, *Adam Smith's Politics: An Essay in Historiographic Revision* (Cambridge, 1978), 18; John Robertson, "Scottish Political Economy beyond the Civic Tradition: Government and Economic Development in the *Wealth of Nations*," *History of Political Thought* 4 (1983): 463, 467.

19. JTC, *Short History of Excise Laws*, 5–6.

20. JTC, *History of 1796*, 198.

21. JTC, *Sketches*, 37–38; Adam Smith, *Wealth of Nations* bk. 4, chap. 7, pt. 2.

22. JTC, *Sketches*, 207, 185.

23. JTC, *Sedgwick and Co.; or, A Key to the Six Per Cent Cabinet* (Philadelphia, 1798), 87; JTC, *Sketches*, 186–87.

24. *Exam.*, 21 Nov. 1800.

25. JTC, *Sketches*, 68. In *History of 1796*, 226–27, JTC wrote that the Federalists "had no more warrant for erecting banks than for erecting pyramids."

26. JTC, *Sketches*, 189, 184. By supporting paper money in moderate amounts, JTC was again following Adam Smith (see McDonald, *Novus Ordo Seclorum*, 130–31).

27. JTC, *Sketches*, 190, 185.

28. Ibid., 181–82.

29. Ibid., 209.

30. William M. Gavre, "Republicanism in the American Revolution: The Collapse of the Classical Ideal" (Ph.D. diss., University of California, Los Angeles, 1978), 587–94; Drew M. McCoy, *The Elusive Republic: Political Economy in Jeffersonian America* (Chapel Hill, N.C., 1980), chap. 7; Twomey, "Jacobins and Jeffersonians," 146–70; Durey, "Thomas Paine's Apostles," 678–81.

31. Joyce Appleby, "What Is Still American in the Political Philosophy of Thomas Jefferson?" *WMQ*, 3d ser. 39 (1982): 287–309; Foner, *Writings of Paine* 1:357; JTC, *Sedgwick and Co.*, 87; JTC, *Prospect* 1:73. There are clear echoes of Paine in the passage; compare with "Useful and Entertaining Hints" (1775), in Foner, *Writings of Paine* 2:1022–23.

32. JTC, *History of 1796*, 287, 25–26.

33. JTC, *Deformities*, vii.

34. *Aurora*, 18 Oct. 1794; JTC, *Sketches*, 84.

35. JTC, *Short History of Excise Laws*, 45–46.

36. *Exam.*, 21 June 1799; *Aurora*, 9 Nov. 1796.

37. JTC, *Prospect* 2:vi–vii. For Madison's view see Douglass Adair, "'That Politics May be Reduced to a Science': David Hume, James Madison, and the Tenth *Federalist*," in *Fame and the Founding Fathers: Essays by Douglass Adair*, ed. Trevor Colbourn (New York, 1974), 101–3; *The Federalist Papers*,

122–28. There is no evidence that JTC ever read the *Federalist Papers*, although he was familiar with Hume's writings, the inspiration for Madison's ideas.

38. JTC, *Prospect* 2:143, 89–90; *Exam.*, 21 June 1799.

39. JTC, *Prospect* 2:143, *Aurora*, 21 March 1798.

40. JTC, *History of 1796*, 294.

41. JTC, *Prospect* 2:144, 1:11; *Aurora*, 28 April, 15 March 1796, 17 Feb. 1798.

42. JTC, *Prospect* 2:56, 91, 144; Richard C. Ellis, "The Persistence of Antifederalism after 1789," in *Beyond Confederation*, ed. Beeman et al., 298–303.

43. JTC to Jefferson, 22 Sept., 26 Oct. 1798, Jefferson Papers, LC.

44. Richard C. Ellis, *The Jeffersonian Crisis: Courts and Politics in the Young Republic* (New York, 1971), 21–22.

45. Ibid., 20; see also Ashworth, "The Jeffersonians: Classical Republicans or Liberal Capitalists?" 425–35.

46. JTC, *Sketches*, 224; JTC, *History of 1796*, 270.

47. JTC, *History of 1796*, 234, 28; JTC, *Prospect* 2:73; Spurlin, *French Enlightenment*, 64–65; Appleby, *Capitalism and a New Social Order*, 77; *Rec.*, 1 Dec. 1802.

48. JTC, *Deformities*, 87; *Bee*, 20 June 1792, p. 243, 14 March 1792, p. 46; JTC, *History of 1796*, 169–70; *Exam.*, 7 Feb. 1800.

49. [William Cobbett], *Observations on the Emigration of Dr. Priestley* (Philadelphia, 1794), preface; JTC, *Prospect*, quoted in Ray Boston, "The Impact of 'Foreign Liars' on the American Press (1790–1800)," *Journalism Quarterly* 50 (1973): 726; *Aurora*, 30 March 1795.

50. Steven H. Hochman, "On the Liberty of the Press in Virginia: From Essay to Bludgeon, 1798–1803," *VMHB* 84 (1976): 431; Ford, "Jefferson and Callender," 5; JTC to Jefferson, 26 Oct. 1798, ibid., 12; JTC, *Prospect* 1:145.

51. *Exam.*, 7 Feb. 1800; JTC, *Prospect* 2:145, 1:3; JTC, *Political Register*, 32; JTC, *History of 1796*, 29; JTC, *Critical Review*, 50.

52. *Aurora*, 3, 15 March, 11, 16 April, 3 May, 9, 20, 21, 22, 23 Dec. 1796, 6 Feb., 6 March 1797; Tagg, "Benjamin Franklin Bache," 526.

53. Manning J. Dauer, *The Adams Federalists* (Baltimore, 1968), 112, 116; JTC, *Sketches*, 232–33.

54. JTC, *Prospect* 2:34–35; Dauer, *Adams Federalists*, 116–17, 128; *Aurora*, 14, 20 March 1797; Mitchell, *New Letters of Abigail Adams*, 94.

55. *Aurora*, 15 Nov. 1796, 4 Feb., 19, 23, 25 May 1797; JTC, *History of 1796*, 3.

56. *The Papers of Alexander Hamilton*, ed. Harold C. Syrett and Jacob E. Cooke, 26 vols. (New York, 1960–79), 19:121–44; Forrest McDonald, *Alexander Hamilton: A Biography* (New York, 1979), 227–30; Broadus Mitchell, *Alexander Hamilton: The National Adventure, 1788–1804* (New York, 1962), 399–421; *The Papers of Thomas Jefferson*, ed. Julian P. Boyd et al, 22 vols. to date

(Princeton, N.J., 1950–), 18:613–88; Harry Ammon, *James Monroe: The Quest for National Identity* (New York, 1971), 158–60.

57. Statement of Oliver Wolcott, 12 July 1797, in Alexander Hamilton, *Observations on Certain Documents Contained in No. V & VI of "The History of the United States for the Year 1796"* . . . , in Syrett, *Papers of Hamilton* 21:279.

58. Ibid., 270. The best accounts of this very complicated episode are Syrett's and Boyd's editorial essays.

59. Boyd, *Papers of Jefferson* 18:649; *Aurora*, 23 Oct. 1795, 11 June 1796; JTC, *History of 1796*, 208.

60. JTC, *History of 1796*, 204–5, 223, 249; *Exam.*, 16 Oct. 1802; Berkeleys, *Beckley*, 161.

61. The documents numbered I to IV and Hamilton's notes to Reynolds, numbered VI, were printed in JTC, *History of 1796*, 209–16, 218–21.

62. Cooke, *Coxe*, 283 n. 18. The note is in the Tench Coxe Papers.

63. Syrett, *Papers of Hamilton* 21:134.

64. Boyd, *Papers of Jefferson* 18:631 n. 62; Syrett, *Papers of Hamilton* 21:136–38.

65. The copies given to Hamilton are in the McLean-Hamilton Papers. I have used photocopies of these.

66. *Rec.*, 3 Nov. 1802; Ford, "Jefferson and Callender," 6. The publication dates of parts 5 and 6 of the pamphlet version cannot be confirmed (indeed, no copies are extant). But an advertisement in the *Aurora*, 24 June 1797, says part 5 would be published on 26 June. Part 6 was published on or just before 7 July (Walcott to Hamilton, 7 July 1797, in Syrett, *Papers of Hamilton* 21:151). The book version of *History of 1796* was published on 27 July; see the *Aurora* for that date, where it is advertised under the heading "Memoirs of Modern Innocence."

67. Boyd, *Papers of Jefferson* 18:631 n. 62.

68. JTC, *Sketches*, 101–2.

69. JTC, *History of 1796*, 220, 229; Document No. III, ibid., 211.

70. JTC, *Sketches*, 97–100; JTC, *History of 1796*, 205.

71. JTC to Jefferson, 28 Sept. 1797, in Ford, "Jefferson and Callender," 8; JTC to Mathew Carey, 6 Oct. 1797, Lea and Febiger Collection, HSP.

72. Cobbett, *Bone to Gnaw* 2:4, 1:4–5; *Porc. Gaz.*, 6 June, 18 April 1798, 10 Aug. 1797; *Gaz. U.S.*, 7 March 1798; *Porcupine's Works* 9:216.

73. *Porc. Gaz.*, 19 July 1797, 6 June 1798; *Exam.*, 11 Feb. 1800.

74. Berkeleys, *Beckley*, 159; Cooke, *Coxe*, 302–7; John C. Miller, *Crisis in Freedom: The Alien and Sedition Laws* (Boston, 1951), 39.

75. Mathew Carey to James Carey, 16 May 1797, James Carey to Mathew Carey, 23 Sept. 1797, Lea and Febiger Collection, HSP; Carter, "Mathew Carey," 254–55.

76. Baumann, "Swanwick," 178–80; *Carey's United States Recorder*, 2 Aug. 1798.

77. James Carey to Mathew Carey, 8 July 1797, JTC to Mathew Carey, 6 Oct. 1797, Lea and Febiger Collection, JTC to James Carey, 22 Feb. 1799, Edward Carey Gardiner Collection, HSP; *Exam.*, 25 Sept. 1802; JTC to Jefferson, 28 Sept. 1797, in Ford, "Jefferson and Callender," 8.

78. JTC, *History of 1796*, 29–30; JTC to Jefferson, 28 Sept. 1797, 21 March, 26 Oct., 19 Nov. 1798, in Ford, "Jefferson and Callender," 8, 9, 14.

79. *Gaz. U.S.*, 24 April 1798; *Porc. Gaz.*, 24 April 1798.

80. Jefferson to Madison, 26 April 1798, in Ford, "Jefferson and Callender," 9; *Rec.*, 26 May, 4 Aug., 25 Aug. 1802.

81. JTC to Jefferson, 21 March 1798, in Ford "Jefferson and Callender," 9; *Gaz. U.S.*, 8 March 1798. Fenno headed one paragraph, "HELP! OH! HELP!" (ibid., 4 June 1798).

82. *Aurora*, 30 April 1798 (in reply to *Porc. Gaz.*, 27 April 1798, and *Gaz. U.S.*, 24 April 1798), 14, 21 March 1798.

83. Ibid., 13, 16, 27 April 1798.

84. *Gaz. U.S.*, 24 April 1798, quoted in James Morton Smith, *Freedom's Fetters: The Alien and Sedition Laws and American Civil Liberties* (1956; rept. Ithaca, N.Y., 1966), 336; *Carey's U.S. Rec.*, 14 June 1798; see also "An American," in *Porc. Gaz.*, 24 March 1798.

85. George Spater, *William Cobbett: The Poor Man's Friend*, 2 vols. (Cambridge, 1982), 2:95–99; *Porc. Gaz.*, 30 Dec. 1797.

86. JTC, *Sedgwick and Co.*, 18; *Rec.*, 20 Oct. 1802.

87. *Aurora*, 20 Aug. 1798; Naturalization Petition, filed 4 June 1798, Pennsylvania Records, Harrisburg.

CHAPTER SIX

1. *Porc. Gaz.*, 14 July 1798; JTC to Jefferson, 19 Nov. 1798, Jefferson Papers, LC.

2. *Porcupine's Works* 9:215–21; *Massachusetts Spy*, 22 Aug. 1798, quoted in Brown, "Adams and the Press," 85.

3. JTC to Jefferson, 19 Nov., 22 Sept. 1798, Jefferson Papers, LC.

4. Jefferson to Madison, 29 May 1801, Jefferson to Abigail Adams, 22 July 1804, Jefferson to Monroe, 15 July 1802, in Ford, "Jefferson and Callender," 157, 326–27, 158.

5. JTC to Jefferson, 26 Oct., 19 Nov. 1798, Jefferson Papers, LC.

6. JTC to Jefferson, 22 Sept. 1798, ibid.

7. Jefferson to JTC, 11 Oct. 1798, JTC to Jefferson, 19 Nov. 1798, Jefferson to S. T. Mason, 11 Oct. 1798, ibid.

8. JTC to Jefferson, 19 Nov., 22 Sept. 1798, ibid.

9. Ibid.; Smith, *Freedom's Fetters*, 338.

10. JTC to James Carey, 22 Feb. 1799, Edward Carey Gardiner Collection, HSP; Donald H. Stewart, *The Opposition Press of the Federalist Period* (Albany, 1969), 617. One account claims 62 workers in newspaper offices died in the epidemic (Scharf and Westcott, *Philadelphia* 1:495).

11. JTC to Meriwether Jones, 16, 21 March 1798, qutoed in *Exam.*, 29 May 1802; Stewart, *Opposition Press*, 479; Smith, *Freedom's Fetters*, 398–404.

12. JTC to Jefferson, 22 Sept. 1798, Jefferson Papers, LC; Stewart, *Opposition Press*, 29–30. For Matthew Lyon, see Aleine Austin, *Matthew Lyon; "New Man" of the Democratic Revolution, 1749–1822* (University Park, Pa., 1981).

13. *The Papers of Benjamin Henry Latrobe*, ed. Edward C. Carter II et al. (New Haven, 1977—), ser. 1:544; Clarence S. Brigham, *History and Bibliography of American Newspapers, 1690–1820*, 2 vols (Worcester, Mass., 1947), 2:1139–40; *Exam.*, 29 May 1802.

14. *Rec.*, 5 May 1802.

15. Virginius Dabney, *Richmond: The Story of a City* (New York, 1976), 34; W. Asbury Christian, *Richmond: Her Past and Present* (Richmond 1912), 72; Loth, *Marshall*, 111.

16. Christian, *Richmond*, 41; *Rec.*, 9 March 1803; *A Richmond Reader, 1783–1983*, ed. Maurice Duke and Daniel P. Jordan (Chapel Hill, N.C., 1983), 24–25.

17. Duke and Jordan, *Richmond Reader*, 15; Christian, *Richmond*, 50–51.

18. Duke and Jordan, *Richmond Reader*, 26.

19. *Rec.*, 24 April 1802; *Exam.*, 11 Nov., 21 Oct. 1800, 21 Feb. 1801; Norman K. Risjord, *Chesapeake Politics, 1781–1800* (New York, 1978), 550–52; Fischer, *The Revolution of American Conservatism*, 421.

20. Brigham, *American Newspapers* 2:1142–43; *Evans' American Bibliography*, 14 vols. (New York, 1942), 13:1; *Exam.*, 2 June 1802.

21. *Exam.*, 21 June 1799.

22. Ibid., 30 July, 9 Aug. 1799; Smith, *Freedom's Fetters*, 338.

23. *Exam.*, 30 July 1799. In fact, the Federalists rightly regarded JTC as the editor (see *Va. Fed.*, 20 July 1799).

24. *The Constitutional Diary and Philadelphia Evening Advertiser*, 1 Jan. 1800; JTC to Jefferson, 10 Aug. 1798, Jefferson Papers, LC. The *Diary* was James Carey's latest attempt to break into the Philadelphia newspaper market.

25. *Exam.*, 9 Aug. 1799.

26. JTC to Jefferson, 10 Aug. 1799, Jefferson Papers, LC.

27. Jefferson to JTC, 6 Sept. 1799, ibid.

28. *Exam.*, 29 May 1802; JTC to Jefferson, 26 Sept. 1799, Jefferson to JTC, 6 Oct. 1799, Jefferson Papers, LC.

29. *Rec.*, 18 June 1803.

30. Appleby, *Captialism and a New Social Order*, 78.

31. Durey, "Thomas Paine's Apostles," 681–87; *Rec.*, 12 May 1802; *Exam.*, 3 Dec. 1799, 7 Jan. 1800.

32. JTC to Jefferson, 14 March 1800, 10 Aug. 1799, Jefferson Papers, LC.

33. *Rec.*, 3 Nov. 1802.

34. *Exam.*, 9 May 1800; Smith, *Freedom's Fetters*, 341–42.

35. JTC, *Prospect* 1:3–4.

36. Ibid., 149–50.

37. *Exam.* 14 Feb. 1800.

38. Smith, *Freedom's Fetters*, 338–39; *Exam.*, 1 Nov. 1799; JTC, *Prospect* 1:148.

39. *Exam.*, 29 May 1802, 17 Jan. 1800.

40. *Rec.*, 5 May 1802; *Exam.*, 11 Feb. 1800.

41. *Exam.*, 1, 11 April 1800.

42. Ibid., 18 Feb. 1800; JTC to Jefferson, 10 March 1800, Jefferson Papers, LC.

43. *Exam.*, 11 Feb. 1800; JTC to Duane, 27 April 1800, in Ford, "Jefferson and Callender," 22. Ford mistakenly transcribed "treaty" instead of "treasury" (see Boston, "Foreign Liars," 723). JTC's letter was published in *Am. Pat.*, 7 May 1800.

44. Smith, *Freedom's Fetters*, 340, 345–46. Meriwether Jones later claimed Chase deliberately set low bail in the hope that JTC would flee (*Exam.*, 23 Sept. 1800); but this seems unlikely because Chase was determined to implement the Sedition Act in Virginia, Republicanism's stronghold.

45. *Exam.*, 27 May 1800.

46. Jellison, "That Scoundrel Callender," 300; Levy, *Emergence of a Free Press*, 300–301.

47. Lance Banning, *The Jeffersonian Persuasion: Evolution of a Party Ideology* (Ithaca, N.Y., 1978), 206.

48. Robert E. Shalhope, *John Taylor of Caroline: Pastoral Republican* (Columbia, S.C. 1980), 96–99, 102.

49. Quoted in James Haw et al., *Stormy Patriot: The Life of Samuel Chase* (Baltimore, 1980), 248.

50. Ibid. 206–7; Smith, *Freedom's Fetters*, 257–68, 307–33.

51. Haw, *Chase*, 202–3.

52. Quoted in Smith, *Freedom's Fetters*, 343.

53. Jefferson to Philip N. Nicholas, 7 April 1800, Jefferson to Monroe, 16 March 1800, Jefferson Papers, LC.

54. Jefferson to Monroe, 13 April 1800, ibid.

55. Monroe to Jefferson, 25 May 1800, ibid.

56. Ibid.; Notes of Jefferson to Monroe, 26 May 1800, ibid.; Smith, *Freedom's Fetters*, 345–46. The quotation was from counsel George Hay.

57. Smith, *Freedom's Fetters*, 441–42; Francis Wharton, ed., *State Trials of the United States during the Administrations of Washington and Adams* (1849; rept. New York, 1970), 688–90; Levy, *Emergence of a Free Press*, 297.

58. *Exam.*, 10 June 1800; Haw, *Chase*, 183, 197.

59. *Exam.*, 10 June 1800.

60. Wharton, *State Trials*, 692–93.

61. Hochman, "Liberty of the Press," 432; Haw, *Chase*, 312–14.

62. Haw, *Chase*, p. 192; Wharton, *State Trials*, 694–95; *Exam.*, 10 June 1800.

63. Smith, *Freedom's Fetters*, 348; Wharton, *State Trials*, 696–97; Haw, *Chase*, 204.

64. Smith, *Freedom's Fetters*, 348–49.

65. Wharton, *State Trials*, 698–700.

66. Ibid., 700–704.

67. Shalhope, *Taylor*, 86; Wharton, *State Trials*, 708.

68. Haw, *Chase*, 205; Wharton, *State Trials*, 712.

69. *Exam.*, 29 May 1802; *Rec.*, 5 July 1802.

70. *Exam.*, 18 July 1800; JTC to Jefferson, 11 Oct. 1800, Jefferson Papers, LC.

71. Dabney, *Richmond*, 48; *Exam.*, 4 Oct. 1800, 2 June 1802; JTC to Jefferson, 14 Aug. 1800, Jefferson Papers, LC; JTC, *Prospect* 2:138.

72. JTC to Jefferson, 11, 27 Oct. 1800, 23 Jan. 1801, Jefferson Papers, LC. JTC mischievously used the visits of Wythe and Monroe to blacken the Republicans after his break with the party. "But far above all," he wrote of his time in prison, "the marked kindness of THE GOVERNOR shall never be erased from [my] memory" (*Rec.*, 5 May 1802).

73. JTC to Jefferson, 11 Oct. 1800, Jefferson Papers, LC; *Exam.*, 10 Oct. 1800.

74. Austin, *Matthew Lyon*, 135–37; Stephen L. Newman, "Thomas Cooper, 1759–1839: The Political Odyssey of a Bourgeois Ideologue," *Southern Studies* 24 (1985): 295–305; *Aurora*, 26 July 1794; JTC, *History of 1796*, 24; JTC, *Prospect* 1:112; *Exam.*, 1 April, 10 Nov. 1800; *Rec.*, 25 Aug. 1802, 3 June 1803.

75. *Exam.*, 18 Nov. 1800; *Rec.*, 10 Nov. 1802. JTC's position was very similar to Jefferson's, though expressed in coarser language (Thomas Jefferson, *Notes on the State of Virginia*, in *Basic Writings of Thomas Jefferson*, ed. Philip S. Foner [New York, 1944], 144–45). Jefferson's hopes of transporting slaves to Africa were lessened by reading contemporary works on Africa. (Jefferson to Rush, 23 Sept. 1800, Jefferson Papers, LC).

76. *Rec.*, 3 June 1803.

77. JTC, *Prospect* 2:130; *Exam.*, 6 Feb. 1801.

78. JTC to Jefferson, 13 Sept., 11 Oct., 1 Nov. 1800, Jefferson Papers, LC; Fawn Brodie, *Thomas Jefferson: An Intimate History* (New York, 1974), 342; Gilbert Chinard, *Thomas Jefferson: The Apostle of Americanism* 2d ed. (Ann Arbor, 1975), 357–58.

79. Sisson, *American Revolution of 1800*, 368; Jefferson to Rush, 23 Sept. 1800, Jefferson Papers, LC; Chinard, *Jefferson*, 367.

80. *Exam.*, 5 Aug., 28 Oct., 11 Nov. 1800, 2 June 1802; JTC *Prospect* 2:104; JTC to Jefferson, 13 Sept. 1800, Jefferson Papers, LC.

81. JTC to Jefferson, 23 Feb. 1801, Jefferson Papers, LC.

82. JTC, *The Conduct of Meriwether Jones, in a Series of Letters to the Public* (Richmond, 1802), 55; JTC to Jefferson, 14 March 1800, Jefferson Papers, LC; *Rec.*, 12 May 1802; *Exam.*, 25 Nov. 1800.

83. *Exam.*, 25, 11 Nov. 1800.

84. Ibid., 14, 18, 21 Nov. 1800.

85. Ibid., 14, 25 Nov. 1800. JTC was right to suggest that Jefferson had major reservations about the Constitution. But, as usual, Jefferson had voiced his concerns only privately, to trusted friends. JTC in effect was publicizing opinions that Jefferson preferred to remain hidden. He also exaggerated them, for there is no evidence that Jefferson considered, in practice rather than in theory, amending the Constitution (Hannah Arendt, *On Revolution* [New York, 1963], 235; Richard K. Matthews, *The Radical Politics of Thomas Jefferson: A Revisionist View* [Lawrence, Kans., 1984], 77).

86. *Exam.*, 25 Nov., 31 Oct. 1800.

87. Ibid., 6 Jan. 1801.

88. *Rec.*, 12 May 1802.

89. *Exam.*, 27 March, 10 April 1801.

CHAPTER SEVEN

1. JTC to Jefferson, Oct., 17 Nov. 1800, Jefferson Papers, LC; *Exam.*, 3 Jan., 23 Sept. 1800, 17 April 1801. For McKean's nepotism, see Kim T. Phillips, "William Duane, Philadelphia's Democratic Republicans, and the Origins of Modern Politics," *PMHB* 101 (1977): 371.

2. Carl E. Prince, "The Passing of the Aristocracy: Jefferson's Removal of the Federalists, 1801–1805," *Journal of American History* 57 (1970): 565; see also Noble E. Cunningham Jr., *The Process of Government under Jefferson* (Princeton, N.J., 1978), 165–87; Robert M. Johnstone, Jr., *Jefferson and the Presidency: Leadership in the Young Republic* (Ithaca, N.Y., 1978), 102–13. Both Cunningham and Johnstone believe political circumstances forced Jefferson into a more partisan policy than he personally wished.

3. Dumas Malone, *Jefferson and His Time*, 6 vols. (Boston, 1948–81), 4:89; *Am. Cit.*, 6 June 1801; David Denniston and James Cheetham to Jefferson, 1 June 1801, in "Letters of James Cheetham," ed. Worthington C. Ford, *Proceedings of the Massachusetts Historical Society*, 3d ser., 1 (1907): 42–43; *Am. Pat.*, 25 Sept. 1802.

4. Albert Gallatin to Jefferson, 15 Dec. 1801, in "Letters of William Duane," ed. Worthington C. Ford, *Proceedings of the Massachusetts Historical Society*, 2d ser., 20 (May 1906): 258–59; Phillips, "William Duane, Revolutionary Editor"; Boston, "Foreign Liars," 730; Carter, "Mathew Carey," 270–71; Sanford W. Higginbotham, *The Keystone in the Democratic Arch: Pennsylvania Politics, 1800–16* (Harrisburg, 1952), 43.

5. JTC to Jefferson, 12 April 1801, Jefferson Papers, LC.

6. Jellison, "That Scoundrel Callender," 300–301; Virginius Dabney, *The Jefferson Scandals: A Rebuttal* (New York, 1981), 8; Jefferson to Monroe, 29, 26 May 1801, Jefferson Papers, LC; *Exam.*, 2 July, 21 Aug. 1802.

7. JTC to Madison, 27 April 1801, in Ford, "Jefferson and Callender," 35; *Rec.*, 11 Aug. 1802; *Exam.*, 29 May 1802; David Randolph to Levi Lincoln, 25 March 1801, Lincoln to Randolph, 20 April 1801, in *Exam.*, 21 Aug. 1802.

8. JTC to Jefferson, 12 April 1801, Jefferson Papers, LC.

9. JTC to Madison, 27 April 1801, in Ford, "Jefferson and Callender," 153–55.

10. Ibid.

11. *Exam.*, 28 July 1802. Jones was a staunch supporter of Jefferson's moderate removals policy (ibid., 19 June 1801).

12. Ibid., 21 Aug. 1801; JTC to Madison, 7 May 1801, in Ford, "Jefferson and Callender," 156.

13. *Rec.*, 3 Nov. 1802; Jefferson to Monroe, 29 May 1801, in Ford, "Jefferson and Callender," 157; Madison to Monroe, 1 June 1801, quoted in Jellison, "That Scoundrel Callender," 302.

14. *Rec.*, 9 Feb. 1803; *Aurora*, 18 Aug. 1802.

15. *Exam.*, 21 Aug. 1802, 18 Sept. 1801.

16. Ibid., 4, 29 Sept. 1801.

17. Ibid., 18 Sept. 1802, 1 Jan., 6 July 1803; *Rec.*, 21 Nov. 1801, 12 May 1802.

18. *Rec.*, 18 June 1803.

19. Ibid., 13, 6 March 1802, 9 March 1803.

20. See, for example, Jellison, "That Scoundrel Callender," 303, where he writes of JTC quickly finding new Federalist friends in 1802; Dabney, *Jefferson Scandals*, 9, and Brodie, *Jefferson*, 348, both call the *Recorder* a Federalist newspaper. *Rec.*, 5 May 1802.

21. *Rec.*, 9 June, 28 July, 18 Aug., 27 Oct., 3 Nov., 1 Dec. 1802, 9 Feb. 1803.

22. Ibid., 5, 19 May, 28 July, 3 Nov. 1802.

23. Ibid., 27 Oct. 1802.

24. Ibid., 6, 27 March, 5 May, 9 June 1802; *Exam.*, 5 May, 19 June 1802; Smith, *Freedom's Fetters*, 343.

25. *Rec.*, 5, 26 May 1802; *Exam.*, 23 June, 8 May 1802; *DAB*, s.v. "Harvie John."

26. Rhys Isaac, *The Transformation of Virginia, 1740–1790* (Chapel Hill, N.C., 1982); T. H. Breen, "Horses and Gentlemen: The Cultural Significance of Gambling among the Gentry of Virginia," in *Puritans and Adventurers* (New York, 1981), 148–63.

27. Quoted in Duke and Jordan, *Richmond Reader*, 27–28; see also Jack P. Greene, "Society, Ideology, and Politics: An Analysis of the Political Culture of Mid–Eighteenth-Century Virginia," in *Society, Freedom and Conscience: The Coming of the Revolution in Virginia, Massachusetts, and New York*, ed. Richard M. Jellison (New York, 1976), 71–75.

28. Duke and Jordan, *Richmond Reader*, 28; Dabney, *Richmond*, 66–67; *Va. Fed.*, 24 Aug. 1799.

29. *Rec.*, 23 April 1802; *Exam.*, 27 April 1802; JTC, *Conduct of Meriwether Jones*, 7.

30. *Exam.*, 15 May 1801; *Rec.* 5, 19 May, 9 June 1802.

31. *Exam.*, 28 April 1802; *Rec.*, 26 May 1802; JTC, *Conduct of Meriwether Jones*, 50–52.

32. *Exam.*, 17 July, 29 May 1802.

33. *Rec.*, 5 May, 21 July, 20 Oct. 1802; *Exam.*, 11 April 1800.

34. *Exam.*, 25 Sept. 1802.

35. Ibid., 19, 12 May 1802; New York *Herald*, quoted ibid., 14 July 1802.

36. *Exam.*, 9 Jan. 1800, 9, 23 June, 11, 21 Aug. 1802; *Rec.*, 21 July, 4 Aug. 1802.

37. *Rec.*, 23 June, 5 July 1802; New York *Herald*, 5 Aug. 1802, quoted ibid., 18 Aug. 1802.

38. *Exam.*, 24 July, 18, 28 Aug. 1802; *Aurora*, 16 July, 4, 18, 25 Aug. 1802; JTC, *Conduct of Meriwether Jones*, 104–5.

39. *Exam.*, 11 Aug. 1802; *Rec.*, 22 Sept. 1802; *Aurora*, 25 Aug. 1802.

40. Dabney, *Jefferson Scandals*, 15–19; Douglass Adair, "The Jefferson Scandals," in Colbourn, *Fame and the Founding Fathers*, 166–69; Brodie, *Jefferson*.

41. Adair, "Jefferson Scandals"; Dabney, *Jefferson Scandals*; Malone, *Jefferson*, 4:chap. 12; Dumas Malone and Steven H. Hochman, "A Note on Evidence: The Personal History of Madison Hemings," *Journal of Southern History* 41 (1975): 523–28; John Chester Miller, *The Wolf by the Ears: Thomas Jefferson and Slavery* (New York, 1977), chap. 20.

42. Malone, *Jefferson* 4:214; see also Adair, "Jefferson Scandals," 161, 164, 181; Miller, *Wolf*, 165.

43. Brodie, *Jefferson*, 73–79, 199–227.

44. *Rec.*, 1 Sept. 1802.

45. Ibid., 15 Sept., 20 Oct., 3 Nov. 1802; Adair, "Jefferson Scandals," 174.

46. *Rec.*, 10 Nov., 8 Dec. 1802.

47. Ibid., 22 Sept., 13, 27 Oct. 1802, 19 March, 28 May 1803.

48. Malone, *Jefferson* 4:213; Adair, "Jefferson Scandals," 174–79; Dabney, *Jefferson Scandals*, 47; Miller, *Wolf by the Ears*, 156; Brodie, *Jefferson*, 287.

49. *Rec.*, 10, 17 Nov. 1802.

50. *Exam.*, 1, 15 Sept., 6 Nov. 1802.

51. Ibid., 25 Sept. 1802.

52. Adair, "Jefferson Scandals," 187; *Exam.*, 22, 25 Sept. 1802.

53. *Rec.*, 13, 27 Oct., 17 Nov. 1802; Brodie, *Jefferson*, 352–54; Malone, *Jefferson* 4:216–20; Jellison, "That Scoundrel Callender," 304. Jellison claims that Jefferson sought no more than a kiss.

54. *Rec.*, 27 Oct., 17 Nov. 1802. Letters written by Jefferson after the exposure of the affair were circulated in 1803; JTC seems to have had access to these (ibid., 2 Feb. 1803).

55. Ibid., 17 Nov. 1802, 28 May 1803; Jellison, "That Scoundrel Callender," 304; Brodie, *Jefferson*, 351.

56. Malone, *Jefferson* 4:138–39; Brodie, *Jefferson*, 353–54; Merrill D. Peterson, *The Jeffersonian Image in the American Mind* (New York, 1962), 182, 186. Historians who believe it may be true include T. Harry Williams, "On the Couch at Monticello," *Reviews in American History* 2 (1974): 528; Max Lerner, "We Are All Federalists, All Republicans," in *Portrait of America*, ed. Stephen B. Oates, 2 vols., 3d ed. (Boston, 1983), 1:158–59.

57. *Rec.*, 2 Feb. 1803.

58. Ibid., 1 Sept., 20 Oct., 1 Dec. 1802; *Frederick-Town Herald*, 30 Oct. 1802, quoted ibid., 17 Nov. 1802.

59. *Exam.*, 9 Jan. 1800; *Rec.*, 21 July, 4 Aug. 1802, 12 Jan., 11 June 1803.

60. *Rec.*, 1, 15 Dec. 1802, 12 Jan. 1803.

61. Ibid., 15, 22 Dec. 1802; Hochman, "Liberty of the Press," 436. I have relied heavily on Hochman's essay in the following paragraphs, although my interpretation has a different focus.

62. Hochman, "Liberty of the Press," 437; *Exam.*, 29 Dec. 1802.

63. Richmond *Republican Argus*, reprinted in *Aurora*, 5 Jan. 1803; Hochman, "Liberty of the Press," 438.

64. *Rec.*, 29 Dec. 1802. Meriwether Jones derided JTC's attempts to prove the existence of a mob waiting to assault him (*Exam.*, 1 Jan. 1803).

65. Hochman, "Liberty of the Press," 439; *Aurora*, 5 Jan. 1803.

66. *Aurora*, 5 Jan. 1803; Hochman, "Liberty of the Press," 439–40. For the democrats' attacks on the common law, see Higginbotham, *Keystone in the Democratic Arch*, 79; Twomey, "Jacobins and Jeffersonians," 201; Ellis, *Jeffersonian Crisis*, 112.

67. *Aurora*, 5 Jan. 1803 and passim; Brown, "Adams and the Press," 79–80; Phillips, "William Duane: Revolutionary Editor," chaps. 3–8.

68. Hochman, "Liberty of the Press," 441; *Rec.*, 3 March 1803.

69. *Rec.*, 2 Feb., 16, 23 March, 6 April 1803; Elizabeth D. Coleman, "Peter Carr of Carr's Brook (1770–1815)," *Papers of the Albermarle County Historical Society* 4 (1943–44): 5–23.

70. *Rec.*, 9 Feb. 1803.

71. Ibid., 12 Jan., 2 Feb., 2 April 1803.

72. Ibid., 30 March, 2, 20 April 1803.

73. Richmond *Virginia Gazette*, 15 June 1803; *Rec.*, 18 June 1803.

74. *Exam.*, 6 July 1803; *Rec.*, 28 May, 18 June 1803.

75. *Virginia Gazette*, 15 June 1803; *Rec.*, 18 June 1803; *Exam.*, 29 June 1803. In Virginia real property could not be seized to pay debts. For the "feigned selling" of movable goods and the holding of them "as hired," see Duke and Jordan, *Richmond Reader*, 27.

76. *Rec.*, 18 June 1803.

77. *Exam.*, 6 July 1803.

78. Ibid., 13, 6 July 1803; *Rec.*, 13 July 1803.

79. *Republican Argus*, 15 Aug. 1803; *Rec.*, 20 July 1803; Jellison, "That Scoundrel Callender," 305.

EPILOGUE

1. *Exam.*, 27 Aug. 1803.

2. Ford, "Jefferson and Callender," 321; Jellison, "That Scoundrel Callender," 306; Dabney, *Jefferson Scandals*, 65.

3. A. J. Youngson, *The Prince and the Pretender: A Study in the Writing of History* (Beckenham, 1985), 23.

4. *Rec.*, 1 Dec., 18 Aug. 1802; *Exam.*, 6 July 1803; Brigham, *American Newspapers* 2:1141.

5. *Rec.*, 15 June 1803.

6. Ibid., 23 March 1803.

7. Speer, *Prominent Tennesseans*, 59–61.

Bibliography

PRIMARY SOURCES

Manuscript Collections

Court of the Lord Lyon, Edinburgh
    Court Book, vol. 5, 1770–1818
    Records of Messengers' Admissions, 1778–1815
Historical Society of Pennsylvania
    Tench Coxe Papers
    Edward Carey Gardiner Collection
    Lea and Febiger Collection
Library of Congress
    Thomas Jefferson Papers (microfilm)
    McLean-Hamilton Papers
Pennsylvania Historical and Museum Commission, Harrisburg
    Naturalization Records, 1798
    Navigation Commission Records, 1792–94
National Library of Scotland, Edinburgh
    Account Books of Andrew Stuart: MS 5398
    Cash Books of Andrew Stuart: MSS 5394–95
    Correspondence of Thomas Muir: MS 3825
    Correspondence of Andrew Stuart: MS 8621
Public Record Office, London
    Foreign Office: FO 5/14
    Home Office, Scotland: HO 102/5, 102/6, 102/7
Sasine Office, Edinburgh
    General Register of Sasines, Edinburgh
Scottish Record Office, Edinburgh
    Lord Clerk Register: SRO 6/1/2
    Scottish Correspondence: RH 2/4/74
    Scottish Papers: SRO 1/109
University of Edinburgh, Special Collections
    Davidson Correspondence
    Forbes Correspondence

Parliamentary and Congressional Records

Debates and Proceedings in the Congress of the United States. 42 vols. Washington, D.C., 1834–56.
First Annual Report of the Deputy Clerk Register of Scotland. Edinburgh, 1807.
The Parliamentary History of England, from the Earliest Period to 1803. 34 vols. London, 1816–18.
Returns of Salaries, *Parliamentary Papers* 14 (1821).
Returns, Scottish Offices, *Parliamentary Papers* 39 (1837).
Second Annual Report of the Deputy Clerk Register of Scotland. Edinburgh, 1808.

Newspapers

Scotland
  Edinburgh Evening Courant
  Glasgow Courier
United States
  Baltimore *American Patriot*
  Boston *Polar Star*
  Charleston, S.C., *Daily Evening Gazette*
  New York *American Citizen*
  Philadelphia *American Daily Advertiser*
  Philadelphia *Aurora*
  Philadelphia *Carey's United States Recorder*
  Philadelphia *The Constitutional Diary and Philadelphia Evening Advertiser*
  Philadelphia *Gazette of the United States*
  Philadelphia *Porcupine's Gazette*
  Richmond *Examiner*
  Richmond *Recorder*
  Richmond *Republican Argus*
  Richmond *Virginia Federalist*
  Richmond *Virginia Gazette*

Periodicals

The Annual Biography and Obituary for the Year 1818. 2 vols. London, n.d.
The Bee, or Literary Weekly Intelligencer. Edinburgh, 1792.
European Magazine and London Review 6 (London, 1784).
Gentleman's Magazine 87 (London, 1817).
Scots Magazine. Edinburgh, 1789.

Trials

Howell, T. B. and T. J., eds. *A Complete Collection of State Trials.* 34 vols. London, 1817.
Wharton, Francis, ed. *State Trials of the United States during the Administration of Washington and Adams.* Washington, D.C., 1849; rept. New York: Burt Franklin, 1970.

Directories and Dictionaries

Bell, William. *A Dictionary and Digest of the Laws of Scotland.* Edinburgh, 1861.
A Biographical Dictionary of Eminent Scotsmen. Ed. Robert Chambers. 4 vols. Edinburgh, 1835.
Brigham, Clarence S. *History and Bibliography of American Newspapers, 1690–1820.* Worcester, Mass.: American Antiquarian Society, 1947.
Cross, F. L, and E. A. Livingstone. *The Oxford Dictionary of the Christian Church.* 2d ed. London: Oxford University Press, 1974.
Darling, James J. *The Powers and Duties of Messengers at Arms, Sheriffs, and Burgh Officers.* Edinburgh, 1840.
Edinburgh and Leith Trade Directory. Edinburgh, 1786–88, 1790–92.

Evans, Charles. *American Bibliography*. 14 vols. Worcester, Mass.: American Antiquarian Society, 1925–55.
Horne, Colin J., ed. *Swift on His Age: Selected Prose and Verse*. London: Harrap, 1953.
Johnson, Allen, and Dumas Malone, eds. *Dictionary of American Biography*. 12 vols. New York: Scribner's, 1927–58.
Livingstone, M. *A Guide to the Public Records of Scotland Deposited in H.M. General Register House, Edinburgh*. Glasgow, 1905.
Stephen, Sir Leslie, and Sir Sidney Lee, eds. *Dictionary of National Biography*. 22 vols. Oxford: Oxford University Press, 1967–68.
Williamson's Edinburgh Directory. Edinburgh, 1788–90.

Collected Letters and Writings

Allen, W. B., ed. *Works of Fisher Ames as Published by Seth Ames*. 2 vols. Indianapolis: Liberty Press, 1983.
Boyd, Julian P., et al. eds. *The Papers of Thomas Jefferson*. 22 vols. to date. Princeton, N.J.: Princeton University Press, 1950—.
[Cobbett, William.] *Porcupine's Works*. 12 vols. London, 1801.
Foner, Philip S., ed. *Basic Writings of Thomas Jefferson*. New York: Wiley, 1944.
——, ed. *The Life and Major Writings of Thomas Paine*. 2 vols. Secaucus, N.J.: Citadel Press, 1974.
Ford, Worthington C., ed. "Letters of James Cheetham." *Proceedings of the Massachusetts Historical Society*, 3d ser., 1 (1907): 41–64.
——, ed. "Letters of William Duane." *Proceedings of the Massachusetts Historical Society*, 2d ser., 20 (1906–7): 258–394.
——, ed. "Thomas Jefferson and James Thomson Callender." *New England Historical and Genealogical Register* 51 (1896): 321–33, 445–58; 52 (1897): 19–25, 153–58, 323–28.
Mitchell, Stewart, ed. *New Letters of Abigail Adams, 1788–1801*. 2d ed. New York: Greenwood Press, 1973.
Syrett, Harold C., and Jacob E. Cooke, eds. *The Papers of Alexander Hamilton*. 26 vols. New York: Columbia University Press, 1960–79.

Contemporary Pamphlets

Callender, James Thomson. *British Honour and Humanity; or, The Wonders of American Patience*. Philadelphia, 1796.
——. *The Conduct of Meriwether Jones, in a Series of Letters to the Public*. Richmond, 1802.
[——.] *A Critical Review of the Works of Dr. Samuel Johnson*. Edinburgh, 1783.
[——.] *Deformities of Dr. Samuel Johnson, Selected from His Works*. 2d ed. London, 1782.
[——.] *The History of the United States for 1796; Including a Variety of Interesting Particulars Relative to the Federal Government* . . . . Philadelphia, 1797.
[——.] *An Impartial Account of the Conduct of the Excise towards the Breweries of Scotland*. Edinburgh, 1791.
[——,] ed. *Miscellanies in Prose and Verse; Including Remarks on English Plays, Operas, and Farces, and on a Variety of Other Modern Publications, by the Honourable Lord Gardenstone*. 2d ed. Edinburgh, 1792.

[——.] *The Political Progress of Britain* . . . . [Part 1.] Edinburgh, 1792. 2d ed. Philadelphia, 1794.

[——.] *The Political Progress of Britain* . . . . Part 2. Philadelphia, 1795.

[——.] *The Political Register; or, Proceedings in the Session of Congress, Commencing in November 3d, 1794, and Ending March 3d, 1795.* Philadelphia, 1795.

[——.] *The Prospect before Us.* 2 vols. Richmond, 1800.

——. *Sedgwick and Co.; or, A Key to the Six Per Cent Cabinet.* Philadelphia, 1798.

[——.] *A Short History of the Nature and Consequences of Excise Laws* . . . . Philadelphia, 1795.

——. *Sketches of the History of America.* Philadelphia, 1798.

[Cobbett, William.] *A Bone to Gnaw for the Democrats: or, Observations on a Pamphlet, Entitled the Political Progress of Britain.* [Vol. 1.] Philadelphia, 1795.

[——.] *A Bone to Gnaw for the Democrats.* Vol. 2. Philadelphia, 1795.

[——.] *The Life and Adventures of Peter Porcupine.* Philadelphia, 1796.

[——.] *Observations on the Emigration of Dr. Priestley.* Philadelphia, 1794.

[——.] *The Political Censor* . . . . No. 2. Philadelphia, 1796.

Dwight, Jasper [William Duane]. *A Letter to President Washington.* Philadelphia, 1796.

Kennedy, James. *Treason!!! or Not Treason!!! Alias The Weavers Budget.* London, (1795?).

Knox, John. *A View of the British Empire, More Especially Scotland* . . . . London, 1784.

SECONDARY SOURCES

Books

Ammon, Harry. *James Monroe: The Quest for National Identity.* New York: McGraw-Hill, 1971.

Anderson, Dice R. *William Branch Giles: A Study in the Politics of Virginia and the Nation from 1790 to 1830.* 1914; rept. Gloucester, Mass: Peter Smith, 1965.

Anderson, Robert. *Life of Samuel Johnson, LLD.* 3d ed. Edinburgh, 1815.

Anon. *History of the Society of Writers to His Majesty's Signet.* Edinburgh, 1936.

Appleby, Joyce. *Capitalism and a New Social Order: The Republican Vision of the 1790s.* New York: New York University Press, 1984.

Arendt, Hannah. *On Revolution.* New York: Viking, 1963.

Austin, Aleine. *Matthew Lyon: "New Man" of the Democratic Revolution, 1749–1822.* University Park: Pennsylvania State University Press, 1981.

Axelrad, Jacob. *Philip Freneau: Champion of Democracy.* Austin: University of Texas Press, 1967.

Bailyn, Bernard. *The Ideological Origins of the American Revolution.* Cambridge, Mass.: Belknap Press, 1967.

Banning, Lance. *The Jeffersonian Persuasion: Evolution of a Party Ideology.* Ithaca, N.Y.: Cornell University Press, 1978.

Berkeley, Edmund, and Dorothy S. Berkeley. *John Beckley: Zealous Partisan in a Nation Divided.* Philadelphia: American Philosophical Society, 1973.

Bewley, Christina. *Muir of Huntershill*. Oxford: Oxford University Press, 1981.
Bloom, Allan. *The Closing of the American Mind*. New York: Simon and Schuster, 1987.
Breen, T. H. *Puritans and Adventurers: Change and Persistence in Early America*. New York: Oxford University Press, 1980.
Brock, W. R. and C. H. *Scotus Americanus*. Edinburgh: Edinburgh University Press, 1982.
Brodie, Fawn. *Thomas Jefferson: An Intimate History*. New York: Norton, 1974.
Burleigh, J.H.S. *A History of the Church of Scotland*. Edinburgh, 1960.
Cannon, John. *Parliamentary Reform, 1640–1832*. Cambridge: Cambridge University Press, 1973.
Cantwell, Robert. *Alexander Wilson: Naturalist and Pioneer*. Philadelphia: Lippincott, 1961.
Chinard, Gilbert. *Thomas Jefferson: The Apostle of Americanism*. 2d ed. Ann Arbor: University of Michigan Press, 1975.
Chitnis, Anand C. *The Scottish Enlightenment: A Social History*. London: Croom Helm, 1976.
Christian, W. Asbury. *Richmond: Her Past and Present*. Richmond, 1912.
Clark, J. C. D. *English Society, 1688–1832*. Cambridge: Cambridge University Press, 1985.
——. *Revolution and Rebellion: State and Society in England in the Seventeenth and Eighteenth Centuries*. Cambridge: Cambridge University Press, 1986.
Cockburn, Henry. *Memorials of His Time*. Edinburgh, 1856; rept. Edinburgh: Mercat Press, 1971.
Cook, Richard I. *Jonathan Swift as a Tory Pamphleteer*. Seattle: University of Washington Press, 1967.
Cooke, Jacob E. *Tench Coxe and the Early Republic*. Chapel Hill: University of North Carolina Press, 1978.
Cragg, Gerald R. *The Church and the Age of Reason, 1648–1789*. 2d ed. London: Penguin, 1983.
Cunningham, Noble E., Jr. *The Process of Government under Jefferson*. Princeton, N.J.: Princeton University Press, 1978.
Dabney, Virginius. *The Jefferson Scandals: A Rebuttal*. New York: Dodd, Mead, 1981.
——. *Richmond: The Story of a City*. New York: Doubleday, 1976.
Darnton, Robert. *The Literary Underground of the Old Regime*. Cambridge, Mass.: Harvard University Press, 1982.
Dauer, Manning J. *The Adams Federalists*. Baltimore: Johns Hopkins University Press, 1968.
Dickinson, Harry T. *Liberty and Property: Political Ideology in Eighteenth-Century Britain*. New York: Holmes and Meier, 1977.
Duke, Maurice, and Daniel P. Jordan, eds. *A Richmond Reader, 1783–1983*. Chapel Hill: University of North Carolina Press, 1983.
Ellis, P. Beresford, and Seumas MacA'Ghobhainn. *The Scottish Insurrection of 1820*. London: Gollancz, 1970.
Ellis, Richard C. *The Jeffersonian Crisis: Courts and Politics in the Young Republic*. New York: Oxford University Press, 1971.
Erdman, David V. *Commerce des Lumières: John Oswald and the British in Paris, 1790–1793*. Columbia: University of Missouri Press, 1986.

Fergusson, Sir James. *Balloon Tytler.* London: Faber and Faber, 1972.

Fischer, David Hackett. *The Revolution of American Conservatism: The Federalist Party in the Era of Jeffersonian Democracy.* New York: Harper and Row, 1965.

Foner, Eric. *Tom Paine and Revolutionary America.* New York: Oxford University Press, 1976.

Foner, Philip, ed. *The Democratic Republican Societies, 1790–1800.* Westport, Conn.: Greenwood, 1976.

Fraser, William R. *History of the Parish and Burgh of Laurencekirk.* Edinburgh, 1880.

Goodwin, Albert. *The Friends of Liberty: The English Democratic Movement in the Age of the French Revolution.* London: Hutchinson, 1979.

Hatch, Nathan O. *The Sacred Cause of Liberty: Republican Thought and the Millennium in Revolutionary New England.* New Haven: Yale University Press, 1977.

Haw, James, et al. *Stormy Patriot: The Life of Samuel Chase.* Baltimore: Maryland Historical Society, 1980.

Hawke, David F. *Paine.* New York: Harper and Row, 1974.

Hazlitt, William. *Table-Talk: Essays on Men and Manners.* London, 1905.

Higginbotham, Sanford W. *The Keystone in the Democratic Arch: Pennsylvania Politics, 1800–16.* Harrisburg: Pennsylvania Historical and Museum Commission, 1952.

Hofstadter, Richard. *The Paranoid Style in American Politics and Other Essays.* New York: Knopf, 1965.

Hook, Andrew. *Scotland and America: A Study of Cultural Relations, 1750–1835.* Glasgow: Blackie, 1975.

Hunt, Lynn. *Politics, Culture, and Class in the French Revolution.* Berkeley: University of California Press, 1984.

Hunter, Clark, ed. *The Life and Letters of Alexander Wilson.* Philadelphia: American Philosophical Society, 1983.

Hurstfield, Joel. *Freedom, Corruption, and Government in Elizabethan England.* London: Jonathan Cape, 1973.

Isaac, Rhys. *The Transformation of Virginia, 1740–1790.* Chapel Hill: University of North Carolina Press, 1982.

Jacob, Margaret, and James Jacob, eds. *The Origins of Anglo-American Radicalism.* London: Allen and Unwin, 1984.

Janson, Charles W. *The Stranger in America, 1793–1806.* 1806; rept. New York: Lenox Hill, 1971.

Johnson, Samuel. *Lives of the Poets.* 2 vols. London, 1964.

Johnstone, Robert M., Jr. *Jefferson and the Presidency: Leadership in the Young Republic.* Ithaca, N.Y.: Cornell University Press, 1978.

Kay, John. *Original Portraits.* 2 vols. Edinburgh, 1877.

Kenyon, John. *The History Men.* London: Weidenfeld and Nicolson, 1983.

Kerber, Linda K. *Federalists in Dissent: Image and Ideology in Jeffersonian America.* Ithaca, N.Y.: Cornell University Press, 1980.

Knox, J. Wendell. *Conspiracy in American Politics, 1787–1815.* New York: Arno Press, 1972.

Lenman, Bruce. *Integration, Enlightenment, and Industrialisation: Scotland, 1746–1832.* London: Arnold, 1981.

Levy, Leonard W. *Emergence of a Free Press.* New York: Oxford University Press, 1985.

Loth, David. *Chief Justice: John Marshall and the Growth of the Republic.* New York: Greenwood Press, 1949.

McCoy, Drew M. *The Elusive Republic: Political Economy in Jeffersonian America.* Chapel Hill: University of North Carolina Press, 1980.

McDonald, Forrest. *Alexander Hamilton: A Biography.* New York: Norton, 1979.

——. *Novus Ordo Seclorum: The Intellectual Origins of the Constitution.* Lawrence: University of Kansas Press, 1985.

McElroy, David D. *Scotland's Age of Improvement: A Survey of Eighteenth-Century Literary Clubs and Societies.* Pullman: Washington State University Press, 1969.

Malone, Dumas. *Jefferson and His Time.* 6 vols. Boston: Little, Brown, 1948–81.

Matthews, Richard K. *The Radical Politics of Thomas Jefferson: A Revisionist View.* Lawrence: University of Kansas Press, 1984.

Meikle, Henry W. *Scotland and the French Revolution.* 2d ed. London: Frank Cass, 1969.

Miller, John C. *Crisis in Freedom: The Alien and Sedition Laws.* Boston: Little, Brown, 1951.

——. *The Federalist Era, 1789–1801.* New York: Harper and Row, 1963.

——. *The Wolf by the Ears: Thomas Jefferson and Slavery.* New York: Free Press, 1977.

Miller, Richard G. *Philadelphia: The Federalist City.* Port Washington, N.Y.: Kennikat Press, 1976.

Mitchell, Broadus. *Alexander Hamilton: The National Adventure, 1788–1804.* New York: Macmillan, 1962.

Murdoch, Alexander. *"The People Above": Politics and Administration in Mid–Eighteenth Century Scotland.* Edinburgh: John Donald, 1980.

Ockrent, Lewis. *Land Rights: An Enquiry into the History of Registration for Publication in Scotland.* London, 1942.

Peterson, Merrill D. *The Jeffersonian Image in the American Mind.* New York: Oxford University Press, 1962.

Pocock, J. G. A. *The Machiavellian Moment: Florentine Republican Thought and the Atlantic Republican Tradition.* Princeton, N.J.: Princeton University Press, 1975.

——. *Virtue, Commerce, and History.* Cambridge: Cambridge University Press, 1985.

Porter, Roy. *English Society in the Eighteenth Century.* London: Penguin, 1982.

Powell, John H. *Bring Out Your Dead: The Great Plague of Yellow Fever in Philadelphia in 1793.* Philadelphia: University of Pennsylvania Press, 1949.

Ramsay, John. *Scotland and Scotsmen in the Eighteenth Century.* 2 vols. Edinburgh, 1888.

Raphael, D. D. *Adam Smith.* Oxford: Oxford University Press, 1985.

Risjord, Norman K. *Chesapeake Politics, 1781–1800.* New York: Columbia University Press, 1978.

Rogers, George C., Jr. *Evolution of a Federalist: William Loughton Smith of Charleston (1758–1812).* Columbia: University of South Carolina Press, 1962.

Ross, P. *The Scot in America.* New York, 1896.

Scharf, Thomas, and Thompson Westcott. *History of Philadelphia, 1609–1884*. 3 vols. Philadelphia, 1884.

Scott, H. *Fasti Ecclesiae Scoticanae*. 4 vols. Edinburgh, 1923.

Shalhope, Robert E. *John Taylor of Caroline: Pastoral Republican*. Columbia: University of South Carolina Press, 1980.

Sisson, David. *The American Revolution of 1800*. New York: Alfred A. Knopf, 1974.

Smith, James Morton. *Freedom's Fetters: The Alien and Sedition Laws and American Civil Liberties*. 1956; rept. Ithaca, N.Y.: Cornell University Press, 1966.

"Society of Ancient Scots." *Lives of the Scottish Poets*. 3 vols. London, 1822.

Spater, George. *William Cobbett: The Poor Man's Friend*. 2 vols. Cambridge: Cambridge University Press, 1982.

Speer, William S., ed. *Sketches of Prominent Tennesseans*. Nashville, 1888.

Spurlin, Paul M. *The French Enlightenment in America*. Athens: University of Georgia Press, 1984.

Stauffer, Vernon. *New England and the Bavarian Illuminati*. New York, 1918; rept. New York: Columbia University Press, 1967.

Stewart, Donald H. *The Opposition Press of the Federalist Period*. Albany: State University of New York Press, 1969.

Sunter, Ronald M. *Patronage and Politics in Scotland 1707–1832*. Edinburgh: John Donald, 1986.

Sutherland, D. M. G. *France, 1789–1815: Revolution and Counterrevolution*. London: Fontana, 1985.

Thomas, William. *The Philosophic Radicals: Nine Studies in Theory and Practice, 1817–1841*. Oxford: Oxford University Press, 1979.

Thompson, J. Maitland. *The Public Records of Scotland*. Glasgow; 1922.

Tucker, Bernard. *Jonathan Swift*. Dublin: Gill and Macmillan, 1983.

Warren, Charles. *Jacobin and Junto: or Early American Politics Viewed in the Diary of Dr. Nathaniel Ames, 1758–1822*. New York: AMS, 1970.

Webster, Grace. *Memoir of Dr. Charles Webster*. Edinburgh, 1853.

Werkmeister, Lucyle. *A Newspaper History of England, 1792–1793*. Lincoln: University of Nebraska Press, 1969.

Wexler, Victor G. *David Hume and the History of England*. Philadelphia: American Philosophical Society, 1979.

Wills, Garry. *Inventing America: Jefferson's Declaration of Independence*. New York: Viking, 1979.

Winch, Donald. *Adam Smith's Politics: An Essay in Historiographic Revision*. Cambridge: Cambridge University Press, 1978.

Youngson, A. J. *After the Forty-Five: The Economic Impact on the Scottish Highlands*. Edinburgh: Edinburgh University Press, 1973.

——. *The Prince and the Pretender: A Study in the Writing of History*. Beckenham: Croom Helm, 1985.

Zvesper, John. *Politics, Philosophy, and Rhetoric: A Study of the Origins of American Party Politics*. Cambridge: Cambridge University Press, 1977.

Articles

Adair, Douglass. "The Jefferson Scandals." In *Fame and the Founding Fathers: Essays by Douglass Adair*, ed. Trevor Colbourn, pp. 160–91. New York: Norton, 1974.

——. "'That Politics May Be Reduced to a Science': David Hume, James Madison, and the Tenth *Federalist*." In *Fame and the Founding Fathers: Essays by Douglass Adair*, ed. Trevor Colbourn, pp. 93–106. New York: Norton, 1974.

Appleby, Joyce. "The New Republican Synthesis and the Changing Political Thought of John Adams." *American Quarterly* 25 (1973): 578–95.

——. "What Is Still American in the Political Philosophy of Thomas Jefferson?" *William and Mary Quarterly*, 3d ser., 39 (1982): 287–309.

Ashworth, John. "The Jeffersonians: Classical Republicans or Liberal Capitalists?" *Journal of American Studies* 18 (1984): 425–35.

Banning, Lance. "Republican Ideology and the Triumph of the Constitution, 1789–1793." *William and Mary Quarterly*, 3d ser., 21 (1974): 167–88.

Baumann, Roland M. "John Swanwick: Spokesman for 'Merchant-Republicanism' in Philadelphia, 1790–1798." *Pennsylvania Magazine of History and Biography* 97 (1973): 131–82.

——. "Philadelphia's Manufacturers and the Excise Taxes of 1794: The Forging of the Jeffersonian Coalition." *Pennsylvania Magazine of History and Biography* 106 (1982): 3–39.

Boston, Ray. "The Impact of 'Foreign Liars' on the American Press (1790–1800)." *Journalism Quarterly* 50 (1973): 722–30.

Coleman, Elizabeth D. "Peter Carr of Carr's Brook (1770–1815)." *Papers of the Albemarle County Historical Society* 4 (1943–44): 5–23.

Durey, Michael. "Thomas Paine's Apostles: Radical Emigrés and the Triumph of Jeffersonian Republicanism." *William and Mary Quarterly*, 3d ser., 44 (1987): 661–88.

——. "Transatlantic Patriotism: Political Exiles and America in the Age of Revolutions." In *Artisans, Peasants, and Proletarians, 1760–1860: Essays Presented to Gwyn A. Williams*, ed. Clive Emsley and James Walvin, pp. 7–31. London: Croom Helm, 1985.

Dwyer, John, and Alexander Murdoch. "Paradigms and Politics: Manners, Morals, and the Rise of Henry Dundas, 1770–1784." In *New Perspectives on the Politics and Culture of Early Modern Scotland*, ed. John Dwyer et al., pp. 210–48. Edinburgh: John Donald, 1982.

Ellis, Richard E. "The Persistence of Antifederalism after 1789." In *Beyond Confederation: Origins of the Constitution and American National Identity*, ed. Richard Beeman, Stephen Botein, and Edward C. Carter II, pp. 295–314. Chapel Hill: University of North Carolina Press, 1987.

Fairley, John A. "The Pantheon: An Old Edinburgh Debating Society." *The Book of the Old Edinburgh Club* 1 (1908): 47–75.

Ferguson, William. "The Electoral System in the Scottish Counties before 1832." *Stair Society* 35 (1984): 261–94.

Greene, Jack P. "Society, Ideology, and Politics: An Analysis of the Political Culture of Mid–Eighteenth-Century Virginia." In *Society, Freedom, and Conscience: The Coming of the Revolution in Virginia, Massachusetts, and New York*, ed. Richard M. Jellison, pp. 14–76. New York: Norton, 1976.

Hochman, Steven H. "On the Liberty of the Press in Virginia: From Essay to Bludgeon, 1798–1803." *Virginia Magazine of History and Biography* 84 (1976): 431–45.

Howe, John R. "Republican Thought and the Political Violence of the 1790s." *American Quarterly* 19 (1967): 147–65.

Hughes, Edward. "The Scottish Reform Movement and Charles Grey, 1792–94." *Scottish Historical Review* 35 (1956): 26–41.

Jellison, Charles A. "That Scoundrel Callender." *Virginia Magazine of History and Biography* 64 (1959): 295–306.

Lee, Janice. "Political Antiquarianism Unmasked: The Conservative Attack on the Myth of the Ancient Constitution." *Bulletin of the Institute of Historical Research* 55 (1982): 166–79.

Lerner, Max. "We Are All Federalists, All Republicans." In *Portrait of America,* ed. Stephen B. Oates. 2 vols. 3d ed. Boston: Houghton Mifflin, 1983.

McGuffie, Helen L. "Dr. Johnson and the Little Dogs: The Reaction of the London Press to 'Taxation No Tyranny.'" In *Newsletters to Newspapers: Eighteenth-Century Journalism,* ed. Donovan H. Bond and W. Reynolds McLeod, pp. 191–206. Morgantown, W.Va.: University of West Virginia Press, 1977.

Malone, Dumas, and Steven H. Hochman. "A Note on Evidence: The Personal History of Madison Hemings." *Journal of Southern History* 41 (1975): 522–28.

Miles, Michael. "'A Haven for the Privileged': Recruitment into the Profession of Attorney in England, 1709–92." *Social History* 11 (1986): 197–210.

Mitchinson, Rosalind. "Nineteenth Century Scottish Nationalism: The Cultural Background." In *The Roots of Nationalism: Studies in Northern Europe,* ed. Rosalind Mitchinson, pp. 131–42. Edinburgh: John Donald, 1980.

Murray, W. J. "Poetry and Politics: Burns and Revolution." *Studies in the Eighteenth Century* 4 (1979): 57–82.

Newman, Stephen L. "Thomas Cooper, 1759–1839: The Political Odyssey of a Bourgeois Ideologue." *Southern Studies* 24 (1985): 295–305.

Parker, Peter J. "Asbury Dickins, Bookseller, 1798–1801, or the Brief Career of a Careless Youth." *Pennsylvania Magazine of History and Biography* 94 (1970): 464–83.

Pernick, Martin S. "Politics, Parties, and Pestilence: Epidemic Yellow Fever and the Rise of the First Party System." *William and Mary Quarterly,* 3d ser., 29 (1972): 559–86.

Phillips, Kim T. "William Duane, Philadelphia's Democratic Republicans, and the Origins of Modern Politics," *Pennsylvania Magazine of History and Biography* 101 (1977): 365–87.

Phillipson, Nicholas. "Adam Smith as Civic Moralist." In *Wealth and Virtue: The Shaping of Political Economy in the Scottish Enlightenment,* ed. Istvan Holt and Michael Ignatieff, pp. 179–202. Cambridge: Cambridge University Press, 1983.

——. "The Scottish Enlightenment." In *The Enlightenment in National Context,* ed. Roy Porter and Mikulas Teich, pp. 19–40. Cambridge: Cambridge University Press, 1981.

——. "Towards a Definition of the Scottish Enlightenment." In *City and Society in the Eighteenth Century,* ed. Paul Fritz and David Williams, pp. 125–47. Toronto: University of Toronto Press, 1973.

Prince, Carl E. "The Passing of the Aristocracy: Jefferson's Removal of the Federalists, 1801–1805." *Journal of American History* 57 (1970): 563–75.

Robertson, John. "Scottish Political Economy beyond the Civic Tradition: Government and Economic Development in the *Wealth of Nations.*" *History of Political Thought* 4 (1983): 451–82.

Rubinstein, William D. "The End of 'Old Corruption' in Britain, 1780–1860." *Past and Present* 101 (1984): 55–86.

Sher, Richard B. "Moderates, Managers, and Popular Politics in Mid–Eighteenth Century Edinburgh: The 'Drysdale Bustle' of the 1760s." In *New Perspectives in the Politics and Culture of Early Modern Scotland*, ed. John Dwyer et al., pp. 179–209. Edinburgh: John Donald, 1982.

Tinling, Marion. "Thomas Lloyd's Reports of the First Federal Congress." *William and Mary Quarterly*, 3d ser., 18 (1961): 519–45.

Twomey, Richard J. "Jacobins and Jeffersonians: Anglo–American Radical Ideology, 1790–1810." In *The Origins of Anglo–American Radicalism*, ed. Margaret Jacob and James Jacob, pp. 284–99. London: George Allen and Unwin, 1984.

Williams, T. Harry. "On the Couch at Monticello." *Reviews in American History* 2 (1974): 523–29.

Wood, Gordon S. "Conspiracy and the Paranoid Style." *William and Mary Quarterly*, 3d ser., 39 (1982): 401–41.

———. "Interests and Disinterestedness in the Making of the Constitution." In *Beyond Confederation: Origins of the Constitution and American National Identity*, ed. Richard Beeman, Stephen Botein, and Edward C. Carter II, pp. 69–109. Chapel Hill: University of North Carolina Press, 1987.

Dissertations

Baumann, Roland M. "The Democratic-Republicans of Philadelphia: The Origins, 1776–97." Ph.D. diss., Pennsylvania State University, 1970.

Brims, John D. " The Scottish Democratic Movement in the Age of the French Revolution." Ph.D. diss., University of Edinburgh, 1983.

Brown, Walter F., Jr. "John Adams and the American Press, 1797–1801: The First Full-Scale Confrontation between the Executive and the Media." Ph.D. diss., University of Notre Dame, 1974.

Carter, Edward C., II. "The Political Activities of Mathew Carey, Nationalist, 1760–1814." Ph.D. diss., Bryn Mawr College, 1962.

Dearmont, Nelson S. "Secrecy in Government: The Public Debate in Congress during the Formative Years of the American Republic." Ph.D. diss., City University of New York, 1975.

Gallin, Richard G. "Scottish Radicalism, 1792–1794." Ph.D. diss., Columbia University, 1979.

Gavre, William M. "Republicanism in the American Revolution: The Collapse of the Classical Ideal." Ph.D. diss., University of California, Los Angeles, 1978.

McCue, Daniel L. "Daniel Isaac Eaton and *Politics for the People*." 2 vols. Ph.D. diss., Columbia University, 1974.

Pendleton, Gayle T. "English Conservative Propaganda during the French Revolution, 1789–1802." Ph.D. diss., Emory University, 1976.

Phillips, Kim T. "William Duane, Revolutionary Editor." Ph.D. diss., University of California, Berkeley, 1968.

Rasmussen, Ethel. "Capital on the Delaware: A Study of Philadelphia's Upper Class, 1789–1800." Ph.D. diss., Brown University, 1962.

Tagg, James D. "Benjamin Franklin Bache and the Philadelphia *Aurora*." Ph.D. diss., Wayne State University, 1973.

Twomey, Richard J. "Jacobins and Jeffersonians: Anglo-American Radicalism in the United States, 1790–1820." Ph.D. diss., Northern Illinois University, 1974.

Wheeler, William B. "Urban Politics in Nature's Republic: The Development of Political Parties in the Seaport Cities in the Federalist Era." Ph.D. diss., University of Virginia, 1967.

Index